SOURCES FOR *FORGING AMERICA*

SOURCES FOR FORGING AMERICA

A CONTINENTAL HISTORY OF THE UNITED STATES

VOLUME ONE: TO 1877

EDITED BY

Alexandra E. Stern
THE CITY COLLEGE OF NEW YORK

Stefan Lund
UNIVERSITY OF VIRGINIA

OXFORD
UNIVERSITY PRESS

OXFORD
UNIVERSITY PRESS

Oxford University Press is a department of the University of Oxford.
It furthers the University's objective of excellence in research, scholarship,
and education by publishing worldwide. Oxford is a registered trade mark
of Oxford University Press in the UK and in certain other countries.

Published in the United States of America by Oxford University Press
198 Madison Avenue, New York, NY 10016, United States of America.

© 2024 by Oxford University Press

Library of Congress Cataloging-in-Publication Data

Names: Stern, Alexandra E., editor. | Lund, Stefan (Writer on the Civil
   War), editor. | Viator, Felicia Angeja, 1978—editor.
Title: Sources for "Forging America" : a continental history of the United
   States / edited by Alexandra E. Stern, The City College of New York;
   Stefan Lund, University of Virginia; Felicia Angeja Viator, San
   Francisco State University.
Other titles: Continental history of the United States
Identifiers: LCCN 2023017235 (print) | LCCN 2023017236 (ebook) | ISBN
   9780197657072 (v. 1 ; paperback) | ISBN 9780197657119 (v. 2 ; paperback)
   | ISBN 9780197657102 (v. 1 ; ebook) | ISBN 9780197657140 (v. 2 ; ebook)
Subjects: LCSH: United States—History—Sources.
Classification: LCC E173 .S689 2024 (print) | LCC E173 (ebook) | DDC
   973—dc23/eng/20230419
LC record available at https://lccn.loc.gov/2023017235
LC ebook record available at https://lccn.loc.gov/2023017236

Printed by Integrated Books International, United States of America

CONTENTS

HOW TO READ A PRIMARY SOURCE

This sourcebook is composed of ninety-four primary sources. A primary source is any text, image, or other source of information that gives us a first-hand account of the past by someone who witnessed or participated in the historical events in question. While such sources can provide significant and fascinating insight into the past, they must also be read carefully to limit modern assumptions about historical modes of thought. Here are a few elements to keep in mind when approaching a primary source.

AUTHORSHIP

Who produced this source of information? A male or a female? A member of the elite or of the lower class? An outsider looking in at an event or an insider looking out? What profession or lifestyle does the author pursue, which might influence how they are recording their information?

GENRE

What type of source are you examining? Different genres—categories of material—have different goals and stylistic elements. For example, a personal letter meant exclusively for the eyes of a distant cousin might include unveiled opinions and relatively trivial pieces of information, like the writer's vacation plans. On the other hand, a political speech intended to convince a nation of a leader's point of view might subdue personal opinions beneath artful rhetoric and focus on large issues like national welfare or war. Identifying genre can be useful for deducing how the source may have been received by an audience.

AUDIENCE

Who is reading, listening to, or observing the source? Is it a public or private audience? National or international? Religious or nonreligious? The source may be geared toward the expectations of a particular group; it may be recorded in a language that is specific to a particular group. Identifying audience can help us understand why the author chose a certain tone or why they included certain types of information.

HISTORICAL CONTEXT

When and why was this source produced? On what date? For what purposes? What historical moment does the source address? It is paramount that we approach primary sources in context to avoid anachronism (attributing an idea or habit to a past era where it does not belong) and faulty judgment. For example, when considering a medieval history, we must take account of the fact that in the Middle Ages, the widespread understanding was that God created the world and could still interfere in the activity of humankind—such as sending a terrible storm when a community had sinned. Knowing the context (Christian, medieval views of the world) helps us to avoid importing modern assumptions—like the fact that storms are caused by atmospheric pressure—into historical texts. In this way we can read the source more faithfully, carefully, and generously.

BIAS AND FRAMING

Is there an overt argument being made by the source? Did the author have a particular agenda? Did any political or social motives underlie the reasons for writing the document? Does the document exhibit any qualities that offer clues about the author's intentions?

STYLISTIC ELEMENTS

Stylistic features such as tone, vocabulary, word choice, and the manner in which the material is organized and presented should also be considered when examining a source. They can provide insight into the writer's perspective and offer additional context for considering a source in its entirety.

SOURCES FOR *FORGING AMERICA*

CHAPTER 1

BEGINNINGS TO 1519

1.1 THE SPLENDORS OF HANGZHOU, CHINA (c. 1235)*

Hangzhou was the capital of the Southern Song empire. Located near the coast, in the heart of a fertile rice-growing region, Hangzhou flourished as the commercial as well as political center of China. Its population swelled to more than a million people by 1200, and the city became a hub of domestic and international trade. The following excerpts are taken from a memoir of life in Hangzhou published in 1235. The unknown author lavishes attention on the city's marketplaces, restaurants, teahouses, entertainment quarters, social clubs, religious life, and pastimes.

MARKETPLACES

During the morning hours, pearls and jades, rare and exotic goods, newly picked flowers and fruits, fresh fish and wild game, and marvelous items found nowhere else in the empire all are gathered for sale in New Street, which runs northward from the imperial palace's Gate of Peace and Tranquility. From there to Heaven-Gazing Gate, Pure Stream Ward, Central Mall,[1] Ba Creek Landing, Government Lane, Canopy Square, and Contented Populace Bridge throngs of people overflow the food stalls and commercial shops.

At night the markets continue to hum in all of these places—except in front of the imperial palace—but none more so than the Central Mall, where exquisite porcelains and lacquer dishes as well as a hundred kinds of merchandise are set out for sale, just as in daytime. Other marketplaces throughout the lanes and alleys of the city echo with the calls of shopkeepers and peddlers hawking their wares. Taverns and music halls quiet down only after the fourth watch [2 a.m.]. By the fifth watch [4 a.m.], the officials are astir, hastening to the morning audience at the court, and the shopkeepers getting ready for the early morning business have already opened their shutters. All year round it is like this. . . .

The liveliest time of year comes during the Lantern Festival.[2] Row upon row of businesses and homes are gaily decorated, and tents are set up for various displays and spectacles too numerous to describe in

---

1 *Central Mall:* Hangzhou was famous for its malls or entertainment quarters where the brothels were located and opera troupes, puppet masters, storytellers, and other entertainers plied their trades.

2 *Lantern Festival:* Occurring on the fifteenth day of the first lunar month, it marks the end of the New Year season.

---

* Translation by Richard von Glahn.

full. During the Longxing era [1163–1164], the Imperial Ancestral Temple and the Six Palaces of the imperial harem were located at the Central Mall, directly opposite the present dyeworks of the Imperial Workshops. Once, after performing the New Year's sacrifices to his ancestors, Emperor Xiaozong [r. 1162–1189] stopped to see the lantern displays and sample the rare foodstuffs. Columns of imperial attendants stood in order of rank before the emperor's carriage. They spent piles of cash to purchase fancy delicacies, and with shouts and huzzahs handed out coins and gifts to onlookers. Some were fortunate enough to get gold and silver coins. At that time, one could still find some of the gourmet shops—such as Mama Li's Porridges and Zhang's Rice Pastries in the South Mall—of merchants who had come to Hangzhou from the old capital at Kaifeng.

On occasions of imperial processions or the spring and autumn religious festivals the carriages are lined up in long files with their canopies overlapping each other, like rows of fish scales. . . .

In the vacant plaza beneath the capital magistrate's hall various kinds of entertainers and actors are always performing and great crowds gather to watch. The same is true of the boulevard in front of the offices of the imperial constabulary. During the summer months, acrobats also put on amazing performances at the army training ground outside the Tide-Facing Gate. In other marketplaces and anywhere where there is sufficient open space—such as the meat market in the Great Mall, the medicine market at Coal Bridge, the booksellers' lane at the Orange Grove Pavilion, the vegetable market on the east side, and the rice market on the north side—you will also see people engaged in all kinds of entertainments. There are many other popular gathering places like the shops of the Fujian candied fruit sellers at the Five Span Tower, but I cannot name them all.

GUILDS

Commercial establishments are grouped into "guilds," a name given to them because each trade is required to provide the government with goods and services. Whether they are petty shopkeepers or great merchants, all must pool their resources to meet the officials' demands, and thus they are organized into guilds. Even physicians and fortunetellers must share this duty. Some trades that are not designated guilds by the government nonetheless refer to themselves as guilds, such as the wine guild and the food vendors' guild. Some merchant groups are called "circles," such as the south side flower circle, the fresh fruit circle of Muddy Street, the Riverbank dried-fish circle, and the Back Street Market tangerine circle. Artisans and craftsmen sometimes refer to themselves as "crafts," such as the comb and cutlery craft, the belt and sash makers' craft, and the gold-and-silver plating craft.

Some trades also have unusual names: dealers in the seven kinds of treasures [antiques] call themselves the "Bone Brokers Guild,"[3] while the bathhouses have taken the name "Fragrant Waters Guild."

In general, the capital attracts goods of every variety and the finest quality. In the flower market of Government Lane, for example, one finds caps, combs, hairpins, and bracelets of exquisite craftsmanship surpassing anything that existed in past times. Among the famous shops of the capital known far and wide one can mention the honey locust soaps sold in the Central Mall; the sweet bean soup vendors of the Sundry Goods Bazaar; Ge Family Pickled Dates; Guang Family Porridges in Government Lane; the fruit vendors of the Great Mall; the cured meats sold in front of the Temple of Perpetual Mercy; Fifth Sister Song's Fish Broth outside the Qian River Gate; the juicy gizzards of Gushing Gold Gate; Zhi Family Lamb Stew and Peng Family Boots in the Central Mall; Xuan Family Tailors and Zhang Family Rice Pastries in the South Mall; Gu the Fourth's Piccolos at Tide-Facing Gate; and Qiu Family Flutes at the Great Mall. . . .

---

3   *Bone Brokers Guild:* "Bone" is a pun; the word rhymes with a rare word for "antiques."

QUESTIONS TO CONSIDER

1. What sorts of merchants and businesses does the writer describe? What might this indicate about thirteenth-century China?
2. How does this description of Hangzhou compare with European societies during this same time period?

1.2 HOPI ORIGIN STORY: THE EMERGENCE (N.D.)*

The Hopi, commonly called the Pueblo after the Spanish term for their villages, are an American Indigenous people from what is now the southwestern United States. The Hopi developed a distinctive architectural style, including circular subterranean rooms called *kivas* that were used for a variety of sacred functions. Despite the arid conditions of their homeland, the Hopi successfully practiced agriculture supporting villages of over ten thousand people. The Hopi experienced their first contact with Europeans when they were visited by Spanish explorer Francisco Vásquez de Coronado in 1540. The Spanish attempted to convert the Hopi to Catholicism and Spanish culture during the 1600s, but in 1680 the Hopi launched a massive revolt that removed Spanish influence for over a decade.

This excerpt describes a portion of the Hopi explanation of the origins of the world, including the origins of animals on earth. The story reflects Hopi knowledge of the Spanish and their understanding that Europeans were difficult, avaricious, and violent neighbors.

1. ORIGIN MYTH[1]

A very long time ago there was nothing but water. In the east Hurúing Wuhti,[2] the deity of all hard substances, lived in the ocean. Her house was a kiva like the kivas of the Hopi of to-day. To the ladder leading into the kiva were usually tied a skin of a gray fox and one of a yellow fox. Another Hurúing Wuhti lived in the ocean in the west in a similar kiva, but to her ladder was attached a turtle-shell rattle.

The Sun also existed at that time. Shortly before rising in the east the Sun would dress up in the skin of the gray fox, whereupon it would begin to dawn—— the so-called white dawn of the Hopi. After a little while the Sun would lay off the gray skin and put on the yellow fox skin, whereupon the bright dawn of the morning—the so-called yellow dawn of the Hopi— would appear. The Sun would then rise, that is, emerge from an opening in the north end of the kiva in which Hurúing Wuhti lived. When arriving in the west again, the sun would first announce his arrival by fastening the rattle on the point of the ladder beam, whereupon he would enter the kiva, pass through an opening in the north end of the kiva, and continue his course eastward under the water and so on.

By and by these two deities caused some dry land to appear in the midst of the water, the waters receding eastward and westward. The Sun passing over this dry land constantly took notice of the fact, that no living being of any kind could be seen anywhere, and mentioned this fact to the two deities. So one time the Hurúing Wuhti of the west sent word through the Sun to the Hurúing Wuhti in the east to come over to her

---

1   Told by Qöyáwaima (Oraíbi). The events here related are supposed to have happened in the lower world. The increasing of the various peoples and tribes, and the constant contentions among them, finally led to the emigration from the nether world through the sípapu into this world, the account of which is related by variant traditions of the Hopi.

2   The nearest *literal* translation that can be given of this name, which appears so frequently in Hopi mythology and ceremonies is Hard Being Woman, i.e., woman of that which is hard, and the Hopi say she is the owner of such hard objects as shells, corals, turquoise, beads, etc.

---

* H. R. Voth, "Origin Myth," in *The Traditions of the Hopi* (Chicago: Columbian Field Museum, 1905), 1–5, https://archive.org/details/traditionsofhopi08voth/page/n13/mode/2up?view=theater.

as she wanted to talk over this matter. The Hurúing Wuhti of the east complied with this request and proceeded to the West over a rainbow. After consulting each other on this point the two concluded that they would create a little bird; so the deity of the east made a wren of clay, and covered it up with a piece of native cloth (möchápu). Hereupon they sang a song over it, and after a little while the little bird showed signs of life. Uncovering it, a live bird came forth, saying: "Úma hínok pas nui kitâ' náwakna?" (why do you want me so quickly). "Yes," they said, "we want you to fly all over this dry place and see whether you can find anything living." They thought that as the Sun always passed over the middle of the earth, he might have failed to notice any living beings that might exist in the north or the south. So the little Wren flew all over the earth, but upon its return reported that no living being existed anywhere. Tradition says, however, that by this time Spider Woman (Kóhk'ang Wuhti), lived somewhere in the south-west at the edge of the water, also in a kiva, but this the little bird had failed to notice.

Hereupon the deity of the west proceeded to make very many birds of different kinds and form, placing them again under the same cover under which the Wren had been brought to life. They again sang a song over them. Presently the birds began to move under the cover. The goddess removed the cover and found under it all kinds of birds and fowls. "Why do you want us so quickly?" the latter asked. "Yes, we want you to inhabit this world." Hereupon the two deities taught every kind of bird the sound that it should make, and then the birds scattered out in all directions.

Hereupon the Hurúing Wuhti of the west made of clay all different kinds of animals, and they were brought to life in the same manner as the birds. They also asked the same question: "Why do you want us so quickly?" "We want you to inhabit this earth," was the reply given them, whereupon they were taught by their creators their different sounds or languages, after which they proceeded forth to inhabit the different parts of the earth. They now concluded that they would create man. The deity of the east made of clay first a woman and then a man, who were brought to life in exactly the same manner as the birds and animals before them. They asked the same question, and were told that they should live upon this earth and

should understand everything. Hereupon the Hurúing Wuhti of the east made two tablets of some hard substance, whether stone or clay tradition does not say, and drew upon them with the wooden stick certain characters, handing these tablets to the newly created man and woman, who looked at them, but did not know what they meant. So the deity of the east rubbed with the palms of her hands, first the palms of the woman and then the palms of the man, by which they were enlightened so that they understood the writing on the tablets. Hereupon the deities taught these two a language.[3] After they had taught them the language, the goddess of the east took them out of the kiva and led them over a rainbow, to her home in the east. Here they stayed four days, after which Hurúing Wuhti told them to go now and select for themselves a place and live there. The two proceeded forth saying that they would travel around a while and wherever they would find a good field they would remain. Finding a nice place at last, they built a small, simple house, similar to the old houses of the Hopi. Soon the Hurúing Wuhti of the west began to think of the matter again, and said to herself: "This is not the way yet that it should be. We are not yet done," and communicated her thoughts to the Hurúing Wuhti of the east. By this time Spider Woman had heard about all this matter and she concluded to anticipate the others and also create some beings. So she also made a man and woman of clay, covered them up, sang over them, and brought to life her handiwork. But these two proved to be Spaniards. She taught them the Spanish language, also giving them similar tablets and imparting knowledge to them by rubbing their hands in the same manner as the woman of the East had done with the "White Men." Hereupon she created two burros, which she gave to the Spanish man and woman. The latter settled down close by. After this, Spider Woman continued to create people in the same manner as she had created the Spaniards, always a man and a woman, giving a different language to each pair. But all at once she found that she had forgotten to create a woman for a certain

---

3   Some Hopi say that these two people were the ancestors of what are now called the White Man, and the people say that they believe this language taught to these two people was the language of the present White Man.

man, and that is the reason why now there are always some single men.

She continued the creating of people in the same manner, giving new languages as the pairs were formed. All at once she found that she had failed to create a man for a certain woman, in other words, it was found that there was one more woman than there were men. "Oh my!" she said, "How is this?" and then addressing the single woman she said: "There is a single man somewhere, who went away from here. You try to find him and if he accepts you, you live with him. If not, both of you will have to remain single. You do the best you can about that." The two finally found each other, and the woman said, "Where shall we live?" The man answered: "Why here, anywhere. We shall remain together." So he went to work and built a house for them in which they lived. But it did not take very long before they commenced to quarrel with each other. "I want to live here alone," the woman said. "I can prepare food for myself." "Yes, but who will get the wood for you? Who will work the fields?" the man said. "We had better remain together." They made up with each other, but peace did not last. They soon quarreled again, separated for a while, came together again, separated again, and so on. Had these people not lived in that way, all the other Hopi would now live in peace, but others learned it from them, and that is the reason why there are so many contentions between the men and their wives. These were the kind of people that Spider Woman had created. The Hurúing Wuhti of the west heard about this and commenced to meditate upon it. Soon she called the goddess from the east to come over again, which the latter did. "I do not want to live here alone," the deity of the west said, "I also want some good people to live here." So she also created a number of other people, but always a man and a wife. They were created in the same manner as the deity of the east had created hers. They lived in the west. Only wherever the people that Spider Woman had created came in contact with these good people there was trouble. The people at that time led a nomadic life, living mostly on game. Wherever they found rabbits or antelope or deer they would kill the game and eat it. This led to a good many contentions among the people. Finally the Woman of the west said to her people: "You

remain here; I am going to live, after this, in the midst of the ocean in the west. When you want anything from me, you pray to me there." Her people regretted this very much, but she left them. The Hurúing Wuhti of the east did exactly the same thing, and that is the reason why at the present day the places where these two live are never seen.

Those Hopi who now want something from them deposit their prayer offerings in the village. When, they say their wishes and prayers they think of those two who live in the far distance, but of whom the Hopi believe that they still remember them.

The Spanish were angry at Hurúing Wuhti and two of them took their guns and proceeded to the abiding place of the deity. The Spaniards are very skillful and they found a way to get there. When they arrived at the house of Hurúing Wuhti the latter at once surmised what their intentions were. "You have come to kill me," she said; "don't do that; lay down your weapons and I shall show you something; I am not going to hurt you." They laid down their arms, whereupon she went to the rear end of the kiva and brought out a white lump like a stone and laid it before the two men, asking them to lift it up. One tried it, but could not lift it up, and what was worse, his hands adhered to the stone. The other man tried to assist him, but his hands also adhered to the stone, and thus they were both prisoners. Hereupon Hurúing Wuhti took the two guns and said: "These do not amount to anything," and then rubbed them between her hands to powder. She then said to them: "You people ought to live in peace with one another. You people of Spider Woman know many things, and the people whom we have made also know many, but different, things. You ought not to quarrel about these things, but learn from one another; if one has or knows a good thing he should exchange it with others for other good things that they know and have. If you will agree to this I shall release you. They said they did, and that they would no more try to kill the deity. Then the latter went to the rear end of the kiva where she disappeared through an opening in the floor, from where she exerted a secret influence upon the stone and thus released the two men. They departed, but Hurúing Wuhti did not fully trust them, thinking that they would return, but they never did.

QUESTIONS TO CONSIDER

1. What does this excerpt explain about the Hopi understanding of their place in the world? What relation do the Hopi have to other living things and to supernatural forces?
2. What role do the Spanish play in this story?

1.3 CHRISTOPHER COLUMBUS, LETTER TO LUIS DE ST. ANGEL ON HIS FIRST VOYAGE (1493)*

Christopher Columbus (1451–1506) was a sailor from the Italian city of Genoa who, with the support of the Spanish monarchs Isabella and Ferdinand, embarked on a voyage across the Atlantic in 1492. Columbus hoped to discover a sea route to China (Cathay) across the Atlantic based on his erroneous belief that the circumference of the earth was considerably smaller than it really is. As a result, when he made landfall in the Caribbean Sea, he assumed that he was in Asia and that the people he met were an Indian people.

Columbus's first letter to Europe describing what he found on his voyage is addressed to Luis de St. Angel, an advisor to Isabella and Ferdinand. He describes how he claimed the land he discovered in the name of the king and queen, his impression of the people he met, and his hopes of discovering large cities and other states.

SIR:

As I know you will be rejoiced at the glorious success that our Lord has given me in my voyage, I write this to tell you how in thirty-three days I sailed to the Indies with the fleet that the illustrious King and Queen, our Sovereigns, gave me, where I discovered a great many islands inhabited by numberless people; and of all I have taken possession for their Highnesses by proclamation and display of the Royal Standard [Spanish flag] without opposition. To the first island I discovered I gave the name of San Salvador in commemoration of His Divine Majesty, who has wonderfully granted all this. The Indians call it Guanaham. The second I named the Island of Santa Maria de Concepcion; the third, Fernandina; the fourth, Isabella; the fifth, Juana; and thus to each one I gave a new name.

When I came to Juana, I followed the coast of that isle toward the west and found it so extensive that I thought it might be the mainland, the province of Cathay [China]; and as I found no towns nor villages on the seacoast, except a few small settlements, where it was impossible to speak to the people because they fled at once, I continued the said route, thinking I could not fail to see some great cities or towns; and finding at the end of many leagues that nothing new appeared and that the coast led northward, contrary to my wish, because the winter had already set in, I decided to make for the south, and as the wind also was against my proceeding, I determined not to wait there longer and turned back to a certain harbor whence I sent two men to find out whether there was any king or large city. They explored for three days and found countless small communities and people, without number, but with no kind of government, so they returned.

I heard from other Indians I had already taken that this land was an island, and thus followed the eastern

---

* Charles W. Eliot, ed., *American Historical Documents, 1000–1904*, Harvard Classics, vol. 43 (New York: Collier, 1910).

coast for one hundred and seven leagues until I came to the end of it. From that point I saw another isle to the eastward, at eighteen leagues' distance, to which I gave the name of Hispaniola. I went thither and followed its northern coast to the east, as I had done in Juana, one hundred and seventy-eight leagues eastward, as in Juana. This island, like all the others, is most extensive. It has many ports along the seacoast excelling any in Christendom—and many fine, large, flowing rivers. The land there is elevated, with many mountains and peaks incomparably higher than in the centre isle. They are most beautiful, of a thousand varied forms, accessible, and full of trees of endless varieties, so high that they seem to touch the sky, and I have been told that they never lose their foliage. I saw them as green and lovely as trees are in Spain in the month of May. Some of them were covered with blossoms, some with fruit, and some in other conditions, according to their kind. The nightingale and other small birds of a thousand kinds were singing in the month of November when I was there. There were palm trees of six or eight varieties, the graceful peculiarities of each one of them being worthy of admiration as are the other trees, fruits and grasses. There are wonderful pine woods, and very extensive ranges of meadow land. There is honey, and there are many kinds of birds, and a great variety of fruits. Inland there are numerous mines of metals and innumerable people.

Hispaniola is a marvel. Its hills and mountains, fine plains and open country, are rich and fertile for planting and for pasturage, and for building towns and villages. The seaports there are incredibly fine, as also the magnificent rivers, most of which bear gold. The trees, fruits and grasses differ widely from those in Juana. There are many spices and vast mines of gold and other metals in this island. They have no iron, nor steel, nor weapons, nor are they fit for them, because although they are well-made men of commanding stature, they appear extraordinarily timid. The only arms [weapons] they have are sticks of cane, cut when in seed with a sharpened stick at the end, and they are afraid to use these. Often I have sent two or three men ashore to some town to converse with them, and the natives came out in great numbers, and as soon as they saw our men arrive, fled without a moment's delay although I protected them from all injury.

At every point where I landed and succeeded in talking to them, I gave them some of everything I had—cloth and many other things—without receiving anything in return, but they are a hopelessly timid people. It is true that since they have gained more confidence and are losing this fear, they are so unsuspicious and so generous with what they possess, that no one who had not seen it would believe it. They never refuse anything that is asked for. They even offer it themselves, and show so much love that they would give their very hearts. Whether it be anything of great or small value, with any trifle of whatever kind, they are satisfied. I forbade worthless things being given to them, such as bits of broken bowls, pieces of glass, and old straps, although they were as much pleased to get them as if they were the finest jewels in the world. One sailor was found to have got for a leathern strap, gold of the weight of two and a half castellanos, and others for even more worthless things much more; while for a new blancas they would give all they had, were it two or three castellanos [thirteen to nineteen ounces] of pure gold or an arroba or two [twenty-five to fifty pounds] of spun cotton. Even bits of the broken hoops of wine casks they accepted, and gave in return what they had, like fools, and it seemed wrong to me. I forbade it, and gave a thousand good and pretty things that I had to win their love and to induce them to become Christians, and to love and serve their Highnesses and the whole Castilian nation, and help to get for us things they have in abundance, which are necessary to us.

They have no religion nor idolatry, except that they all believe power and goodness to be in heaven. They firmly believed that I, with my ships and men, came from heaven, and with this idea I have been received everywhere, since they lost fear of me. They are, however, far from being ignorant. They are most ingenious men, and navigate these seas in a wonderful way and describe everything well, but they never before saw people wearing clothes, nor vessels like ours. Directly I reached the Indies in the first isle I discovered, I took by force some of the natives, that from them we might gain some information of what there was in these parts; and so it was that we immediately understood each other, either by words or signs. They are still with me and still believe that I come from heaven. They were the first to declare this wherever I went, and the others ran from house to house, and to the towns around, crying out, "Come! come! and see the men from heaven!" Then all, both men and women, as soon as they were reassured about us, came, both small and great, all bringing something to eat and to drink, which they presented with marvelous kindness.

In these isles there are a great many canoes, something like rowing boats, of all sizes, and most of them are larger than an eighteen-oared galley. They are not so broad, as they are made of a single plank, but a galley could not keep up with them in rowing, because they go with incredible speed, and with these they row about among all these islands, which are innumerable, and carry on their commerce. I have seen some of these canoes with seventy and eighty men in them, and each had an oar. In all the islands I observed little difference in the appearance of the people, or in their habits and language, except that they understand each other, which is remarkable. Therefore I hope that their Highnesses will decide upon the conversion of these people to our holy faith, to which they seem much inclined.

I have already stated how I sailed one hundred and seven leagues along the seacoast of Juana [Cuba] in a straight line from west to east. I can therefore assert that this island is larger than England and Scotland together, since beyond these one hundred and seven leagues there remained at the west point two provinces where I did not go, one of which they call Avan, the home of men with tails. These provinces are computed to be fifty or sixty leagues in length, as far as can be gathered from the Indians with me, who are acquainted with all these islands. This other, Hispaniola, is larger in circumference than all Spain from Catalonia to Fuentarabia in Biscay, since upon one of its four sides I sailed one hundred and eighty- eight leagues from west to east. This is worth having, and must on no account be given up. I have taken possession of all these islands for their Highnesses, and all may be more extensive than I know or can say, and I hold them for their Highnesses, who can command them as absolutely as the kingdoms of Castile.

In Hispaniola, in the most convenient place, most accessible for the gold mines and all commerce with the mainland on this side or with that of the great Khan on the other, with which there would be great trade and profit, I have taken possession of a large town, which I have named the City of Navidad. I began fortifications there which should be completed by this time, and I have left in it men enough to hold it, with arms, artillery, and provisions for more than a year; and a boat with a master seaman skilled in the arts necessary to make others. I am so friendly with the king of that country that he was proud to call me his brother and hold me as such. Even should he change his mind and wish to quarrel with my men, neither he nor his subjects know what arms are nor wear clothes, as I have said. They are the most timid people in the world, so that only the men remaining there could destroy the whole region, and run no risk if they know how to behave themselves properly.

In all these islands the men seem to be satisfied with one wife, except they allow as many as twenty to their chief or king. The women appear to me to work harder than the men, and so far as I can hear they have nothing of their own, for I think I perceived that what one had others shared, especially food. In the islands so far I have found no monsters, as some expected, but, on the contrary, they are people of very handsome appearance. They are not black as in Guinea, though their hair is straight and coarse, as it does not grow where the sun's rays are too ardent. And in truth the sun has extreme power here, since it is within twenty-six degrees of the equinoctial line [equator]. In these islands there are mountains where the cold this winter was very severe, but the people endure it from habit, and with the aid of the meat they eat with very hot spices.

As for monsters, I have found no trace of them except at the point in the second isle as one enters the Indies, which is inhabited by a people considered in all the isles as most ferocious, who eat human flesh. They possess many canoes, with which they overrun all the isles of India [West Indies], stealing and seizing all they can. They are not worse looking than the others, except that they wear their hair long like women, and use bows and arrows of the same cane, with a sharp stick at the end for want lack of iron, of which they have none. They are ferocious compared to these other races, who are extremely cowardly, but I only hear this from the others. They are said to make treaties of marriage with the women in the first isle to be met with coming from Spain to the Indies, where there are no men. These women have no feminine oc-cupation, but use bows and arrows of cane like those before mentioned, and cover and arm themselves with plates of copper, of which they have a great quantity. Another island, I am told, is larger than Hispaniola, where the natives have no hair, and where there is countless gold; and from them all I bring Indians to testify to this.

To speak, in conclusion, only of what has been done during this hurried voyage, their Highnesses will see that I can give them as much gold as they desire, if they will give me a little assistance, spices, cotton, as much as their Highnesses may command to be shipped, and mastic as much as their Highnesses choose to send for, which until now has only been found in Greece, in the isle of Chios, and the Signoria can get its own price for it; as much lign-aloe as they command to be shipped, and as many slaves as they choose to send for, all heathens. I think I have found rhubarb and cinna-mon. Many other things of value will be discovered by the men I left behind me, as I stayed nowhere when the wind allowed me to pursue my voyage, except in the City of Navidad, which I left fortified and safe. Indeed,

I might have accomplished much more, had the crews served me as they ought to have done.

The eternal and almighty God, our Lord, it is Who gives to all who walk in His way, victory over things apparently impossible, and in this case signally so, because although these lands had been imagined and talked of before they were seen, most men listened incredulously to what was thought to be but an idle tale. But our Redeemer has given victory to our most illustrious King and Queen, and to their kingdoms rendered famous by this glorious event, at which all Christendom should rejoice, celebrating it with great festivities and solemn Thanksgivings to the Holy Trin-ity, with fervent prayers for the high distinction that will accrue to them from turning so many peoples to our holy faith; and also from the temporal bene-fits that not only Spain but all Christian nations will obtain. Thus I record what has happened in a brief note written on board the Caravel, off the Canary Isles, on the 15th of February, 1493.

Yours to command,
THE ADMIRAL.

QUESTIONS TO CONSIDER

1. How does Columbus's religious faith inform his world view? What role does the Catholic Church play in Columbus's hopes for the West Indies?
2. How does Columbus describe the people whom he meets on his voyage?

1.4 KING NZINGA MBEMBA (AFONSO I), EXCERPTS FROM LETTERS TO THE KING OF PORTUGAL (1526)*

Nzinga Mbemba (c. 1460–1542), sometimes known by his baptismal name Afonso, ruled the Kingdom of Kongo in central Africa in the early to mid-1500s. Kongo had been in contact with Portugal since the 1480s and Nzinga was a zealous convert to Catholicism, working to help establish the church in Kongo after ascending to the throne in 1509.

* "Excerpt of Letter from Nzinga Mbemba to Portuguese King João III," World History Commons, accessed January 26, 2023, https://worldhistorycommons.org/excerpt-letter-nzinga-mbemba-portuguese-king-joao-iii.

In this letter to King João III of Portugal, he details the misfortune that had resulted from the Portuguese slave trade on the coast of Kongo. Although Kongo had practiced slavery before the arrival of the Portuguese, Nzinga describes how the Portuguese desire to buy enslaved people had led to a breakdown in order as people were captured and rushed to be sold in order to acquire Portuguese goods. Nzinga requests that João restrict his merchants (factors) from buying enslaved people, believing Kongo was already becoming "depopulated" due to the work of "men of bad conscience."

Sir, Your Highness should know how our Kingdom is being lost in so many ways that it is convenient to provide for the necessary remedy, since this is caused by the excessive freedom given by your agents and officials to the men and merchants who are allowed to come to this kingdom to set up shops with goods and many things which have been prohibited by us, and which they spread through our Kingdoms and Domains in such an abundance that many of our vassals, whom we had in obedience, do not comply because they have the things in greater abundance than we ourselves; and it was with these things that we had them content and subjected under our vassalage and jurisdiction, so it is doing a great harm not only to the service of God, but the security and peace of our Kingdoms and State as well.

And we cannot reckon how great the damage is, since the mentioned merchants are taking every day our natives, sons of the land and the sons of our noblemen and vassals and our relatives, because the thieves and men of bad conscience grab them wishing to have the things and wares of this Kingdom which they are ambitious of, they grab them and get them to be sold; and so great, Sir, is the corruption and licentiousness that our country is being completely depopulated, and Your Highness should not agree with this nor accept it as in your service. And to avoid it we need from those Kingdoms no more than some priests and a few people to reach in schools, and no other goods except wine and flour for the holy sacrament.

That is why we beg of Your Highness to help and assist us in this matter, commanding your factors that they should not send here either merchants or wares, because it is our will that in these Kingdoms there should not be any trade of slaves nor outlet for them. Concerning what is referred to above, again we beg of Your Highness to agree with it, since otherwise we cannot remedy such an obvious damage, Pray Our Lord in His mercy to have Your Highness under His guard and let you do forever the things of His service, I kiss your hands many times. . . .

Many of our people, keenly desirous as they are of the wares and things of your Kingdoms, which are brought here by your people, and in order to satisfy their voracious appetite, seize many of our people, freed and exempt men, and very often it happens that they kidnap even noblemen and the sons of noblemen, and our relatives, and take them to be sold to the white men who are in our Kingdoms; and for this purpose they have concealed them; and others are brought during the night so that they might not be recognized.

And as soon as they are taken by the white men they are immediately ironed and branded with fire, and when they are carried to be embarked, if they are caught by our guards' men the whites allege that they have bought them but they cannot say from whom, so that it is our duty to do justice and to restore to the freemen their freedmen, but it cannot be done if your subjects feel offended, as they claim to be. . . .

QUESTIONS TO CONSIDER

1. How has the slave trade destabilized Kongo, according to Nzinga Mbemba? What motivates people in Kongo to participate in this trade?
2. What upsets Nzinga Mbemba about how the Portuguese practice slavery?

1.5 VISUAL SOURCE: THE SIGÜENZA MAP (c. 1500)*

The Sigüenza map is a pictorial history of the migration of the Mexica people from their homeland in Aztlán to the valley of central Mexico. It is unclear whether Aztlán was a real place or part of a mythological origin story of the Mexica. The map tells a narrative of how the Aztecs arrived at the island of Tenochtitlan in Lake Texcoco, where they built one of the largest cities in pre-Columbian America. The map depicts their departure from Aztlán, the deeds of various heroes, leaders, and gods, and their eventual arrival at the lake. Footprint symbols trace the journey across the map, and glyphs at each major location indicate how long the Mexica remained before moving onward.

It is uncertain who created the map or when. It is believed to date from the sixteenth century and may have been created in Chapultepec, near Tenochtitlan.

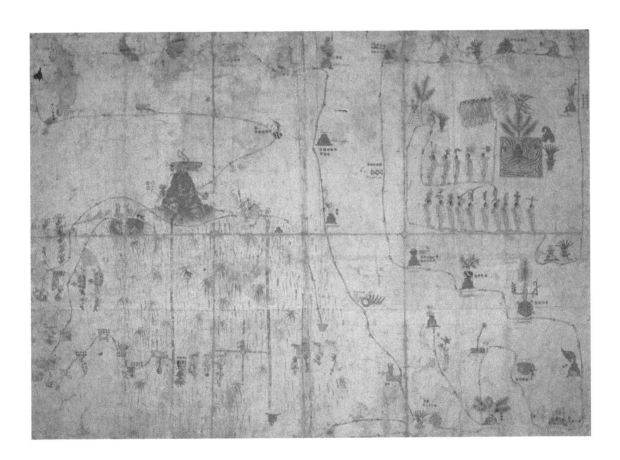

* Courtesy of the Library of Congress

QUESTIONS TO CONSIDER

1. How does the map visually depict time as well as space?
2. What symbols can you identify on this map? Why might these objects or animals have been important to the Mexica?

1.6 VISUAL SOURCE: BENIN PLAQUE OF THE OBA WITH EUROPEANS (c. 1500s)*

This brass plaque originates from the Kingdom of Benin, a West African kingdom of the Edo people who, beginning in the late fifteenth century, carried on extensive commercial relations with the Portuguese, Dutch, and other Europeans. The Oba, or king, ruled from Benin City, a large walled settlement near the Atlantic coast that some Europeans compared favorably with European cities. Between the fifteenth and nineteenth centuries, Benin sold tropical goods as well as enslaved people to European merchants, until the British conquered the kingdom in 1897. This plaque is now held by the British Museum in London after it was seized when the British captured Benin City.

This plaque depicts the seated Oba, flanked by two guards or followers. The Oba holds a hammer in his right hand and both he and his companions wear beaded collars and cylindrical headdresses. At the top two Portuguese men are depicted in profile with long hair and helmets.

---

* © The Trustees of the British Museum

QUESTIONS TO CONSIDER

1. Compare and contrast the depiction of Edo and Portuguese people in this plaque. What does the depiction of the Portuguese suggest about what this Edo artist associated with them?
2. How is this scene composed to make it clear that the Oba is an authority figure? What about how he is positioned, how he is dressed, and how other figures are positioned around him makes his royal position clear?

CHAPTER 2

CONTACT ZONES, 1450–1600

2.1 AN AZTEC ACCOUNT OF THE CONQUEST OF MEXICO (1520)*

The Aztec Empire was an alliance of city states in the Valley of Mexico made up of Nahuatl-speaking Mexica people. Its island capital of Tenochtitlan was the largest city in the Americas and was ruled by the emperor Moctezuma (1466–1520), sometimes styled as Montezuma, in the early sixteenth century. In 1519 the Spanish conquistador Hernán Cortés (1485–1547) set out to conquer the Aztecs, securing alliances with their rivals such as the nearby city of Tlaxcala to supplement a small Spanish force. Although Moctezuma welcomed Cortés and his forces into Tenochtitlan, Cortés's men quickly turned on their hosts, capturing Moctezuma and slaughtering many of the city's inhabitants.

This account of Cortés's arrival in Tenochtitlan and the violence that followed comes from a series of contemporary descriptions by Nahuatl-speaking Mexicans. As relatively few written accounts of the sixteenth century survive, especially from a Native perspective, this narrative offers valuable insight into how the Aztecs understood the Spanish conquest.

SPEECHES OF MOTECUHZOMA AND CORTÉS

When Motecuhzoma [Montezuma] had given necklaces to each one, Cortés asked him: "Are you Motecuhzoma? Are you the king? Is it true that you are the king Motecuhzoma?"

And the king said: "Yes, I am Motecuhzoma." Then he stood up to welcome Cortés; he came forward, bowed his head low and addressed him in these words: "Our lord, you are weary. The journey has tired you, but now you have arrived on the earth. You have come to your city, Mexico. You have come here to sit on your throne, to sit under its canopy.

"The kings who have gone before, your representatives, guarded it and preserved it for your coming. The kings Itzcoatl, Motecuhzoma the Elder, Axayacatl, Tizoc and Ahuitzol ruled for you in the City of Mexico. The people were protected by their swords and sheltered by their shields.

* Miguel Leon-Portilla, ed., *The Broken Spears: The Aztec Account of the Conquest of Mexico*, trans. Lysander Kemp (Boston: Beacon Press, 1962), 64–66, 129–31.

Used with permission of Beacon Press, from *The Broken Spears: The Aztec Account of the Conquest of Mexico*, Miguel Leon-Portilla, 1962; permission conveyed through Copyright Clearance Center, Inc.

"Do the kings know the destiny of those they left behind, their posterity? If only they are watching! If only they can see what I see!

"No, it is not a dream. I am not walking in my sleep. I am not seeing you in my dreams. . . . I have seen you at last! I have met you face to face! I was in agony for five days, for ten days, with my eyes fixed on the Region of the Mystery. And now you have come out of the clouds and mists to sit on your throne again.

"This was foretold by the kings who governed your city, and now it has taken place. You have come back to us; you have come down from the sky. Rest now, and take possession of your royal houses. Welcome to your land, my lords!"

When Motecuhzoma had finished, La Malinche translated his address into Spanish so that the Captain could understand it. Cortés replied in his strange and savage tongue, speaking first to La Malinche: "Tell Motecuhzoma that we are his friends. There is nothing to fear. We have wanted to see him for a long time, and now we have seen his face and heard his words. Tell him that we love him well and that our hearts are contented."

Then he said to Motecuhzoma: "We have come to your house in Mexico as friends. There is nothing to fear."

. . .

MASSACRE IN THE MAIN TEMPLE

During this time, the people asked Motecuhzoma how they should celebrate their god's fiesta. He said: "Dress him in all his finery, in all his sacred ornaments."
During this same time, The Sun commanded that Motecuhzoma and Itzcohuatzin, the military chief of Tlatelolco, be made prisoners. The Spaniards hanged a chief from Acolhuacan named Nezahualquentzin. They also murdered the king of Nauhtla, Cohualpopocatzin,

by wounding him with arrows and then burning him alive.

For this reason, our warriors were on guard at the Eagle Gate. The sentries from Tenochtitlan stood at one side of the gate, and the sentries from Tlatelolco at the other. But messengers came to tell them to dress the figure of Huitzilopochtli. They left their posts and went to dress him in his sacred finery: his ornaments and his paper clothing.

When this had been done, the celebrants began to sing their songs. That is how they celebrated the first day of the fiesta. On the second day they began to sing again, but without warning they were all put to death. The dancers and singers were completely unarmed. They brought only their embroidered cloaks, their turquoises, their lip plugs, their necklaces, their clusters of heron feathers, their trinkets made of deer hooves. Those who played the drums, the old men, had brought their gourds of snuff and their timbrels.

The Spaniards attacked the musicians first, slashing at their hands and faces until they had killed all of them. The singers—and even the spectators—were also killed. This slaughter in the Sacred Patio went on for three hours. Then the Spaniards burst into the rooms of the temple to kill the others: those who were carrying water, or bringing fodder for the horses, or grinding meal, or sweeping, or standing watch over this work.

The king Motecuhzoma, who was accompanied by Itzcohuatzin and by those who had brought food for the Spaniards, protested: "Our lords, that is enough! What are you doing? These people are not carrying shields or macanas. Our lords, they are completely unarmed!"

The Sun had treacherously murdered our people on the twentieth day after the captain left for the coast. We allowed the Captain to return to the city in peace. But on the following day we attacked him with all our might, and that was the beginning of the war.

QUESTIONS TO CONSIDER

1. How would you characterize the behavior of Hernán Cortés as described in this narrative? What stands out to you about his behavior toward the Aztec people?
2. How do you think Cortés portrayed these events to other Spaniards? Why is it important that this Native account has survived?

2.2 GIOVANNI DA VERRAZZANO, EXCERPTS FROM LETTER TO KING FRANCIS I OF FRANCE (1524)*

Giovanni da Verrazzano (1485–1528) was a Florentine sailor who, on behalf of King Francis I of France, set out in 1522 to chart parts of the Americas and find a sea route to Asia. Verrazzano became the first European to lead an expedition of what is now the eastern seaboard of the United States, following the coastline from modern-day North Carolina north past the Chesapeake Bay, Long Island, and Narragansett Bay, and possibly as far north as Maine. He describes several major geographical features of what became the early United States, such as the bay of Newport in what is now Rhode Island.

Verrazzano described numerous interactions with Native people of the Americas, including attempts to trade and barter some of the objects that the crew had on hand. Although Verrazzano and his crew did not share any common language with the Native Americans they encountered, Verrazzano made insightful observations of their behavior such as their movable housing, agricultural practices, and generosity within their group.

... We reached another land 15 leagues from the island, where we found an excellent harbor [almost certainly Newport in lower Narragansett Bay]; before entering it, we saw about twenty boats full of people who came around the ship uttering various cries of wonderment. They did not come nearer than fifty paces but stopped to look at the structure of our ship, our persons, and our clothes; then all together they raised a loud cry which meant that they were joyful. We reassured them somewhat by imitating their gestures, and they came near enough for us to throw them a few little bells and mirrors and many trinkets, which they took and looked at, laughing, and then they confidently came on board ship. Among them were two kings, who were as beautiful of stature and build as I can possibly describe. The first was about 40 years old, the other a young man of 24, and they were dressed thus: the older man had on his naked body a stag skin, skillfully worked like damask with various embroideries; the head was bare, the hair tied back with various bands, and around the neck hung a wide chain decorated with many different-colored stones. The young

man was dressed in almost the same way. These people are the most beautiful and have the most civil customs that we have found on this voyage. They are taller than we are; they are a bronze color, some tending more toward whiteness, others to a tawny color; the face is clear-cut; the hair is long and black, and they take great pains to decorate it; the eyes are black and alert, and their manner is sweet and gentle, very like the manner of the ancients I shall not speak to Your Majesty of the other parts of the body, since they have all the proportions belonging to any well-built man.

Their women are just as shapely and beautiful; very gracious, of attractive manner and pleasant appearance; their customs and behavior follow womanly custom as far as befits human nature; they go nude except for stag skin embroidered like the men's, and some wear rich lynx skins on their arms; their bare heads are decorated with various ornaments made of braids of their own hair which hang down over their breasts on either side. Some have other hair arrangements such as the women of Egypt and Syria wear, and these women are older and have been joined in wedlock. Both men and

---

* Lawrence C. Wroth, ed., *The Voyages of Giovanni da Verrazzano, 1524–1528*, trans. Susan Tarrow of the Cellere Codex (New Haven: Yale University Press, 1970), 133–43. Yale University Press.

women have various trinkets hanging from their ears as the Orientals do; and we saw that they had many sheets of worked copper which they prize more than gold. They do not value gold because of its color; they think it the most worthless of all, and rate blue and red above all other colors. The things we gave them that they prized the most were little bells, blue crystals, and other trinkets to put in the ear or around the neck. They did not appreciate cloth of silk and gold, nor even of any other kind, nor did they care to have them; the same was true for metals like steel and iron, for many times when we showed them some of our arms, they did not admire them, nor ask for them, but merely examined the workmanship. They did the same with mirrors; they would look at them quickly, and then refuse them, laughing.

They are very generous and give away all they have. We made great friends with them, and one day before we entered the harbor with the ship, when we were lying at anchor one league out to sea because of unfavorable weather, they came out to the ship with a great number of their boats; they had painted and decorated their faces with various colors, showing us that it was a sign of happiness. They brought us some of their food, and showed us by signs where we should anchor in the port for the ship's safety, and then accompanied us all the way until we dropped anchor.

We stayed there for 15 days, taking advantage of the place to refresh ourselves. . . .

We frequently went five to six leagues into the interior, and found it as pleasant as I can possibly describe, and suitable for every kind of cultivation-grain, wine, or oil. For there the fields extend for 25 to 30 leagues; they are open and free of any obstacles or trees, and so fertile that any kind of seed would produce excellent crops. Then we entered the forests, which could be penetrated even by a large army; the trees there are oaks, cypresses, and others unknown in our Europe. We found Lucullian apples, plums, and filberts, and many kinds of fruit different from ours. There is an enormous number of animals-stags, deer, lynx, and other species; these people, like the others, capture them with snares and bows, which are their principal weapons. Their arrows are worked with great beauty, and they tip them not with iron but with emery, jasper, hard marble, and other sharp stones. They use the same kind of stone instead of iron for cutting trees, and make their little boats with a single log of wood, hollowed out with admirable skill; there is ample room in them for fourteen to fifteen men; they operate a short oar, broad at the end, with only the strength of their arms, and they go to sea without any danger, and as swiftly as they please. When we went farther inland we saw their houses, which are circular in shape, about 14 to 15 paces across, made of bent saplings; they are arranged without any architectural pattern, and are covered with cleverly worked mats of straw which protect them from wind and rain. There is no doubt that if they had the skilled workmen that we have, they would erect great buildings, for the whole maritime coast is full of various blue rocks, crystals, and alabaster, and for such a purpose it has an abundance of ports and shelter for ships.

They move these houses from one place to another according to the richness of the site and the season. They need only carry the straw mats, and so they have new houses made in no time at all. In each house there lives a father with a very large family, for in some we saw 25 to 30 people. They live on the same food as the other people—pulse (which they produce with more systematic cultivation than the other tribes, and when sowing they observe the influence of the moon, the rising of the Pleiades, and many other customs derived from the ancients), and otherwise on game and fish. They live a long time, and rarely fall sick; if they are wounded, they cure themselves with fire without medicine; their end comes with old age. We consider them very compassionate and charitable toward their relatives, for they make great lamentations in times of adversity, recalling in their grief all their past happiness. At the end of their life, the relatives perform together the Sicilian lament, which is mingled with singing and lasts a long time. This is all that we could learn of them.

This country is situated on a parallel with Rome at $40^{2/3}$ degrees, but is somewhat colder, by chance and not by nature, as I shall explain to Your Majesty at another point; I will now describe the position of the aforementioned port. The coast of this land runs from west to east. The harbor mouth [Verrazzano footnote: which we called "refugio" because of its beauty] faces south, and is half a league wide; from its entrance it extends for 12 leagues in a northeasterly direction, and then widens out to form a large bay of about 20 leagues in circumference. In this bay there are five small islands, very fertile and beautiful, full of tall spreading trees, and any large fleet could ride safely among them without fear of tempest or other dangers. Then, going southward to the entrance of the harbor, there are very pleasant hills on either side, with many streams of clear water flowing from the high land into the sea. In the middle of this estuary there is a rock of "viva pietra" [a nonporous rock] formed by nature, which is suitable for building any kind of machine or bulwark for the defense of the harbor. [Verrazzano footnote: which we called "La Petra Viva," on account of both the nature of the stone and the family of a gentlewoman; on the right side of the harbor mouth there is a promontory which we call "Jovius promontory."]

Having supplied all our needs, we left this port on the sixth day of May and continued along the coast, never losing sight of land. [Likely along the southern coast of Cape Cod, first past Martha's Vineyard and then Nantucket] We sailed one hundred and fifty leagues [Verrazzano footnote: within this distance we found sandbanks which stretch from the continent fifty leagues out to sea. Over them the water was never less than three feet deep; thus there is great danger in sailing there. We crossed them with difficulty and called them "Armellini"] and found the land similar in nature, but somewhat higher, with several mountains which all showed signs of minerals. We did not land there because the weather was favorable and helped us in sailing along the coast: we think it resembles the other. The shore ran eastward. At a distance of fifty leagues, keeping more to the north, we found high country full of very dense forests, composed of pines, cypresses, and similar trees which grow in cold regions. [This is likely along the coast of southern Maine.]

The people were quite different from the others, for while the previous ones had been courteous in manner, these were full of crudity and vices, and were so barbarous that we could never make any communication with them, however many signs we made to them. They were clothed in skins of bear, lynx, sea-wolf and other animals. As far as we could judge from several visits to their houses, we think they live on game, fish, and several fruits which are a species of root which the earth produces itself. They have no pulse, and we saw no sign of cultivation, nor would the land be suitable for producing any fruit or grain on account of its sterility. If we wanted to trade with them for some of their things, they would come to the seashore on some rocks where the breakers were most violent, while we remained in the little boat, and they sent us what they wanted to give on a rope, continually shouting to us not to approach the land; they gave us the barter quickly, and would take in exchange only knives, hooks for fishing and sharp metal. We found no courtesy in them, and when we had nothing more to exchange and left them, the men made all the signs of scorn and shame that any brute creature would make [GV footnote: such as showing their buttocks and laughing]. Against their wishes, we penetrated two or three leagues inland with 25 armed men, and when we disembarked on the shore, they shot at us with their bows and uttered loud cries before fleeing into the woods. We did not find anything of great value in this land, except for the vast forests and some hills which could contain some metal: for we saw many natives with "paternostri" beads of copper in their ears.

. . .

Due to the lack of [a common] language, we were unable to find out by signs or gestures how much religious faith these people we found possess. We think they have neither religion nor laws, that they do not know of a First Cause or Author, that they do not worship the sky, the stars, the sun, the moon, or other planets, nor do they even practice any kind of idolatry; we do not know whether they offer any sacrifices or other prayers, nor are there any temples or churches of prayer among their peoples. We consider that they have no religion and that they live in absolute freedom, and that everything they do proceeds from Ignorance; for they are very easily persuaded, and they imitated everything that they saw us Christians do with regard to divine worship, with the same fervor and enthusiasm that we had.

. . .

My intention on this voyage was to reach Cathay and the extreme eastern coast of Asia, but I did not expect to find such an obstacle of new land as I have found; and if for some reason I did expect to find it, I estimated there would be some strait to get through to the Eastern Ocean. This was the opinion of all the ancients, who certainly believed that our Western Ocean was joined to the Eastern Ocean of India without any land in between. Aristotle supports this theory by arguments of various analogies, but this opinion is quite contrary to that of the moderns, and has been proven false by experience. Nevertheless, land has been found by modern man which was unknown to the ancients, another world with respect to the one they knew, which appears to be larger than our Europe, than Africa, and almost larger than Asia. . . .

In the ship *Dauphine* on the 8th day of July, 1524.

Humble servant Janus Verazanus

QUESTIONS TO CONSIDER

1. How might Verrazzano's descriptions of the Native Americans he met be biased or incorrect? Which of his observations seem trustworthy to you and why?
2. How does Verrazzano describe the landscape and geography of America to Francis?

2.3 MICHEL DE MONTAIGNE, EXCERPT FROM "ON CANNIBALS" (c. 1580)*

Michel de Montaigne (1533–1592) was a notable French Renaissance philosopher who was most famous for his personal essays. In this essay he describes some of the cultural mores and practices of the Tupi people of modern Brazil as he understands them. Montaigne pays particular attention to the practice of cannibalism among the Tupi, which he believes to be used as an act of revenge against wartime enemies. Throughout the essay Montaigne cautions against judging these practices too harshly, noting that "every one gives the title of barbarism to everything that is not in use in his own country," and describing tortuous punishments the Portuguese used on captured Tupi. Montaigne also highlights examples from classical Europe to argue that cannibalism is not so foreign as the reader might think. He points out that the philosophers Chrysippus and Zeno endorsed the practice in theory, and that Gauls besieged in the town of Alesia (Alexia) in modern-day France may have resorted to cannibalism.

. . .I long had a man in my house that lived ten or twelve years in the New World, discovered in these latter days, and in that part of it where Villegaignon landed,—[At Brazil, in 1557]. . . .

This man that I had was a plain ignorant fellow, and therefore the more likely to tell truth. . . . I shall therefore content myself with his information, without inquiring what the cosmographers say to the business. . . .

. . . I find that there is nothing barbarous and savage in this nation, by anything that I can gather, excepting, that every one gives the title of barbarism

* Michel de Montaigne, *Essays of Michel de Montaigne*, ed. William Carew Hazlitt, trans. Charles Cotton (1877), First Book, Chapter 30, available on Project Gutenberg.

to everything that is not in use in his own country. As, indeed, we have no other level of truth and reason than the example and idea of the opinions and customs of the place wherein we live: there is always the perfect religion, there the perfect government, there the most exact and accomplished usage of all things. They are savages at the same rate that we say fruits are wild, which nature produces of herself and by her own ordinary progress; whereas, in truth, we ought rather to call those wild whose natures we have changed by our artifice and diverted from the common order. . .

. . . These nations then seem to me to be so far barbarous, as having received but very little form and fashion from art and human invention, and consequently to be not much remote from their original simplicity. The laws of nature, however, govern them still, not as yet much vitiated with any mixture of ours. . . .

As to the rest, they live in a country very pleasant and temperate, so that, as my witnesses inform me, 'tis rare to hear of a sick person, and they moreover assure me, that they never saw any of the natives, either paralytic, bleareyed, toothless, or crooked with age. The situation of their country is along the sea-shore, enclosed on the other side towards the land, with great and high mountains, having about a hundred leagues in breadth between. They have great store of fish and flesh, that have no resemblance to those of ours: which they eat without any other cookery, than plain boiling, roasting, and broiling. The first that rode a horse thither, though in several other voyages he had contracted an acquaintance and familiarity with them, put them into so terrible a fright, with his centaur appearance, that they killed him with their arrows before they could come to discover who he was. Their buildings are very long, and of capacity to hold two or three hundred people, made of the barks of tall trees, reared with one end upon the ground, and leaning to and supporting one another at the top, like some of our barns, of which the covering hangs down to the very ground, and serves for the side walls. They have wood so hard, that they cut with it, and make their swords of it, and their grills of it to broil their meat. Their beds are of cotton, hung swinging from the roof, like our

seamen's hammocks, every man his own, for the wives lie apart from their husbands. They rise with the sun, and so soon as they are up, eat for all day, for they have no more meals but that; they do not then drink, as Suidas reports of some other people of the East that never drank at their meals; but drink very often all day after, and sometimes to a rousing pitch. Their drink is made of a certain root, and is of the colour of our claret, and they never drink it but lukewarm. It will not keep above two or three days; it has a somewhat sharp, brisk taste, is nothing heady, but very comfortable to the stomach; laxative to strangers, but a very pleasant beverage to such as are accustomed to it. They make use, instead of bread, of a certain white compound, like coriander seeds; I have tasted of it; the taste is sweet and a little flat. The whole day is spent in dancing. Their young men go a-hunting after wild beasts with bows and arrows; one part of their women are employed in preparing their drink the while, which is their chief employment. One of their old men, in the morning before they fall to eating, preaches to the whole family, walking from the one end of the house to the other, and several times repeating the same sentence, till he has finished the round, for their houses are at least a hundred yards long. Valour towards their enemies and love towards their wives, are the two heads of his discourse, never failing in the close, to put them in mind, that 'tis their wives who provide them their drink warm and well seasoned. The fashion of their beds, ropes, swords, and of the wooden bracelets they tie about their wrists, when they go to fight, and of the great canes, bored hollow at one end, by the sound of which they keep the cadence of their dances, are to be seen in several places, and amongst others, at my house. They shave all over, and much more neatly than we, without other razor than one of wood or stone. They believe in the immortality of the soul, and that those who have merited well of the gods are lodged in that part of heaven where the sun rises, and the accursed in the west.

They have I know not what kind of priests and prophets, who very rarely present themselves to the people, having their abode in the mountains. At their arrival, there is a great feast, and solemn assembly of many villages: each house, as I have described, makes a village, and they are about a French league distant from one another. This prophet declaims to them in public, exhorting them to virtue and their duty: but all their ethics are comprised in these two articles, resolution in war, and affection to their wives. He also prophesies to them events to come, and the issues they are to expect from their enterprises, and prompts them to or diverts them from war: but let him look to't; for if he fail in his divination, and anything happen otherwise than he has foretold, he is cut into a thousand pieces, if he be caught, and condemned for a false prophet: for that reason, if any of them has been mistaken, he is no more heard of. . . .

They have continual war with the nations that live further within the mainland, beyond their mountains, to which they go naked, and without other arms than their bows and wooden swords, fashioned at one end like the head of our javelins. The obstinacy of their battles is wonderful, and they never end without great effusion of blood: for as to running away, they know not what it is. Every one for a trophy brings home the head of an enemy he has killed, which he fixes over the door of his house. After having a long time treated their prisoners very well, and given them all the regales they can think of, he to whom the prisoner belongs, invites a great assembly of his friends. They being come, he ties a rope to one of the arms of the prisoner, of which, at a distance, out of his reach, he holds the one end himself, and gives to the friend he loves best the other arm to hold after the same manner; which being done, they two, in the presence of all the assembly, despatch him with their swords. After that, they roast him, eat him amongst them, and send some chops to their absent friends. They do not do this, as some think, for nourishment, as the Scythians anciently did, but as a representation of an extreme revenge; as will appear by this: that having observed the Portuguese, who were in league with their enemies, to inflict another sort of death upon any of them they took prisoners, which was to set them up to the girdle in the earth, to shoot at the remaining part till it was stuck full of arrows, and then to hang them, they thought those people of the other world (as being men who had sown the knowledge of a great many vices amongst their neighbours, and who were much greater masters in all sorts of mischief than they) did not exercise this sort of revenge without a meaning, and that it must needs be more painful than theirs, they began to leave their old way, and to follow this. I am not sorry that we should here take notice of the barbarous horror of so cruel an action, but that, seeing so clearly into their faults, we should be so blind to our own. I conceive there is more barbarity in eating a man alive, than when he is dead; in tearing a body limb from limb by racks and torments, that is yet in perfect sense; in roasting it by degrees; in causing it to be bitten and worried by dogs and swine (as we have not only read, but lately seen, not amongst inveterate and mortal enemies, but among neighbours and fellow-citizens, and, which is worse, under colour of piety and religion), than to roast and eat him after he is dead.

Chrysippus and Zeno, the two heads of the Stoic sect, were of opinion that there was no hurt in making use of our dead carcasses, in what way soever for our necessity, and in feeding upon them too;—[Diogenes Laertius, vii. 188.]—as our own ancestors, who being besieged by Caesar in the city Alexia, resolved to sustain the famine of the siege with the bodies of their old men, women, and other persons who were incapable of bearing arms. . . .

QUESTIONS TO CONSIDER

1. Do you think Montaigne's description of Tupi culture and behavior is accurate? Why or why not?

2. Why does Montaigne draw parallels between Tupi and European behavior of violence and cannibalism?

2.4 TOMÁS DE MERCADO, A CRITIQUE OF THE SLAVE TRADE (1587)*

Tomás de Mercado (1525–1575) was a Spanish Dominican friar primarily known as an economist. In this passage, he criticizes the trade in enslaved Africans as it was practiced by the Spanish and Portuguese in the sixteenth century. Common pretexts for slavery at this time were either that the enslaved person was a captured prisoner of war, or that they were the child of an impoverished parent forced to sell their children into servitude. Mercado notes that in reality the high prices that slave traders pay for captives encourage Africans to start wars purely for the purpose of selling captured people, and that parents are induced to sell disobedient children for profit. He notes also that the slave traders employ many tricks of their own, such as enticing Africans on board their ships to kidnap and enslave them. Mercado argues that the slave trade encourages violence and deceit and bears no resemblance in reality to the common justifications for its existence.

It is public opinion and knowledge that no end of deception is practiced and a thousand acts of robbery and violence are committed in the course of bartering and carrying off Negroes from their country and bringing them to the Indies and to Spain. . . . Since the Portuguese and Spaniards pay so much for a Negro, they go out to hunt one another without the pretext of a war, as if they were deer; even the very Ethiopians, who are different, being induced to do so by the profit derived. They make war on one another, their gain being the capture of their own people, and they go after one another in the forests where they usually hunt. . . . In this way, and contrary to all justice, a very great number of prisoners are taken. And no one is horrified that these people are ill-treating and selling one another, because they are considered uncivilized and savage. In addition to the pretext, of parents selling their children as a last resort, there is the bestial practice of selling them without any necessity to do so, and very often through anger or passion, for some displeasure or disrespect they have shown them. . . . The wretched children are taken to the market place for sale, and as the traffic in Negroes is so great, there are Portuguese, or even Negroes themselves, ready everywhere to buy them. There are also among them traders in this bestial and brutal business, who set boundaries in the interior for the natives and carry them off for sale at a higher price on the coasts or in the islands. I have seen many acquired in this way. Apart from these acts of injustice and robberies committed among themselves, there are thousands of other forms of deception practiced in those parts by the Spaniards to trick and carry off the Negroes finally as newly imported slaves, which they are in fact, to the ports, with a few bonnets, gewgaws, beads and bits of paper under which they give them. They put them aboard the ships under false pretenses, hoist anchor, set sail, and make off towards the high seas with their booty. . . . I know a man who recently sailed to one of those Islands and, with less than four thousand ducats for ransom, carried off four hundred Negroes without license or registration. . . . They embark four and five hundred of them in a boat which, sometimes, is not a cargo boat. The very stench is enough to kill most of them, and, indeed, very many die. The wonder is that twenty percent of them are not lost.

---

* David Brion Davis and Steven Mintz, *The Boisterous Sea of Liberty: A Documentary History of America from Discovery Through the Civil War* (New York: Oxford University Press, 1998), 40–41.

QUESTIONS TO CONSIDER

1. How does Mercado describe the Europeans involved in the slave trade?
2. According to Mercado, how have European slave traders changed the African societies they made contact with?

2.5 VISUAL SOURCE: LÁZARO LUÍS, PORTUGUESE MAP OF WEST AFRICA (1563)*

This map was part of an atlas compiled by the Portuguese cartographer Lázaro Luís and published in 1563. The map reflects a quite accurate understanding of world geography, including of the African coastline that Iberian explorers and merchants had charted over the previous century. Each map was also illustrated with plants, animals, people, and coats of arms associated with different parts of the world. Luís illustrated the interior of Africa with the image of a Berber caravan in the north, while West Africa is dominated by Feitoria da Mina or Elmina Castle, a Portuguese trading post on the Gulf of Guinea. Although the Portuguese had reached the southern extent of Africa as early as 1487, the Luís map only depicts the coastline as far as the equator and archipelagos surrounding São Tomé and Príncipe.

* Wikipedia/Photo taken by Alvesgaspar

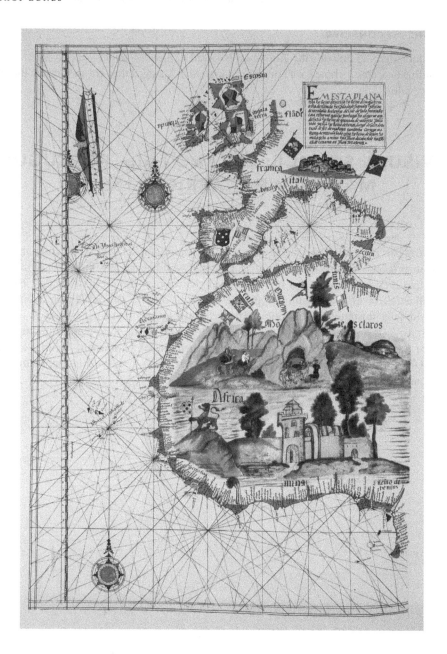

QUESTIONS TO CONSIDER

1. What do Luís's illustrations of the African continent tell us about what sixteenth-century Portuguese associated with Africa?
2. What elements of geography does this map leave out? What does this say about how it was intended to be used?

2.6 VISUAL SOURCE: AZTEC DRAWING OF SMALLPOX VICTIMS (1500s)*

Smallpox was an incredibly infectious disease that arrived in Mexico along with the soldiers of Hernán Cortés in 1519. Although smallpox could be potentially deadly to anyone, Indigenous Americans were particularly vulnerable to it because they had never been exposed to the virus before. As a result, a smallpox epidemic broke out throughout Mexico soon after the arrival of Cortés, spreading quickly among the cities of the Aztec Empire and its neighbors. Although an accurate death toll is impossible to calculate, it is likely that hundreds of thousands of Mexica died in this epidemic.

This image is from the Florentine Codex, a remarkable book illustrated by Mexica artists working with the Spanish friar Bernardino de Sahagún that depicts the history and culture of Mexico in the latter sixteenth century. The illustration depicts victims of smallpox, who bear the distinctive rash that often accompanied the disease.

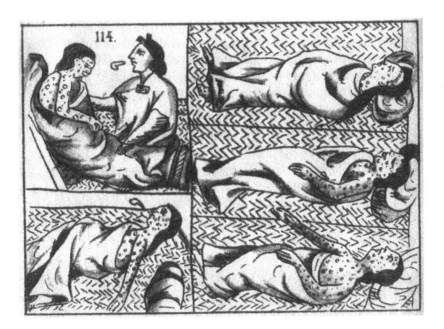

QUESTIONS TO CONSIDER

1. How does the artist convey illness visually? What about the portrayal of the people in this image tells the viewer that they are sick?
2. What does this image tell us about the Mexica understanding of smallpox?

CHAPTER 3

SETTLER COLONIES AND IMPERIAL RIVALRIES, 1565–1681

3.1 RICHARD FRETHORNE, EXPERIENCES OF AN INDENTURED SERVANT IN VIRGINIA (1623)*

Richard Frethorne, an indentured servant in Virginia, sent this letter describing his experiences in the colony to his parents in England. Indentured servants agreed to work as a servant in the American colonies for a certain number of years (usually four to seven) in exchange for their passage to America. When they finished their terms of service, they were entitled to receive certain benefits, usually a set of clothes, tools, and land to farm for their own profit. However, due to the prevalence of illness, violence, and poor nutrition, many indentured servants never lived long enough to claim their reward.

Frethorne, who worked at a plantation near modern-day Williamsburg, Virginia, relates common experiences of hardship and privation that early English colonists experienced. Indentured servants and other colonists found that many of the comforts they were used to in England, including their lodging and diet, were absent in the colony. Colonists also feared attacks from local Native people whom the English frequently angered with violence and demands for foodstuffs.

LOVING AND KIND FATHER AND MOTHER:
My most humble duty remembered to you, hoping in god of your good health, as I myself am at the making hereof. This is to let you understand that I your child am in a most heavy case by reason of the country, [which] is such that it causeth much sickness, [such] as the scurvy and the bloody flux and diverse other diseases, which maketh the body very poor and weak.

And when we are sick there is nothing to comfort us; for since I came out of the ship I never ate anything but peas, and loblollie (that is, water gruel). As for deer or venison I never saw any since I came into this land. There is indeed some fowl, but we are not allowed to go and get it, but must work hard both early and late for a mess of water gruel and a mouthful of bread and beef. A mouthful of bread for a penny loaf must

---

* Richard Frethorne, letter to his father and mother, March 20, April 2 & 3, 1623, in Susan Kingsbury, ed., *The Records of the Virginia Company of London* (Washington, DC: Government Printing Office, 1935), 4:58–62.
Library of Congress, Manuscript Division.

serve for four men which is most pitiful. [You would be grieved] if you did know as much as I [do], when people cry out day and night—Oh! That they were in England without their limbs—and would not care to lose any limb to be in England again, yea, though they beg from door to door. For we live in fear of the enemy every hour, yet we have had a combat with them . . . and we took two alive and made slaves of them. But it was by policy, for we are in great danger; for our plantation is very weak by reason of the death and sickness of our company. For we came but twenty for the merchants, and they are half dead just; and we look every hour when two more should go. Yet there came some four other men yet to live with us, of which there is but one alive; and our Lieutenant is dead, and [also] his father and his brother. And there was some five or six of the last year's twenty, of which there is but three left, so that we are fain to get other men to plant with us; and yet we are but 32 to fight against 3000 if they should come. And the nighest help that we have is ten mile of us, and when the rogues overcame this place [the] last [time] they slew 80 persons. How then shall we do, for we lie even in their teeth? They may easily take us, but [for the fact] that God is merciful and can save with few as well as with many, as he showed to Gilead. And like Gilead's soldiers, if they lapped water, we drink water which is but weak.

And I have nothing to comfort me, nor is there nothing to be gotten here but sickness and death, except [in the event] that one had money to lay out in some things for profit. But I have nothing at all–no, not a shirt to my back but two rags (2), nor clothes but one poor suit, nor but one pair of shoes, but one pair of stockings, but one cap, [and] but two bands [collars]. My cloak is stolen by one of my fellows, and to his dying hour [he] would not tell me what he did with it; but some of my fellows saw him have butter and beef out of a ship, which my cloak, I doubt [not], paid for. So that I have not a penny, nor a penny worth, to help me too either spice or sugar or strong waters, without the which one cannot live here. For as strong beer in England doth fatten and strengthen them, so water here doth wash and weaken these here [and] only keeps [their] life and soul together. But I am not half [of] a quarter so strong as I was in England, and all is for want of victuals; for I do protest unto you

that I have eaten more in [one] day at home than I have allowed me here for a week. You have given more than my day's allowance to a beggar at the door; and if Mr. Jackson had not relieved me, I should be in a poor case. But he like a father and she like a loving mother doth still help me.

For when we go to Jamestown (that is 10 miles of us) there lie all the ships that come to land, and there they must deliver their goods. And when we went up to town [we would go], as it may be, on Monday at noon, and come there by night, [and] then load the next day by noon, and go home in the afternoon, and unload, and then away again in the night, and [we would] be up about midnight. Then if it rained or blowed never so hard, we must lie in the boat on the water and have nothing but a little bread. For when we go into the boat we [would] have a loaf allowed to two men, and it is all [we would get] if we stayed there two days, which is hard; and [we] must lie all that while in the boat. But that Goodman Jackson pitied me and made me a cabin to lie in always when I [would] come up, and he would give me some poor jacks [fish] [to take] home with me, which comforted me more than peas or water gruel. Oh, they be very godly folks, and love me very well, and will do anything for me. And he much marvelled that you would send me a servant to the Company; he saith I had been better knocked on the head. And indeed so I find it now, to my great grief and misery; and [I] saith that if you love me you will redeem me suddenly, for which I do entreat and beg. And if you cannot get the merchants to redeem me for some little money, then for God's sake get a gathering or entreat some good folks to lay out some little sum of money in meal and cheese and butter and beef. Any eating meat will yield great profit. Oil and vinegar is very good; but, father, there is great loss in leaking. But for God's sake send beef and cheese and butter, or the more of one sort and none of another. But if you send cheese, it must be very old cheese; and at the cheesemonger's you may buy very food cheese for twopence farthing or halfpenny, that will be liked very well. But if you send cheese, you must have a care how you pack it in barrels; and you must put cooper's chips between every cheese, or else the heat of the hold will rot them. And look whatsoever you send me—be it never so much—look, what[ever] I make of it, I will deal truly with you. I will send it over and beg the profit to redeem me; and if I die before it come, I have entreated Goodman Jackson to send you the worth of it, who hath promised he will. If you send, you must direct your letters to Goodman Jackson, at Jamestown, a gunsmith. (You must set down his freight, because there be more of his name there.) Good father, do not forget me, but have mercy and pity my miserable case. I know if you did but see me, you would weep to see me; for I have but one suit. (But [though] it is a strange one, it is very well guarded.) Wherefore, for God's sake,

pity me. I pray you to remember my love to all my friends and kindred. I hope all my brothers and sisters are in good health, and as for my part I have set down my resolution that certainly will be; that is, that the answer of this letter will be life or death to me. Therefore, good father, send as soon as you can; and if you send me any thing let this be the mark.

ROT
RICHARD FRETHORNE,
MARTIN'S HUNDRED.

QUESTIONS TO CONSIDER

1. What complaints does Frethorne make about his life in Virginia? How do his experiences there compare with his life in England?
2. Why were the dietary options of Virginians so limited at this time? What decisions and choices might have caused this?

3.2 JOHN WINTHROP, "THE WICKED CAPITALISM OF ROBERT KEAYNE" (1639)*

In his journal, John Winthrop (1588–1649), a key founder and then governor of the Massachusetts Bay colony, commented on the prosecution of Robert Keayne (1595–1656) for corrupt business practices. Keayne was a London merchant who had emigrated with other Puritans to Massachusetts, where he had established a profitable commercial enterprise. His business practices ran him afoul of the expectations of Winthrop and other colonial leaders, however, as they deemed Keayne's methods unchristian and indicative of a "covetous [greedy] and corrupt heart." Keayne was found guilty of overcharging his fellow Puritans by raising his prices because of increased demand, to cover losses in other parts of his business, or to make up for the high prices he had paid for goods in the first place. While Keayne protested his conviction both in life and in his will, he was fined two hundred pounds in 1637, a considerable sum. His experience highlights how Puritan leaders viewed Massachusetts as a noble experiment in godly living and what they expected of fellow Puritans.

---

* John Winthrop, *The History of New England from 1630 to 1649*, 2 vols. (Boston, 1853), 1:377–82.

Mo. 9 [Sept. 1639]

At a general court holden at Boston, great complaint was made of the oppression used in the country in sale of foreign commodities; and Mr. Robert Keaine, who kept a shop in Boston, was notoriously above others observed and complained of, and, being convented, he was charged with many particulars; in some, for taking above six-pence in the shilling profit; in some above eight-pence; and, in some small things, above two for one; and being hereof convict, (as appears by the records,) he was fined £200, which came thus to pass: The deputies considered, apart, of his fine, and set it at £200; the magistrates agreed but to £100. So, the court being divided, at length it was agreed, that his fine should be £200, but he should pay but £100, and the other should be respited to the further consideration of the next general court. By this means the magistrates and deputies were, brought to an accord, which otherwise had not been likely, and so much trouble might have grown, and the offender escaped censure. For the cry of the country was so great against oppression, and some of the elders and magistrates had declared such detestation of the corrupt practice of this man (which was the more observable, because he was wealthy and sold dearer than most other tradesmen, and for that he was of ill report for the like covetous practice in England, that incensed the deputies very much against him). And sure the course was very evil, especial circumstances considered: 1. He being an ancient professor of the gospel: 2. A man of eminent parts: 3. Wealthy, and having but one child: 4. Having come over for conscience' sake, and for the advancement of the gospel here: 5. Having been formerly dealt with and admonished, both by private friends and also by some of the magistrates and elders, and having promised reformation; being a member of a church and commonwealth now in their infancy, and under the curious observation of all churches and civil states in the world. These added much aggravation to his sin in the judgment of all men of understanding. Yet most of the magistrates (though they discerned of the offence clothed with all these circumstances) would have been more moderate in their censure: 1. Because there was no law in force to limit or direct men in point of profit in their trade. 2. Because it is the common practice, in all countries, for men to make use of advantages for raising the prices of their commodities. 3. Because (though he were chiefly aimed at, yet) he was not alone in this fault. 4. Because all men through the country, in sale of cattle, corn, labor, etc., were guilty of the like excess in prices. 5. Because a certain rule could not be found out for an equal rate between buyer and seller, though much labor had been bestowed in it, and divers laws had been made, which, upon experience, were repealed, as being neither safe nor equal. Lastly, and especially, because the law of God appoints no other punishment but double restitution; and, in some cases, as where the offender freely confesseth, and brings his offering, only half added to the principal. After the court had censured him, the church of Boston called him also in question, where (as before he had done in the court) he did, with tears, acknowledge and bewail his covetous and corrupt heart, yet making some excuse for many of the particulars, which were charged upon him, as partly by pretence of ignorance of the true price of some wares, and chiefly by being misled by some false principles, as 1. That, if a man lost in one commodity, he might help himself in the price of another. 2. That if, through want of skill or other occasion, his commodity cost him more than the price of the market in England, he might then sell it for more than the price of the market in New England, etc. These things gave occasion to Mr. Cotton, in his public exercise the next lecture day, to lay open the error of such false principles, and to give some rules of direction in the case.

Some false principles were these:—

1. That a man might sell as dear as he can, and buy as cheap as he can.
2. If a man lose by casualty of sea, etc., in some of his commodities, he may raise the price of the rest.
3. That he may sell as he bought, though he paid too dear, etc., and though the commodity be fallen, etc.
4. That, as a man may take the advantage of his own skill or ability, so he may of another's ignorance or necessity.
5. Where one gives time for payment, he is to take like recompense of one as of another.

The rules for trading were these:—

1. A man may not sell above the current price, i.e., such a price as is usual in the time and place, and as another (who knows the worth of the commodity) would give for it, if he had occasion to use it: as that is called current money, which every man will take, etc.

2. When a man loseth in his commodity for want of skill, etc., he must look at it as his own fault or cross, and therefore must not lay it upon another.

3. Where a man loseth by casualty of sea, or, etc., it is a loss cast upon himself by providence, and he may not ease himself of it by casting it upon another; for so a man should seem to provide against all providences, etc., that he should never lose; but where there is a scarcity of the commodity, there men may raise their price; for now it is a hand of God upon the commodity, and not the person.

4. A man may not ask any more for his commodity than his selling price, as Ephron to Abraham, the land is worth thus much.

QUESTIONS TO CONSIDER

1. How would modern Americans view Keayne's behavior? Would they judge him more or less harshly than Winthrop?

2. What does Winthrop's account of this case tell us about how he expected Puritans in Massachusetts to behave?

3.3 THE FLUSHING REMONSTRANCE (1657)*

The Flushing Remonstrance was a demand for religious toleration in the colony of New Netherland and is commonly regarded as one of the first articulations of the principle of religious liberty in what would become the United States. The town of Vlishing (modern-day Flushing in Queens, New York City), was founded by English settlers in 1645. The Dutch authorities initially granted the town religious tolerance in keeping with common Dutch practice, but a decade later the director-general of New Netherland reversed course, banning religious meetings except those of the Dutch reformed church. Meetings of the Society of Friends, commonly known as Quakers, were deemed particularly dangerous because of their anti-hierarchical principles.

After a Flushing resident was fined and banished in 1657 for holding a Quaker meeting, thirty town residents addressed this letter to the director-general, demanding that he respect freedom of religion in the colony and refusing to engage in any prosecution of Quakers.

---

* New York State Archives. New Netherland. Council. Dutch colonial council minutes, 1638–1665, ser. A1809, vol. 8, https://www.thirteen.org/dutchny/interactives/document-the-flushing-remonstrance.

Right Honorable

You have been pleased to send unto us a certain prohibition or command that we should not receive or entertain any of those people called Quakers because they are supposed to be, by some, seducers of the people. For our part we cannot condemn them in this case, neither can we stretch out our hands against them, for out of Christ God is a consuming fire, and it is a fearful thing to fall into the hands of the living God.

Wee desire therefore in this case not to judge least we be judged, neither to condemn least we be condemned, but rather let every man stand or fall to his own Master. Wee are bounde by the law to do good unto all men, especially to those of the household of faith. And though for the present we seem to be unsensible for the law and the Law giver, yet when death and the Law assault us, if wee have our advocate to seeke, who shall plead for us in this case of conscience betwixt God and our own souls; the powers of this world can neither attach us, neither excuse us, for if God justifye who can condemn and if God condemn there is none can justifye.

And for those jealousies and suspicions which some have of them, that they are destructive unto Magistracy and Ministerye, that cannot bee, for the Magistrate hath his sword in his hand and the Minister hath the sword in his hand, as witnesse those two great examples, which all Magistrates and Ministers are to follow, Moses and Christ, whom God raised up maintained and defended against all enemies both of flesh and spirit; and therefore that of God will stand, and that which is of man will come to nothing. And as the Lord hath taught Moses or the civil power to give an outward liberty in the state, by the law written in his heart designed for the good of all, and can truly judge who is good, who is evil, who is true and who is false, and can pass definitive sentence of life or death against that man which arises up against the fundamental law of the States General; soe he hath made his ministers a savor of life unto life and a savor of death unto death.

The law of love, peace and liberty in the states extending to Jews, Turks and Egyptians, as they are considered sons of Adam, which is the glory of the outward state of Holland, soe love, peace and liberty, extending to all in Christ Jesus, condemns hatred, war and bondage. And because our Saviour sayeth it is impossible but that offences will come, but woe unto him by whom they cometh, our desire is not to offend one of his little ones, in whatsoever form, name or title hee appears in, whether Presbyterian, Independent, Baptist or Quaker, but shall be glad to see anything of God in any of them, desiring to doe unto all men as we desire all men should doe unto us, which is the true law both of Church and State; for our Saviour sayeth this is the law and the prophets.

Therefore if any of these said persons come in love unto us, we cannot in conscience lay violent hands upon them, but give them free egresse and regresse unto our Town, and houses, as God shall persuade our consciences, for we are bounde by the law of God and man to doe good unto all men and evil to noe man. And this is according to the patent and charter of our Towne, given unto us in the name of the States General, which we are not willing to infringe, and violate, but shall houlde to our patent and shall remaine, your humble subjects, the inhabitants of Vlishing.

Written this 27th of December in the year 1657,
by mee.
Edward Hart, Clericus

QUESTIONS TO CONSIDER

1. How do the Flushing residents justify their objections to the director-general?
2. What role does these Flushing residents' Christian faith play in their objections?

3.4 CHRESTIEN LE CLERCQ, A MI'KMAQ RESPONSE TO EUROPEAN CRITICISM (1676)*

Chrestien Le Clercq (1641–c. 1700) was a French friar who spent much of his life as a mission-ary, scholar, and translator in New France. Working in the St. Lawrence River valley, Le Clercq made extensive study of local Indigenous languages and developed a form of writing based on the Mi'kmaq language.

Le Clercq had extensive opportunities to converse with Mi'kmaq and other Native peoples in their own language while pursuing his work as a missionary. He drew from these experiences to write a longer description of the Indigenous peoples of St. Lawrence, in which he also relates many of their responses to French assertions of cultural superiority. As this statement by a Mi'kmaq leader that Le Clercq recorded indicates, Mi'kmaq and other Native peoples often asserted that they had little need for French practices. Since New France had been established for decades, they had witnessed the French mode of living first-hand and, according to Le Clercq, were decidedly unimpressed.

I am greatly astonished that the French have so little cleverness, as they seem to exhibit in the matter of which thou hast just told me on their behalf, in the effort to persuade us to convert our poles, our barks, and our wigwams into those houses of stone and of wood which are tall and lofty, according to their account, as these trees. Very well! But why now, do men of five to six feet in height need houses which are sixty to eighty? For, in fact, as thou knowest very well thyself, Patriarch—do we not find in our own all the conveniences and the advantages that you have with yours, such as reposing, drinking, sleeping, eating, and amusing ourselves with our friends when we wish? This is not all, my brother, hast thou as much ingenuity and cleverness as the Indians, who carry their houses and their wigwams with them so that they may lodge wheresoever they please, independently of any seignior whatsoever? Thou art not as bold nor as stout as we, because when thou goest on a voyage thou canst not carry upon thy shoulders thy buildings and thy edifices. Therefore it is necessary that thou prepares as many lodgings as thou makest changes of residence, or else thou lodgest in a hired house which does not belong to thee. As for us, we find ourselves secure from all these inconveniences, and we can always say, more truly than thou, that we are at home everywhere, because we set up our wigwams with ease wheresoever we go, and with-out asking permission of anybody. Thou reproachest us, very inappropriately, that our country is a little hell in contrast with France, which thou comparest to a terres-trial paradise, inasmuch as it yields thee, so thou safest, every kind of provision in abundance. Thou sayest of us also that we are the most miserable and most unhappy of all men, living without religion, without manners, without honour, without social order, and, in a word, without any rules, like the beasts in our woods and our forests, lacking bread, wine, and a thousand other com-forts which thou hast in superfluity in Europe. Well, my brother, if thou dost not yet know the real feelings which our Indians have towards thy country and towards all thy nation, it is proper that I inform thee at once. I beg thee now to believe that, all miserable as we seem in thine eyes, we consider ourselves nevertheless much happier than thou in this, that we are very content with the little that we have; and believe also once for all, I pray, that thou deceivest thyself greatly if thou thinkest to persuade us that thy country is better than ours. For if France, as thou sayest, is a little terrestrial paradise, art thou sen-sible to leave it? And why abandon wives, children,

---

* Chrestien Le Clercq, *New Relations of Gaspesia with the Customs and Religion of the Gaspesian Indians (1691)*, translated and edited by William F. Ganong (Toronto, 1910), 103–6.

relatives, and friends? Why risk thy life and thy property every year, and why venture thyself with such risk, in any season whatsoever, to the storms and tempests of the sea in order to come to a strange and barbarous country which thou considerest the poorest and least fortunate of the world? Besides, since we are wholly convinced of the contrary, we scarcely take the trouble to go to France, because we fear, with good reason, lest we find little satisfaction there, seeing, in our own experience, that those who are natives thereof leave it every year in order to enrich themselves on our shores. We believe, further, that you are also incomparably poorer than we, and that you are only simple journeymen, valets, servants, and slaves, all masters and grand captains though you may appear, seeing that you glory in our old rags and in our miserable suits of beaver which can no longer be of use to us, and that you find among us, in the fishery for cod which you make in these parts, the wherewithal to comfort your misery and the poverty which oppresses you. As to us, we find all our riches and all our conveniences among ourselves, without trouble and without exposing our lives to the dangers in which you find yourselves constantly through your long voyages. And, whilst feeling compassion for you in the sweetness of our repose, we wonder at the anxieties and cares which you give yourselves night and day in order to load your ship. We see also that all your people live, as a rule, only upon cod which you catch among us. It is everlastingly nothing but cod—cod in the morning, cod at midday, cod at evening, and always cod, until things come to such a pass that if you wish some good morsels, it is at our expense; and you are obliged to have recourse to the Indians, whom you despise so much, and to beg them to go a-hunting that you may be regaled. Now tell me this one little thing, if thou hast any sense: Which of these two is the wisest and happiest— he who labours without ceasing and only obtains, and that with great trouble, enough to live on, or he who rests in comfort and finds all that he needs in the pleasure of hunting and fishing? It is true, that we have not always had the use of bread and of wine which your France produces; but, in fact, before the arrival of the French in these parts, did not the Gaspesians live much longer than now? And if we have not any longer among us any of those old men of a hundred and thirty to forty years, it is only because we are gradually adopting your manner of living, for experience is making it very plain that those of us live longest who, despising your bread, your wine, and your brandy, are content with their natural food of beaver, of moose, of waterfowl, and fish, in accord with the custom of our ancestors and of all the Gaspesian nation. Learn now, my brother, once for all, because I must open to thee my heart: there is no Indian who does not consider himself infinitely more happy and more powerful than the French.

QUESTIONS TO CONSIDER

1. According to Le Clercq, what French claims did the Mi'kmaq express skepticism about?
2. What justifications did the Mi'kmaq Le Clercq met offer for why their ways of living were better than those of the French? Do you find these arguments convincing?

3.5 VISUAL SOURCE: JOHN WHITE, *INDIAN IN BODY PAINT* (c. 1585–1586) AND *PICTISH WARRIOR* (c. 1585–1593)*

John White (d. 1593) was an English colonist, cartographer, and artist who composed notable watercolor illustrations of Native Americans from Virginia and the Carolinas. His dozens of depictions of Algonquin society are an unusually comprehensive record of sixteenth-century English

* Both images: © The Trustees of the British Museum

impressions of Native American life. His other illustrations included this fanciful depiction of a Pictish warrior—the Picts were one of several peoples who inhabited Scotland during antiquity.

White's similar depictions of ancient British tribesmen and modern Algonquin peoples reflected early modern English conceptions of civilization and savagery. It was imagined that although the Picts had been a barbaric people, Britain had, under the influence of the Roman Empire, become a civilized place and the Picts had abandoned their savage behavior. Proponents of British colonization imagined that they might have a similar effect in America, where the Algonquin peoples were already more advanced than the Picts had been, as their use of clothing and other markers of civilization indicated.

QUESTIONS TO CONSIDER

1. Compare and contrast the illustrations of the Pictish and the Algonquin men. In what ways is the Algonquin man depicted as being more civilized?
2. Why might a British colonist like White want to paint an image depicting Britons as a formerly barbaric people?

3.6 VISUAL SOURCE: ENSLAVED BLACK PEOPLE WORKING IN A SUGAR MILL IN HISPANIOLA (1590)*

This illustration of enslaved people working at a sugar mill in a Caribbean colony was one of many by engraver Theodor De Bry (1528–1598) illustrating life in the Americas. It depicts a mill on the island Hispaniola—now shared by Haiti and the Dominican Republic—and shows enslaved Africans at work at all stages of the sugar production process, harvesting and grinding the cane and then boiling the sugar in a large vat.

Colonial sugar plantations in the Americas were both incredibly lucrative and incredibly deadly. The refined sugar that these mills produced could be sold for a high price throughout Europe and the Old World, generating significant wealth for colonial empires. But the sugar production process involved immense labor with many opportunities for maiming and injury. Any misstep with the machetes used for harvesting, the mill wheel that pressed the cane, or the boiling vats of sugar could leave a worker slashed, crushed, or scalded. Many laborers lasted only a few years on a sugar plantation before they died and were replaced by imported enslaved people.

---

* Courtesy of the Library of Congress

QUESTIONS TO CONSIDER

1. How do the enslaved people appear in this illustration? What aspects of enslavement are not pictured here?
2. How does this portrayal of enslaved labor compare with other images you have seen? What is different or the same about the work these enslaved people are doing?

CHAPTER 4

COLONIAL CONVULSIONS AND REBELLIONS, 1640–1700

4.1 JOHN EASTON, METACOM RELATES NATIVE COMPLAINTS ABOUT THE ENGLISH SETTLERS (1675)*

Metacom (1638–1676), sometimes known by his English name King Philip, was a chief of the Wampanoag people of what is today New England. In 1675 he led a confederation of Indigenous peoples of New England in what is known as King Philip's War, an extraordinarily violent conflict between Native peoples and English colonists. Weeks before the war broke out, John Easton (1624–1705), the attorney general of Rhode Island, met with Metacom and recorded the grievances he claimed against the colonists.

Metacom explained that his people found it impossible to live in comfort with the English as neighbors. He stressed the unequal treatment of Native people by English law, English attempts to seize further Native land, and the damage English livestock did to Native crops. Written by Easton close to the outbreak of fighting, the document offers valuable insight into Metacom's reasons for pursuing war against the English.

. . . In the winter in the year 1674 an Indian was found dead, and by a Coroner's inquest of Plymouth Colony judged murdered. . . . And the report came, that the three Indians had confessed and accused Philip so to employ them, and that the English would hang Philip, so the Indians were afraid, and reported that the English had flattered them (or by threats) to belie Philip that they might kill him to have his Land; and that if Philip had done it, it was their Law so to execute whomever their kings judged deserved it, and that he had no cause to hide it.

So Philip kept his Men in Armes. Plimoth Gouverner required him to disband his Men, and informed him his Jealousy was false. Philip answered he would do no Harm, and thanked the Governer for his Information.

---

* John Easton, "A Relation of the Indian War," in *A Narrative of the Causes Which Led to Philip's Indian War* (Albany, NY: J. Munsell, 1858), 5–15.

The three Indians were hungry, to the last denied the Fact; but one broke the Halter as it is reported, then desired to be saved, and so was a littell while, then confessed they three had dun the Fact; and then he was hanged. And it was reported Saussomon before his death had informed of the Indian Plot, and that if the Indians knew it they wold kill him, and that the Heathen might destroy the English for their Wickedness, as God had permitted the Heathen to destroy the Israellites of olde. So the English were afraid and Philip was afraid, and both increased in Arms. But for forty Yeares Time, Reports and jealosys of War had bin very frequent, that we did not think that now a War was breaking forth; but about a Week before it did, we had Cause to think it would. Then to endeavor to prevent it, we lent a Man to Philip, that is he would come to the Ferry we would come over to speak with him. About four Miles we had to come; thither our Messenger come to them; they not aware of it behaved themselves as furious, but suddenly appeased when they understood who he was and what he came for, he called his Counsell and agreed to come to us; came himself unarmed, and about 40 of his Men armed. Then 5 of us went over, 3 were Magistrates. We sate very friendly together. We told him our business was to endeavor that they might not receive or do Rong. They said that was well; they had dun no Rong, the English ronged them. We said we knew the English said the Indians ronged them, and the Indians said the English ronged them, but our Desire was the Quarrell might rightly be decided, in the best Way, and not as Dogs decided their Quarrells. The Indians owned that fighting was the worst Way; then they propounded how Right might take Place. We said, by Arbitration. They said that all English agreed against them, and so by Arbitration they had had much Rong; many Miles square of Land so taken from them, for English would have English Arbitrators; and once they were persuaded to give in their Armes, that thereby Jealousy might be removed, and the English having their Arms wold not deliver them as they had promised, untill they consented to pay a *100po,* (100 pounds) and now they not so much Sum or Muny; that they were as good be Idled as leave all their Livelihode.

We said they might chuse a Indian King and the English might chuse the Governor of New Yorke, that

nether had Case to say either were Parties in the Differance. They said they had not heard of that Way, and said we honestly spoke, so we were perswaided if that Way had been tendered they would have accepted. We did endeavor not to hear their Complaints, said it was not convenient for us now to consider of, but to endeavor to prevent War; said to them when in War against English, Blood was spilt, that engaged all Englishmen, for we were to be all under one King; we knew what their Complaints wold be, and in our Colony had removed some of them in sending for Indian Rulers in what the Crime concerned Indians Lives, which they very lovingly accepted, and agreed with us to their Execution, and said so they were abell to satisfy their Subjects when they knew an Indian sufered duly, but said in what was only between their Indians and not in Towneships, that we had purchased, they wold not have us prosecute, and that that they had a great Fear to have any of their Indians should be called or forced to be Christian Indians. They said that such were in every thing more mischievous; only Disemblers, and then the English made them not subject to their Kings, and by their lying to rong their Kings. We knew it to be true, and we promising them that however in Government to Indians all should be alike, and that we knew it was our King's will it should be so, that altho we were weaker than other Colonies, they having submitted to our King to protect them, Others dared, not otherwise to molest them; so they expressed they took that to be well, that we had littell Case to doubt, but that to us under the King they would have yielded to our Determinations in what any should have complained to us against them.

But Philip charged it to be dishonesty in us to put off the Hearing the just Complaints, therefore we consented to hear them. They said thay had bine the first in doing Good to the English, and the English the first in doing Rong; said when the English first came, their King's Father was as a great Man, and the English as a littell Child; he constrained other Indians from ronging the English, and gave them Corn and shewed them how to plant, and was free to do them any Good, and had let them have a 100 Times more Land than now the King had for his own Peopell. But their King's Brother, [Massasoit] when he was King, came miserably to die by being forced to Court, as they judge poysoned. And another Greavance was, if 20 of their honest Indians testified that a Englishman had dun them Rong, it was as nothing; and if but one of their worst Indians testified against any Indian or their King, when it pleased the English it was sufficient. Another Grievance was, when their King sold Land, the English would say, it was more than they agreed to, and a Writing must be prove against all them, and some of their Kings had dun Rong to sell so much. He left his Peopell none, and some being given to Drunknes the English made them drunk and then cheated them in Bargains, but now their Kings were forewarned not for to part with Land, for nothing in Comparison to the Value thereof. Now home the English had owned for King or Queen, they would disinheret, and make another King that would give or sell them these Lands; that now, they had no Hopes left to keep any Land. Another Grievance, the English Catell and Horses still increased; that when they removed 30 Miles from where English had any thing to do, they could not keep their Corn from being spoiled, they never being used to fence, and thought when the English bought Land of them they would have kept their Catell upon their owne Land. Another Grievance, the English were so eager to sell the Indians Lickers, that most of the Indians spent all in Drunkness, and then ravened upon the sober Indians, and they did believe often did hurt the English Cattel, and their King could not prevent it. We knew before, these were their grand Complaints, but then we only endeavored to persuaid that all Complaints might be righted without War, but could have no other Answer but that they had not heard of that Way for the Governor of Yorke and an Indian King to have the Hearing of it. We had Cause to think in that had bine tendered it would have bine accepted. We endeavored that however they Should lay down the War, for the English were to strong for them; they said, then the English should do to them as they did when they were too strong for the English.

QUESTIONS TO CONSIDER

1. Why does Metacom distrust the English? What experiences in the years leading up to the war have contributed to this?
2. What complaints does Metacom make about English behavior? How might these actions by the English affect the Wampanoag way of life?

4.2 NATHANIEL BACON, "DECLARATION IN THE NAME OF THE PEOPLE" (1676)*

Nathaniel Bacon (1647–1676) was a prominent Virginia colonist, best known as the leader of Bacon's Rebellion, a revolt against the alleged corrupt practices of Virginia governor William Berkeley (1606–1677). Born into a wealthy English family, Bacon emigrated to Virginia, where he became a major landholder. Many of those opposed to Berkeley's policies were smaller landholders and servants, and Bacon likely

---

* "Declaration of Nathaniel Bacon in the Name of the People of Virginia, July 30, 1676," Massachusetts Historical Society Collections, 4th ser. (1871), 9:184–87.

rose to lead the rebellion as he was one of relatively few wealthy Virginians with grievances against Berkeley.

Bacon's "Declaration in the Name of the People," which was promulgated shortly before the beginning of the rebellion, outlined common complaints about Berkeley's leadership. Most notably, the disgruntled colonists felt that Berkeley leveled unjust taxes, offered special treatment to select friends and allies, and failed to protect the colony against attacks by neighboring Native Americans. As poorer planters with smaller landholdings tended to live further west and closer to Virginia's Native peoples, they felt that Berkeley and other wealthy settlers who lived further to the east did not appreciate the danger of conflict with the region's Indigenous population.

---

1. For having, upon specious pretenses of public works, raised great unjust taxes upon the commonalty for the advancement of private favorites and other sinister ends, but no visible effects in any measure adequate; for not having, during this long time of his government, in any measure advanced this hopeful colony either by fortifications, towns, or trade.
2. For having abused and rendered contemptible the magistrates of justice by advancing to places of judicature scandalous and ignorant favorites.
3. For having wronged his Majesty's prerogative and interest by assuming monopoly of the beaver trade and for having in it unjust gain betrayed and sold his Majesty's country and the lives of his loyal subjects to the barbarous heathen.
4. For having protected, favored, and emboldened the Indians against his Majesty's loyal subjects, never contriving, requiring, or appointing any due or proper means of satisfaction for their many invasions, robberies, and murders committed upon us.
5. For having, when the army of English was just upon the track of those Indians, who now in all places burn, spoil, murder and when we might with ease have destroyed them who then were in open hostility, for then having expressly countermanded and sent back our army by passing his word for the peaceable demeanor of the said Indians, who immediately prosecuted their evil intentions, committing horrid murders and robberies in all places, being protected by the said engagement and word past of him the said Sir William Berkeley, having ruined and laid desolate a great part of his Majesty's country, and have now drawn themselves into such obscure and remote places and are

by their success so emboldened and confirmed by their confederacy so strengthened that the cries of blood are in all places, and the terror and consternation of the people so great, are now become not only difficult but a very formidable enemy who might at first with ease have been destroyed.
6. And lately, when, upon the loud outcries of blood, the assembly had, with all care, raised and framed an army for the preventing of further mischief and safeguard of this his Majesty's colony.
7. For having, with only the privacy of some few favorites without acquainting the people, only by the alteration of a figure, forged a commission, by we know not what hand, not only without but even against the consent of the people, for the raising and effecting civil war and destruction, which being happily and without bloodshed prevented; for having the second time attempted the same, thereby calling down our forces from the defense of the frontiers and most weakly exposed places.
8. For the prevention of civil mischief and ruin amongst ourselves while the barbarous enemy in all places did invade, murder, and spoil us, his Majesty's most faithful subjects.

Of this and the aforesaid articles we accuse Sir William Berkeley as guilty of each and every one of the same, and as one who has traitorously attempted, violated, and injured his Majesty's interest here by a loss of a great part of this his colony and many of his faithful loyal subjects by him betrayed and in a barbarous and shameful manner exposed to the incursions and murder of the heathen. And we do further declare these the ensuing persons in this list to have been his wicked and pernicious councilors, confederates, aiders, and assisters against the commonalty in these our civil commotions.

Sir Henry Chichley
Lieut. Coll. Christopher Wormeley
William Sherwood
John Page Clerke
John Cluffe Clerke
John West
Hubert Farrell
Thomas Reade
Matthew Kempe

Joseph Bridger
William Claiburne Junior
Thomas Hawkins
Phillip Ludwell
Robert Beverley
Richard Lee
Thomas Ballard
William Cole
Richard Whitacre
Nicholas Spencer

And we do further demand that the said Sir William Berkeley with all the persons in this list be forthwith delivered up or surrender themselves within four days after the notice hereof, or otherwise we declare as follows.

That in whatsoever place, house, or ship, any of the said persons shall reside, be hid, or protected, we declare the owners, masters, or inhabitants of the said places to be confederates and traitors to the people and the estates of them is also of all the aforesaid persons to be confiscated. And this we, the commons of Virginia, do declare, desiring a firm union amongst ourselves that we may jointly and with one accord defend ourselves against the common enemy. And let not the faults of the guilty be the reproach of the innocent, or the faults or crimes of the oppressors divide and separate us who have suffered by their oppressions.

These are, therefore, in his Majesty's name, to command you forthwith to seize the persons above mentioned as traitors to the King and country and them to bring to Middle Plantation and there to secure them until further order, and, in case of opposition, if you want any further assistance you are forthwith to demand it in the name of the people in all the counties of Virginia.

Nathaniel Bacon
General by Consent of the people.

QUESTIONS TO CONSIDER

1. What redress or solution do Bacon and his allies suggest? What do they want Berkeley to do?
2. How do Bacon and his allies view neighboring Native peoples? What do they hope to change about Virginia's stance toward them?

4.3 PEDRO NARANJO, REASONS FOR THE PUEBLO REVOLT (1680)*

The Pueblo Revolt of 1680 was one of the most successful anticolonial uprisings by Native Americans. The Pueblo peoples of what is today the southwestern United States had been under some form of Spanish colonial domination since the mid-1500s. Spanish missionaries dominated Pueblo towns, extracting tribute in the form of labor, textiles, and food, and demanding conversion to Catholicism. In 1680 numerous Pueblo towns rose in coordinated revolt under the leadership of a man known as

* Charles Wilson Hackett, *Revolt of the Pueblo Indians of New Mexico and Otermin's Attempted Reconquest, 1680–1682* (Albuquerque: University of New Mexico, 1942), 2:245–49.

Popé (d. 1692). Although Popé remains a mysterious figure, it appears that he preached a return to pre-Columbian life—for the Pueblo to recreate their lives before the arrival of the Spanish. The Pueblos consequently rid themselves of anything Spanish, rejecting Spanish names, destroying Catholic idols, releasing Spanish horses, and killing hundreds of Spanish colonists. The revolt rocked the Spanish colonial system, and it proved difficult for the colonial government in New Spain to reassert control over the far-flung Pueblo towns. For over a decade, the Pueblo resisted Spanish authority before the colonial government gradually reclaimed authority. What follows is a record of a statement by the Pueblo prisoner Pedro Naranjo in which he explains what motivated the rebellion.

In the said plaza de armas on the said day, month, and year, for the prosecution of the judicial proceedings of this case his lordship caused to appear before him an Indian prisoner named Pedro Naranjo, a native of the pueblo of San Felipe, of the Queres nation, who was captured in the advance and attack upon the pueblo of La Isleta. He makes himself understood very well in the Castilian language and speaks his mother tongue and the Tegua. He took the oath in due legal form in the name of God, our Lord, and a sign of the cross, under charge of which he promised to tell the truth concerning what he knows and as he might be questioned, and having understood the seriousness of the oath and so signified through the interpreters, he spoke as indicated by the contents of the autos.

Asked whether he knows the reason or motives which the Indians of this kingdom had for rebelling, forsaking the law of God and obedience to his Majesty, and committing such grave and atrocious crimes, and who were the leaders and principal movers, and by whom and how it was ordered; and why they burned the images, temples, crosses, rosaries, and things of divine worship, committing such atrocities as killing priests, Spaniards, women, and children, and the rest that he might know touching the question, he said that since the government of Señor General Hernando Ugarte y la Concha they have planned to rebel on various occasions through conspiracies of the Indian sorcerers, and that although in some pueblos the messages were accepted, in other parts they would not agree to it. . . . Finally, in the past years, at the summons of an Indian named Popé who is said to have communication with the devil, it happened that in an estufa of the pueblo of Los Taos there appeared to the said Popé

three figures of Indians who never came out of the estufa. They gave the said Popé to understand that they were going underground to the lake of Copala. He saw these figures emit fire from all the extremities of their bodies, and that one of them was called Caudi, another Tilini, and the other Tleume; and these three beings spoke to the said Popé, who was in hiding from the secretary, Francisco Xavier, who wished to punish him as a sorcerer. They told him to make a cord of maguey fiber and tie some knots in it which would signify the number of days that they must wait before the rebellion. He said that the cord was passed through all the pueblos of the kingdom so that the ones which agreed to it [the rebellion] might untie one knot in sign of obedience, and by the other knots they would know the days which were lacking; and this was to be done on pain of death to those who refused to agree to it. As a sign of agreement and notice of having concurred in the treason and perfidy they were to send up smoke signals to that effect in each one of the pueblos singly. The said cord was taken from pueblo to pueblo by the swiftest youths under the penalty of death if they revealed the secret. Everything being thus arranged, two days before the time set for its execution, because his lordship had learned of it and had imprisoned two Indian accomplices from the pueblo of Tesuque, it was carried out prematurely that night, because it seemed to them that they were now discovered; and they killed religious, Spaniards, women, and children. This being done, it was proclaimed in all the pueblos that everyone in common should obey the commands of their father whom they did not know, which would be given through El Caydi or El Popé. This was heard by Alonso Catití, who came to the pueblo of this declarant to say that everyone must unite to go to the villa to kill the governor and the Spaniards who had remained with him, and that he who did not obey would, on their return, be beheaded; and in fear of this they agreed to it. Finally the senor governor and those who were with him escaped from the siege, and later this declarant saw that as soon as the Spaniards had left the kingdom an order came from the said Indian, Popé, in which he commanded all the Indians to break the lands and enlarge their cultivated fields, saying that now they were as they had been in ancient times, free from the labor they had performed for the religious and the Spaniards, who could not now be alive. He said that this is the legitimate cause and the reason they had for rebelling, because they had always desired to live as they had when they came out of the lake of Copala. Thus he replies to the question.

Asked for what reason they so blindly burned the images, temples, crosses, and other things of divine worship, he stated that the said Indian, Popé, came down in person, and with him El Saca and El Chato from the pueblo of Los Taos, and other captains and leaders and many people who were in his train, and he ordered in all the pueblos through which he passed that they instantly break up and burn the images of the holy Christ, the Virgin Mary and the other saints, the crosses, and everything pertaining to Christianity, and that they burn the temples, break up the bells, and separate from the wives whom God had given them in marriage and take those whom they desired. In order to take away their baptismal names, the water, and the holy oils, they were to plunge into the rivers and wash themselves with amole, which is a root native to the country, washing even their clothing, with the understanding that there would thus be taken from them the character of the holy sacraments. They did this, and also many other things which he does not recall, given to understand that this mandate had come from the Caydi and the other two who emitted fire from their extremities in the said estufa of Taos, and that they thereby returned to the state of their antiquity, as when they came from the lake of Copala; that this was the better life and the one they desired, because the God of the Spaniards was worth nothing and theirs was very strong, the Spaniard's God being rotten wood. These things were observed and obeyed by all except some who, moved by the zeal of Christians, opposed it, and such persons the said Popé caused to be killed immediately. He saw to it that they at once erected and rebuilt their houses of idolatry which they call estufas, and made very ugly masks in imitation of the devil in order to dance the dance of the cacina; and he said likewise that the devil had given them to understand that living thus in accordance with the law of their ancestors, they would harvest a great deal of maize, many beans, a great abundance of cotton, calabashes, and very large watermelons and cantaloupes; and that they could erect their houses and enjoy abundant health and leisure. As he has said, the people were very much pleased, living at their ease in this life of their antiquity, which was the chief cause of their falling into such laxity. Following what has already been stated, in order to terrorize them further and cause them to observe the diabolical commands, there came to them a pronouncement from the three demons already described, and from El Popé, to the effect that he who might still keep in his heart a regard for the priests, the governor, and the Spaniards would be known from his unclean face and clothes, and would be punished. And he stated that the said four persons stopped at nothing to have their commands obeyed. Thus he replies to the question.

Asked what arrangements and plans they had made for the contingency of the Spaniards' return, he said that what he knows concerning the question is that they were always saying they would have to fight to the death, for they do not wish to live in any other way than they are living at present.

QUESTIONS TO CONSIDER

1. What motivated the Pueblo to revolt? What complaints did they have against the Spanish?
2. How did the Spanish try to change Pueblo culture?

4.4 ANN PUTNAM, CONFESSION (1706)*

In 1692, twelve-year-old Ann Putnam (1679–1716) was one of the primary alleged witnesses to witchcraft that provoked the Salem Witch Trials. Although witch trials had occurred throughout early modern Europe, the Salem Witch Trials are notable for being the deadliest witch trials in the English colonies, and for the rapidity with which accusations were made. Putnam and other young girls leveled over two hundred accusations in the space of fifteen months, leading to dozens of convictions and twenty executions.

In 1706, in her mid-twenties, Putnam wrote a confession and apology for her role in the trials—the only witness to do so. Putnam does not give an explicit reason for her childhood actions, saying that she acted "ignorantly and unwittingly" and due to the "delusion of Satan."

I desire to be humbled before God for that sad and humbling providence that befell my father's family in the year about '92; that I, then being in my childhood, should, by such a providence of God, be made an instrument for the accusing of several persons of a grievous crime, whereby their lives were taken away from them, whom now I have just grounds and good reason to believe they were innocent persons; and that it was a great delusion of Satan that deceived me in that sad time, whereby I justly fear I have been instrumental, with others, though ignorantly and unwittingly, to bring upon myself and this land the guilt of innocent blood; though what was said or done by me against any person I can truly and uprightly say, before God and man, I did it not out of any anger, malice, or ill-will to any person, for I had no such thing against one of them; but what I did was ignorantly, being deluded by Satan. And particularly, as I was a chief instrument of accusing of Goodwife Nurse and her two sisters, I desire to lie in the dust, and to be humbled for it, in that I was a cause, with others, of so sad a calamity to them and their families; for which cause I desire to lie in the dust, and earnestly beg forgiveness of God, and from all those unto whom I have given just cause of sorrow and offence, whose relations were taken away or accused.

[Signed]

This confession was read before the congregation, together with her relation, Aug. 25, 1706; and she acknowledged it. —J. Greene. Pastor.

QUESTIONS TO CONSIDER

1. What does Putnam think about the trials and her own role in them? How does she feel?
2. Why do you think Putnam refrains from offering a specific explanation of why she accused certain people?

---

* Charles Upham, *Salem Witchcraft* (1867), 2:510, available on Project Gutenberg.

4.5 VISUAL SOURCE: MURDEROUS ATTACK ON THE PEQUOT FORT BY ENGLISH SETTLERS (1638)*

This engraving depicts the massacre of hundreds of Pequot civilians by New York and Connecticut militia during the Pequot War. This war was a seventeenth-century conflict in which New England colonies and their Native allies massacred and enslaved the Pequot people, driving them out of what is now the state of Connecticut. In what came to be known as the Mystic Massacre, New England militia and Native allies set fire to a walled Pequot settlement near the modern Connecticut–Rhode Island border and shot anyone who tried to escape.

The Pequot had been the dominant Native people of the Connecticut River Valley, but by the 1630s they had endured internal strife, a devastating smallpox epidemic, and consistent encroachment by New England settlers. Following a series of violent disagreements between Pequots and New Englanders, colonial leaders opted for war. Due to massacres like the pictured one near modern Mystic, Connecticut, the Pequot were nearly destroyed and ceased to be a significant regional power.

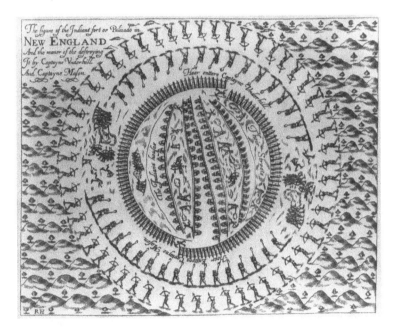

QUESTIONS TO CONSIDER

1. What is happening in this illustration? How can you tell who is a soldier and who a civilian?
2. Why would colonists produce an illustration of their own massacre? What did they imagine the viewer would see?

---

* Courtesy of the Library of Congress

4.6 VISUAL SOURCE: HERMAN MOLL, *A VIEW OF YE INDUSTRY OF YE BEAVERS OF CANADA* (1715)*

The presence of beavers throughout North American rivers and lakes was immensely influential on the course of European colonialism. Beaver fur was ideal for use in cold-weather clothing, in particular hats, but overhunting had caused a significant decline in European beaver populations. Following their discovery of North American beaver European traders began trading manufactured goods to Native peoples in exchange for beaver pelts, leading Native peoples to increase their beaver hunting. The beaver trade led to significant clashes over prime hunting grounds among Indigenous peoples, and these conflicts contributed to several larger wars.

This engraving depicts beavers hard at work building their characteristic dams near Niagara Falls, now at the border between the United States and Canada. At the time of this illustration, beaver would have been considered the primary natural resource of the French colonies in Canada.

QUESTIONS TO CONSIDER

1. The beaver in this illustration are numerous, almost overrunning the picture itself. What would this illustrative choice have conveyed to a contemporary viewer?
2. What impression does this picture give you of the American wilderness?

---

* GRANGER

CHAPTER 5

COLONIAL SOCIETIES AND CONTENTIOUS EMPIRES, 1625–1786

5.1 DOCUMENTS FROM COURT CASES INVOLVING THE JOHNSON FAMILY (1645–1663)*

Anthony Johnson (c. 1600–1670) was a prominent Virginia colonist and one of few Black colonists to achieve substantial wealth or status in the colony. Originally an indentured servant from Angola, Johnson was brought to Virginia, where he served his indenture and afterward acquired 250 acres of land. During his lifetime as a Virginia planter, Johnson employed several indentured servants, some of them serving lifetime indentures, making him one of only few Black colonists in the English colonies to own enslaved people. In the mid-1600s Johnson was involved in a legal dispute involving the indenture of one of his servants, John Casor. In the resulting judgment Johnson won Casor's service for life.

Johnson's life, though unusual, highlights that the social and legal systems of early Virginia treated free men with relative equality, regardless of their race. This would change within Johnson's lifetime. Beginning in the 1660s, Virginia and other English colonies began passing laws designed to keep African servants and their children permanently enslaved and limit the freedoms of free Black colonists.

* Document A: Susie M. Ames, ed., *County Court Records of Accomack-Northampton, Virginia, 1640–1645* (Charlottesville, VA: University Press of Virginia, 1973), 457.
Document B: Frank V. Walczyk, transcriber, *Northampton County Virginia, Orders, Deeds, & Wills, 1651–1654*, Book IV (New York: Peter's Row, 1971), 192–93.
Document C: John H. Russell, "Colored Freemen as Slaveowners in Virginia." *Journal of Negro History*, 1, no. 3 (1916): 234–35.
Document D: Frank V. Walczyk, transcriber, *Northampton County Virginia, Orders, Deeds, & Wills, 1651–1654*, Book IV (New York: Peter's Row, 1971), 137.

DOCUMENT A: ANTHONY ACQUIRES LAND IN NORTHAMPTON COUNTY

The deposition of Edwyn Conaway Clark taken in open court in 1645.

This deposition saith that being at the house of Captain Taylor about the Tenth day of July last past the said Captain Taylor in the morning went into the quartering house and this deponent comeing forth of the dwelling house did see Captain Taylor and Anthony the negro goeing into the Corne Field And when they return'd from the said Corne Field the said Negro told this deponent saying now: "Mr. Taylor and I have devided our corne And I am very glad of it (for) now I know myne owne, hee finds fault with mee that I doe not worke, but now I know myne owne ground and I will worke when I please and play when I please, And the said Captain Taylor asked the said Negro saying are you content with what you have And the negro answered saying I am very well content with what I have or words to that effect, And further not."

(Conaway Clarke, then the clerk of the Northampton County Court)

DOCUMENT B: ANTHONY PETITIONS FOR JOHN CASAR IN 1654.

The deposition of Capt. Sam'll Goldsmyth taken 8th of March 1654 saith that being at the house of Anth. Johnson negro about the beginning of November last, to receive a hog head of tobacco, a negro called John Casar came to this dep't and told him that the came into Virginia for service, or eight years per judgement and that he had demanded his freedom of Anth. Johnson his master and further said that he had kept him his servent and the charge then he should or ought and desired that this dep't would see that he might have no wrong where upon your dep't demanded of Anth. Johnson his indenture the said Johnson answered he never saw any the negro replied when he came in he had an indenture Anth. Johnson said he had the negro for his life, but Mr. Robert and George Parker said they know that the said negro had an indenture in one Mr. Careys hand, on the other side of the bay, further the said Mr. Robert Parker and his brother George said

(of the said Anth. Johnson did not let the negro go free) the said negro John Casar would recover most of his cows from him the said Johnson then Anth. Johnson (as this dep't did suppose) was in fearce (FOLIO 226) (upon this discourse) Anth. Johnsons son in law, his wife, and his own two sons, persuaded the old negro Anth. Johnson to set the said John Casar free more saith not.

Sam'll Goldsmyth

DOCUMENT C: DEPOSITION OF SAMUEL GOLDSMYTH

The deposition of Capt. Samll. Goldsmyth taken in open court 8th of March [16]54 sayeth that being att ye house of Anth. Johnson Negro about ye beginning of November last to receive a Hogsd of tobac, a negro called Jno. Casor came to this depo [nen]t & told him yt hee came into Virginia for seaven or eight years of Indenture; yt hee had demanded his freedome of Antho. Johnson his mayster & further sd yt hee had kept him his serv[ant] seaven years longer than hee should or ought; and desired that this Deponent would see yt hee should or ought; and desired that this Deponent would see yt hee might have noe wronge; whereupon your deponent demanded of Anth. Johnson his Indenture. the sd Johnson answered hee never saw any. The negro Jno. Casor replyed when hee came in he had an Indenture. Anth. Johnson sd hee had ye Negro fro his life, but Mr. Robert & George Parker sd they knewe that ye sd Negro had an Indenture in one Mr. S hand on ye other side of ye Baye. Further sd Mr. Robert Parker & his Brother George sd (if the sd. Anth. Johnson did not let ye negro go free) the said negro Jno Casor

DOCUMENT D: MARY JOHNSON EXEMPTED FROM TAXES AND LEVIES

Upon the pet. of Anth. Johnson negro and Mary his wife, and their information to the court that they have been inhabitants in Virginia (about thirty years) consideration being taken of their hard labor and known service performed by the petitioners in this country, for the obtaining of their livelyhood and the great losses they have sustained (by an unfortunate fire) with their present charge to provide for, its therefore thought fit and ordered that from the day of the date there of (during their natural lives) the said Mary Johnson and two daughters of Anth. Johnson negro be disengaged and freed from payment of taxes and levies in Northampton County for public uses.

QUESTIONS TO CONSIDER

1. What can we learn about Anthony Johnson's life from these documents? How was he similar or different from other prominent Virginians of this time?
2. What is John Casor's grievance with Johnson?

5.2 EXCERPTS FROM LOUISIANA'S CODE NOIR (1724)*

The Code Noir (trans. "Black Law") was a decree by King Louis XIV of France governing the practice of slavery in the French colonial empire. In a list of sixty articles, the code outlined what enslaved people—as well as free Black people—could and could not do in a variety of public and private areas of life. Enslaved people were banned from bearing weapons, marriage (without their enslaver's permission), gathering in large groups, testifying in courts, and escaping enslavement, among other things. The code prescribed punishments for enslaved people who violated these rules, and, in some cases, punishments for enslavers who exhibited too much leniency toward their enslaved people. Unlike the English and Dutch colonies, where some religious pluralism was tolerated, Catholicism was mandated in the French colonies and this is also reflected in the code. Jewish people were barred entirely, as was any non-Catholic worship service. The code reflected that enslavement was an active process; in order to keep people enslaved, colonial authorities were charged with controlling as much of enslaved people's lives as they could.

I. Decrees the expulsion of Jews from the colony.
II. Makes it imperative on masters to impart religious instruction to their slaves.
III. Permits the exercise of the Roman Catholic creed only. Every other mode of worship is prohibited.
IV. Negroes placed under the direction or supervision of any other person than a Catholic, are liable to confiscation.
V. Sundays and holidays are to be strictly observed. All negroes found at work on these days are to be confiscated.

---

* B. F. French, *Historical Collections of Louisiana: Embracing Translations of Many Rare and Valuable Documents Relating to the Natural, Civil, and Political History of that State* (New York: D. Appleton, 1851).

VI. We forbid our white subjects, of both sexes, to marry with the blacks, under the penalty of being fined and subjected to some other arbitrary punishment. We forbid all curates, priests, or missionaries of our secular or regular clergy, and even our chaplains in our navy to sanction such marriages. We also forbid all our white subjects, and even the manumitted or free-born blacks, to live in a state of concubinage with blacks. Should there be any issue from this kind of intercourse, it is our will that the person so offending, and the master of the slave, should pay each a fine of three hundred livres. Should said issue be the result of the concubinage of the master with his slave, said master shall not only pay the fine, but be deprived of the slave and of the children, who shall be adjudged to the hospital of the locality, and said slaves shall be forever incapable of being set free. But should this illicit intercourse have existed between a free black and his slave, when said free black had no legitimate wife, and should said black marry said slave according to the forms prescribed by the church, said slave shall be thereby set free, and the children shall also become free and legitimate; and in such a case, there shall be no application of the penalties mentioned in the present article.

. . .

VIII. We forbid all curates to proceed to effect marriages between slaves without proof of the consent of their masters; and we also forbid all masters to force their slaves into any marriage against their will.

IX. Children, issued from the marriage of slaves, shall follow the condition of their parents, and shall belong to the master of the wife and not of the husband, if the husband and wife have different masters.

X. If the husband be a slave, and the wife a free woman, it is our will that their children, of whatever sex they may be, shall share the condition of their mother, and be as free as she, notwithstanding the servitude of their father; and if the father be free and the mother a slave, the children shall all be slaves.

XI. Masters shall have their Christian slaves buried in consecrated ground.

XII. We forbid slaves to carry offensive weapons or heavy sticks, under the penalty of being whipped, and of having said weapons confiscated for the benefit of the person seizing the same. An exception is made in favor of those slaves who are sent a hunting or a shooting by their masters, and who carry with them a written permission to that effect, or are designated by some known mark or badge.

XIII. We forbid slaves belonging to different masters to gather in crowds either by day or by night, under the pretext of a wedding, or for any other cause, either at the dwelling or on the grounds of one of their masters, or elsewhere, and much less on the highways or in secluded places, under the penalty of corporal punishment, which shall not be less than the whip. In case of frequent offences of the kind, the offenders shall be branded with the mark of the flower de luce, and should there be aggravating circumstances, capital punishment may be applied, at the discretion of our judges. We command all our subjects, be they officers or not, to seize all such offenders, to arrest and conduct them to prison, although there should be no judgment against them.

XIV. Masters who shall be convicted of having permitted or tolerated such gatherings as aforesaid, composed of other slaves than their own, shall be sentenced, individually, to indemnify their neighbors for the damages occasioned by said gatherings, and to pay, for the first time, a fine of thirty livres, and double that sum on the repetition of the offence.

. . .

XXII. We declare that slaves can have no right to any kind of property, and that all that they acquire, either by their own industry or by the liberality of others, or by any other means or title whatever, shall be the full property of their masters; and the children of said slaves, their fathers and mothers, their kindred or other relations, either free or slaves, shall have no pretensions or claims thereto, either through testamentary dispositions or donations inter vivos; which dispositions and donations we declare null and void, and also whatever promises they may have made, or whatever obligations they may have subscribed to, as having been entered into by persons incapable of disposing of any thing, and of participating to any contract.

. . .

XXIV. Slaves shall be incapable of all public functions, and of being constituted agents for any other person than their own masters, with powers to manage or conduct any kind of trade; nor can they serve as arbitrators or experts; nor shall they be called to give their testimony either in civil or in criminal cases, except when it shall be a matter of necessity, and only in default of white people; but in no case shall they be permitted to serve as witnesses either for or against their masters.

. . .

XXXII. The runaway slave, who shall continue to be so for one month from the day of his being denounced to the officers of justice, shall have his ears cut off, and shall be branded with the flower de luce on the shoulder: and on a second offence of the same nature, persisted in during one month from the day of his being denounced, he shall be hamstrung, and be marked with the flower de luce on the other shoulder. On the third offence, he shall suffer death.

. . .

XXXVIII. We also forbid all our subjects in this colony, whatever their condition or rank may be, to apply, on their own private authority, the rack to their slaves, under any pretence whatever, and to mutilate said slaves in any one of their limbs, or in any part of their bodies, under the penalty of the confiscation of said slaves; and said masters, so offending, shall be liable to a criminal prosecution. We only permit masters, when they shall think that the case requires it, to put their slaves in irons, and to have them whipped with rods or ropes.

XXXIX. We command our officers of justice in this colony to institute criminal process against masters and overseers who shall have killed or mutilated their slaves, when in their power and under their supervision, and to punish said murder according to the atrocity of the circumstances; and in case the offence shall be a pardonable one, we permit them to pardon said masters and overseers without its being necessary to obtain from us letters patent of pardon.

XL. Slaves shall he held in law as movables, and as such, they shall be part of the community of acquests between husband and wife; they shall not be liable to be seized under any mortgage whatever; and they shall be equally divided among the co-heirs without admitting from any one of said heirs any claim founded on preciput or right of primogeniture, or dowry.

. . .

XLIII. Husbands and wives shall not be seized and sold separately when belonging to the same master: and their children, when under fourteen years of age, shall not be separated from their parents, and such seizures and sales shall be null and void. The present article shall apply to voluntary sales, and in case such sales should take place in violation of the law, the seller shall be deprived of the slave he has illegally retained, and said slave shall be adjudged to the purchaser without any additional price being required.

. . .

L. Masters, when twenty-five years old, shall have the power to manumit their slaves, either by testamentary dispositions, or by acts inter vivos. But, as there may be mercenary masters disposed to set a price on the liberation of their slaves; and whereas slaves, with a view to acquire the necessary means to purchase their freedom, may be tempted to commit theft or deeds of plunder, no person, whatever may he his rank and condition, shall be permitted to set free his slaves, without obtaining from the Superior Council a decree of permission to that effect; which permission shall be granted without costs, when the motives for the setting free of said slaves, as specified in the petition of the master, shall appear legitimate to the tribunal. All acts for the emancipation of slaves, which, for the future, shall be made without this permission, shall be null; and the slaves, so freed, shall not be entitled to their freedom; they shall, on the contrary, continue to be held as slaves; but they shall be taken away from their former masters, and confiscated for the benefit of the India Company.

LI. However, should slaves be appointed by their masters tutors to their children, said slaves shall be held and regarded as being thereby set free to all intents and purposes.

LII. We declare that the acts for the enfranchisement of slaves, passed according to the forms above described, shall be equivalent to an act of naturalization, when said slaves are not born in our colony of Louisiana, and they shall enjoy all the rights and privileges inherent to our subjects born in our kingdom or in any land or country under our dominion. We declare, therefore, that all manumitted slaves,

and all free-born negroes, are incapable of receiving donations, either by testamentary dispositions, or by acts inter vivos from the whites. Said donations shall be null and void, and the objects so donated shall be applied to the benefit of the nearest hospital.

. . .

LIV. We grant to manumitted slaves the same rights, privileges, and immunities which are enjoyed by free-born persons. It is our pleasure that their merit in having acquired their freedom, shall produce in their favor, not only with regard to their persons, but also to their property, the same effects which our other subjects derive from the happy circumstance of their having been born free.

In the name of the King,
Bienville, De la Chaise.
Fazende, Bruslé, Perry, March, 1724.

QUESTIONS TO CONSIDER

1. The Code Noir devotes three different articles to rules concerning marriage. Why do you think this was such a major concern for those writing the code?
2. Article 14 prescribes a punishment for slaveholders who allowed their enslaved people to gather in large groups. Why do you think this is? What were the authors of the code trying to prevent?

5.3 GOTTLIEB MITTELBERGER, *JOURNEY TO PENNSYLVANIA IN THE YEAR 1750* (PUBLISHED IN ENGLISH IN 1898)*

Transatlantic travel in the early modern world was rarely pleasant and, as Gottlieb Mittelberger describes, could often be horrendous and deadly. Mittelberger and the other Germans he traveled with to Pennsylvania did not have the money to pay for their passage. As a result, they spent the voyage in

* Gottlieb Mittelberger, *Journey to Pennsylvania in the Year 1750*, trans. Carl Theo Eben (Philadelphia: John Jos McVey, 1898), 20–28, https://archive.org/stream/gottliebmittelbeoomitt.

miserable conditions where malnutrition, dehydration, and infectious disease were common. Those who survived the trip were then forced to work a number of years for any colonist who agreed to pay for their travel, a process that could split up families who had made the journey together.

Mittelburger's experience is representative of that of many impoverished Europeans who lacked any prospects in their home country and hoped that the long trials of crossing the ocean and working off their passage would eventually allow them some measure of prosperity and autonomy in the colonies.

When the ships have for the last time weighed their anchors near the city of Kaupp [Cowes] in Old England, the real misery begins with the long voyage. For from there the ships, unless they have good wind, must often sail 8, 9, 10 to 12 weeks before they reach Philadelphia. But even with the best wind the voyage lasts 7 weeks.

But during the voyage there is on board these ships terrible misery, stench, fumes, horror, vomiting, many kinds of sea-sickness, fever, dysentery, headache, heat, constipation, boils, scurvy, cancer, mouth-rot, and the like, all of which come from old and sharply salted food and meat, also from very bad and foul water, so that many die miserably.

Add to this want of provisions, hunger, thirst, frost, heat, dampness, anxiety, want, afflictions and lamentations, together with other trouble, as *c. v.* the lice abound so frightfully, especially on sick people, that they can be scraped off the body. The misery reaches the climax when a gale rages for 2 or 3 nights and days, so that every one believes that the ship will go to the bottom with all human beings on board. In such a visitation the people cry and pray most piteously.

When in such a gale the sea rages and surges, so that the waves rise often like high mountains one above the other, and often tumble over the ship, so that one fears to go down with the ship; when the ship is constantly tossed from side to side by the storm and waves, so that no one can either walk, or sit, or lie, and the closely packed people in the berths are thereby tumbled over each other, both the sick and the well—it will be readily understood that many of these people, none of whom had been prepared for hardships, suffer so terribly from them that they do not survive it.

. . .

Children from 1 to 7 years rarely survive the voyage; and many a time parents are compelled to see their children miserably suffer and die from hunger, thirst and sickness, and then to see them cast into the water. I witnessed such misery in no less than 32 children in our ship, all of whom were thrown into the sea. The parents grieve all the more since their children find no resting-place in the earth, but are devoured by the monsters of the sea. It is a notable fact that children, who have not yet had the measles or small-pocks, generally get them on board the ship, and mostly die of them.

Often a father is separated by death from his wife and children, or mothers from their little children, or even both parents from their children; and sometimes whole families die in quick succession; so that often many dead persons lie in the berths beside the living ones, especially when contagious diseases have broken out on board the ship.

. . .

At length, when, after a long and tedious voyage, the ships come in sight of land, so that the promontories can be seen, which the people were so eager and anxious to see, all creep from below on deck to see the land from afar, and they weep for joy, and pray and sing, thanking and praising God. The sight of the land makes the people on board the ship, especially the sick and the half dead, alive again, so that their hearts leap within them; they shout and rejoice, and are content to bear their misery in patience, in the hope that they may soon reach the land in safety. But alas!

When the ships have landed at Philadelphia after their long voyage, no one is permitted to leave them except those who pay for their passage or can give good security; the others, who cannot pay, must remain on board the ships till they are purchased, and are released from the ships by their purchasers. The sick always fare the worst, for the healthy are naturally preferred and purchased first; and so the sick and wretched must often remain on board in front of the city for 2 or 3 weeks, and frequently die, whereas many a one, if he could pay his debt and were permitted to leave the ship immediately, might recover and remain alive.

. . .

The sale of human beings in the market on board the ship is carried on thus: Every day Englishmen, Dutchmen and High-German people come from the city of Philadelphia and other places, in part from a great distance, say 20, 30, or 40 hours away, and go on board the newly arrived ship that has brought and offers for sale passengers from Europe, and select among the healthy persons such as they deem suitable for their business, and bargain with them how long they will serve for their passage money, which most of them are still in debt for. When they have come to an agreement, it happens that adult persons bind themselves in writing to serve 3, 4, 5 or 6 years for the amount due by them, according to their age and strength. But very young people, from 10 to 15 years, must serve till they are 21 years old.

Many parents must sell and trade away their children like so many head of cattle; for if their children take the debt upon themselves, the parents can leave the ship free and unrestrained; but as the parents often do not know where and to what people their children are going, it often happens that such parents and children, after leaving the ship, do not see each other again for many years, perhaps no more in all their lives.

. . .

It often happens that whole families, husband, wife, and children, are separated by being sold to different purchasers, especially when they have not paid any part of their passage money.

. . .

When both parents have died over half-way at sea, their children, especially when they are young and have nothing to pawn or to pay, must stand for their own and their parents' passage, and serve till they are 21 years old. When one has served his or her term, he or she is entitled to a new suit of clothes at parting; and if it has been so stipulated, a man gets in addition a horse, a woman, a cow. . . .

QUESTIONS TO CONSIDER

1. According to Mittelberger, what role do illness and disease play in the experience of migration?
2. What does Mittelberger think of the "sale of human beings" in Philadelphia? What impact does the sale process have on the life of his fellow travelers?

5.4 GEORGE CATO, ORAL HISTORY OF THE STONO REBELLION, WORKS PROGRESS ADMINISTRATION NARRATIVE (1937)*

The Stono Rebellion was a rebellion by enslaved men in South Carolina that took place over the course of September 9–10, 1739. At the time, it was the largest slave rebellion in the southern English colonies. Led by an enslaved man known as Jeremy or Cato, twenty enslaved people originally from

* Mark Smith, *Stono: Documenting and Interpreting a Southern Slave Revolt* (Columbia: University of South Carolina, 2005), 55–56.

the Kingdom of Kongo gathered near the Stono River near the South Carolina coast and began marching south toward Spanish Florida. The Spanish were known to accept fugitives from English enslavement, and like the Kongolese rebels, were Catholic.

As the rebels marched south, they burned several plantations, killing between twenty or thirty white colonists and recruiting more enslaved people to their cause. The rebels numbered around eighty when they encountered South Carolina militia at the Edisto River on September 10. Dozens were killed on both sides in the ensuing fight, but the rebellion was thwarted and many of the captured rebels were executed. The account of these events given almost two hundred years later by George Cato, a great-great-grandson of the man who led the rebellion, aligns closely with other accounts of the rebellion and ensuing violence.

George Cato, a Negro laborer, residing at the rear of 1010 Lady Street, Columbia, S.C., says he is a great-great-grandson of the late Cato slave who commanded the Stono Insurrection in 1739, in which 21 white people and 44 Negroes were slain. George, now 50 years old, states that this Negro uprising has been a tradition in his family for 198 years.

When asked for the particulars, he smiled, invited the caller to be seated, and related the following story:

"Yes sah! I sho' does come from dat old stock who had de misfortune to be slaves but who decide to be men, at one and de same time, and I's right proud of it. De first Cato slave we knows 'bout, was plum willin' to lay down his life for de right, as he see it. Dat is pow'ful fine for de Catoes who has come after him. My granddaddy and my daddy tell me plenty 'bout it, while we was livin' in Orangeburg County, not far from where de fightin' took place in de long ago.

"My graddaddy was a son of de son of de Stono slave commander. He say his daddy often take him over de route of de rebel slave march, dat time when dere was sho' big trouble all 'bout dat neighborhood. As it come down to me, I thinks de first Cato take a darin' chance on losin' his life, not so much for his own benefit as it was to help others. He was not lak some slaves, much 'bused by deir masters. My kinfolks not 'bused. Da[t] why, I reckons, de captain of de slaves was picked by them. Cato was teached how to read and write by his rich master.

"How it all start? Dat what I ask but nobody ever tell me how 100 slaves between de Combahee and Edisto rivers come to meet in de woods not far from de Stono River on September 9, 1739. And how they elect

a leader, my kinsman, Cato, and late dat day march to Stono town, break in a warehouse, kill two white men in charge, and take all de guns and ammunition they wants. But they do it. Wid dis start, they turn south and march on.

"They work fast, coverin' 15 miles, passin' many fine plantations, and in every single case, stop, and break in de house and kill men, women, and children. Then they take what they want 'cludin' arms, clothes, liquor and food. Near de Combahee swamp, Lieutenant Governor Bull, drivin' from Beaufort to Charleston, see them and he small a rat. Befo' he was seen by de army he detour into de big woods and stay 'til de slave rebels pass.

"Governor Bull and some planters, between de Combahee and Edisto [rivers], ride fast and spread de alarm and it wasn't long 'til de militiamen was on de trail in pursuit of de slave army. When found, many of de slaves was singin' and dancin' and Cap. Cato and some of de other leaders was cussin' at them sumpin awful. From dat day to dis, no Cato has tasted whiskey, 'less he go 'against his daddy's warnin'. Dis war last less than two days but it sho' was pow'ful hot while it last.

"I reckon it was hot, 'cause in less than two days, 21 white men, women, and chillun, and 44 Negroes, was slain. My granddaddy say dat in de woods and at Stono, where de war start, dere was more than 100 Negroes in line. When de militia come in sight of them at Combahee swamp, de drinkin' dancin' Negroes scatter I de brush and only 44 stand deir ground.

"Commander Cato speak for de crowd. He say: 'We don't lak slavery. We start to jine de Spanish in

Florida. We surrender but we not whipped yet and we is not converted." De other 43 men say: 'Amen.' They was taken, unarmed, and hanged by de militia. Long befo' dis uprisin', de Cato slave wrote passes for slaves and do all he can to send them to freedom. He die but he die for doin' de right, as he see it."

QUESTIONS TO CONSIDER

1. What motives does George Cato attribute to the Stono rebels?
2. How is the history of the Stono Rebellion passed on within George Cato's family? What does the rebellion mean to him?

5.5 VISUAL SOURCE: THREE VILLAGES ROBE (c. 1740)*

Buffalo robes were cured buffalo hides used as clothing or blankets by Great Plains Indians. The decoration of these robes could vary significantly. Some included intricate ornamental beading, while others—like the one pictured here—conveyed a story about past events.

This robe was created by people of the Quapaw people of the Arkansas River Valley and appears to commemorate an alliance with the French and subsequent battle with the Chickasaw. Domed huts represent the villages of the Quapaw, while houses bearing a cross represent the French settlement known as the Arkansas Post. The Quapaw are also shown gathering for a ceremony following the battle.

---

* © musée du quai Branly – Jacques Chirac, Dist. RMN-Grand Palais / Art Resource, NY

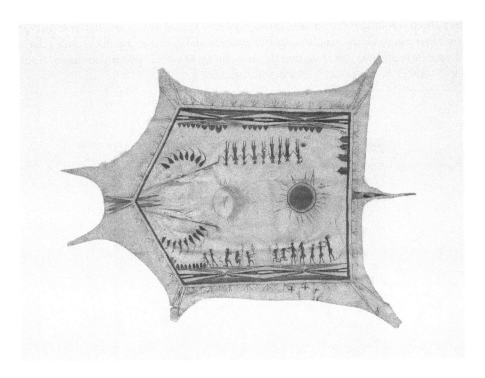

QUESTIONS TO CONSIDER

1. How does the robe represent both time and space? Why might the images on the robe be arranged that way?
2. What evidence is there of the presence of Europeans in this image?

5.6 VISUAL SOURCE: JOHN GREENWOOD, *PORTRAIT OF ANN ARNOLD* (AKA "JERSEY NANNY") (1748)*

This portrait by Boston artist John Greenwood of an enslaved woman is the first individual portrait of a Black woman created in North America. Almost nothing is known about the subject of the painting, an enslaved Boston woman named Ann Arnold. A contemporary advertisement indicated that she may have been known as "Jersey Nanny," which suggests that she may have worked as a wetnurse or as a guardian of children.

---

* Museum of Fine Arts, Boston
Gift of Henry Lee Shattuck

The portrait is relatively devoid of later stereotypes of African Americans that were incorporated into American visual culture. Arnold is presented seated and gazing at the viewer with a flat, undisturbed stare. It is possible, however, that the accompanying poem[1] which encourages "Ladies" to "own that NANNY is your sister" is meant to be mocking.

QUESTIONS TO CONSIDER

1. What emotions do Arnold's face and posture portray?
2. How should this portrait be interpreted in light of the accompanying poem?

---

[1] The short poem underneath the image reads "Nature her various Skill displays/In thousand Shapes, a thousand Ways/Tho' one Form differs from another/She's still of all the common Mother/Then, Ladies, let not Pride resist her/But own that NANNY is your Sister."

CHAPTER 6

GLOBAL WAR AND AMERICAN INDEPENDENCE, 1730–1776

6.1 DELAWARES DISCUSS THE FRENCH & INDIAN WAR (1758)*

The French and Indian War is the name given to the North American theater of the global conflict known as the Seven Years' War (1754–1763). Fighting began over control of the Ohio River and eventually spread throughout the borderlands between the English colonies and New France, including the St. Lawrence River, and along Newfoundland and Nova Scotia. The English captured Quebec in 1760 and eventually seized all of New France, effectively ending France's North American colonial enterprise.

Throughout the war, both the French and English sought and received aid from multiple Native peoples. The French operated sparsely populated colonies and relied primarily on small bands of traders to make their colonies profitable. Meanwhile the population of English colonists grew quickly, and they bought or seized land from nearby Native peoples to consistently expand the borders of their colonies.

Sept. 1. Shingas, King Beaver, Delawar George and Pisquetum, with several other Indians, Captains, said to me, "Brother, we have thought a great deal since God has brought you here, and this is a matter of great consequence, which we can't readily answer, we think on it, and will answer you as soon as we can, our feast hinders us; all our young men, women and children are glad to see you: before you came, they all agreed together to go and join the French; but since they have seen you they all draw back, tho' we have great reason to believe you intend to drive us away and settle the country; or why do you come to fight in the Land that God has given us?" I said we did not intend to take the land from them; but only to drive the French away, they said they knew better for that they were informed so by our Greatest Traders, and several Justices of the Peace had told them the same, and the French tells us much the same thing, that the English intend to

* Samuel Hazard, *Pennsylvania Archives*, vol. 3 (Philadelphia, 1835), 534–37, https://www.google.com/books/edition/Pennsylvania_Archives/3_APAAAAYAAJ?hl=en&gbpv=0.

destroy us, and take our lands from us, but that they come only to defend us and our Lands, that the land is ours, and not theirs, therefore we say if you will be at peace with us, we will send the French home, 'tis you that have begun the war, and 'tis necessary that you hold fast, and be not discouraged, for we love you more than you love us, for when we take any Prisoners from you, we treat them as our own children; we are Poor and yet we clothe them as well as we can, you can see our children are as naked as at the first, by this you may see that our hearts are better than your heart, 'tis plain that you are the cause of this war. Why don't you and the French fight in the old country, and on the sea? Why do you come to fight on our land? This makes everybody believe you only want to take and settle the Land. I told them, "Brothers, as for my Part I have not one foot of Land nor do I desire to have any; and if I had any Land I would rather give it to them than take any from them, Brothers, if I die, you will get a little more ground from me. I will walk on that ground which God has made, we have told you that you should keep nothing in your hearts but bring it before the Council, they will readily hear you, and I promise you, what they answer they will stand to, I further to you what agreements they made about Wioming, and they stand to them."

They said, "Brother, your Heart is good, you speak always very fine; but we know there are always a great many that want to be rich, they never have enough. Look, we do not want to be rich, and take away that which others have. God has given you the tame creatures; we don't want to take them from you. God has given to us the deer, which we must feed on, and we rejoice in that which springs out of the Ground, and thank God for it. Look now my Brother, the white people think we have no brains in our heads, they are so great and big that makes them make war with us, we are but a little handful to what you are. When you look for a Turkey you can't find it it is so little, it hides itself under the Bushes, and when you hunt for a Rattle Snake you cannot find it, and perhaps it will bite you before you see it, and since you are so great and big, and we so little, it is you that must keep on, this is the first time that we saw, or heard of you, and we have great reason to think about it, since such a great body of you comes in our Lands 'tis you and the French have agreed to make this war, it is told us that you and the French contrived the war between you; this was told us by chief of the Indian traders, and they said further, "Brethren this is the last time we shall come among you; for the French and the English intend to join and kill all the Indians, and then divide the land among themselves." Then they addressed themselves to me, and said, "Brother, I suppose you know something about it; or has the Governor stopped your mouth that you should not tell us?"

QUESTIONS TO CONSIDER

1. What concerns do Delaware leaders have about the intentions of the English?
2. Are the Delaware interested in participating in the war? Why or why not?

6.2 KING GEORGE III, ROYAL PROCLAMATION (1763)*

Following the French and Indian War, the English government acquired vast territories in North America from the French, including much of what is now Canada and the midwestern United States. The Proclamation of 1763 was issued to impose new rules and organization for this territory, and

---

* King George III of England, "Royal Proclamation, 1763," Exhibits, University of Toronto Libraries, accessed January 29, 2023, https://exhibits.library.utoronto.ca/items/show/2470.

specifically on how to deal with the numerous Native groups who had previously had commercial and diplomatic ties with the French. In its most important provision, the Proclamation barred English colonial settlement "beyond the Heads or Sources of any of the Rivers which fall into the Atlantic Ocean," effectively banning colonists from moving west beyond the Appalachian Mountains. This measure was intended to prevent rapid settlement of the Ohio Valley by colonists, which could spark conflict with the Native peoples living there and lead to another war. The Proclamation was met with frustration in the colonies as many colonists had hoped to establish new settlements on Native land along the Ohio, which some did in defiance of the Proclamation.

1763, OCTOBER 7.
BY THE KING.
A Proclamation
George r.
Whereas We have taken into Our Royal Consideration the extensive and valuable Acquisitions in America, secured to Our Crown by the late Definitive Treaty of Peace, concluded at Paris the Tenth Day of February last, and being desirous, that all Our loving Subjects, as well of Our Kingdoms as of Our Colonies in America, may avail themselves, with all convenient Speed, of the great Benefits and Advantages which must accrue therefrom to their Commerce, Manufactures, and Navigation; We have thought fit, with the Advice of Our Privy Council, to issue this Our Royal Proclamation, hereby to publish and declare to all Our loving Subjects, that We have, with the Advice of Our said Privy Council, granted Our Letters Patent under Our Great Seal of Great Britain, to erect within the Countries and Islands ceded and confirmed to Us by the said Treaty, Four distinct and separate Governments, stiled and called by the Names of Quebec, East Florida, West Florida, and Grenada, and limited and bounded as follows; viz.

First. The Government of Quebec, bounded on the Labrador Coast by the River St. John, and from thence by a Line drawn from the Head of that River through the Lake St. John to the South End of the Lake nigh Pissin; from whence the said Line crossing the River St. Lawrence and the Lake Champlain in Forty five Degrees of North Latitude, passes along the High Lands which divide the Rivers that empty themselves into the said River St. Lawrence, from those which fall into the Sea; and also along the North Coast of the Baye des Chaleurs, and the Coast of the Gulph of St. Lawrence to Cape Rosieres, and from thence crossing the Mouth of the River St. Lawrence by the West End of the Island of Antiocosti, terminates at the aforesaid River of St. John.

Secondly. The Government of East Florida, bounded to the Westward by the Gulph of Mexico, and the Apalachicola River; to the Northward, by a Line drawn from that Part of the said River where the Chatahouchee and Flint Rivers meet, to the Source of St. Mary's River, and by the Course of the said River to the Atlantick Ocean; and to the Eastward and Southward, by the Atlantick Ocean, and the Gulph of Florida, including all Islands within Six Leagues of the Sea Coast.

Thirdly. The Government of West Florida, bounded to the Southward by the Gulph of Mexico, including all Islands within Six Leagues of the Coast from the River Apalachicola to Lake Pentchartain; to the Westward, by the said Lake, the Lake Mauripas, and the River Mississippi; to the Northward, by a Line drawn due East from that Part of the River Mississippi which lies in Thirty one Degrees North Latitude, to the River Apalachicola or Chatahouchee; and to the Eastward by the said River.

Fourthly. The Government of Grenada, comprehending the Island of that Name, together with the Grenadines, and the Islands of Dominico, St. Vincents and Tobago. And, to the End that the open and free Fishery of Our Subjects may be extended to and carried on upon the Coast of Labrador and the adjacent Islands, We have thought fit, with the Advice of Our said Privy Council, to put all that Coast, from the River St. John's to Hudson's Straights, together with the Islands of Anticosti and Madelaine, and all other smaller Islands lying upon the said Coast, under the Care and Inspection of Our Governor of Newfoundland.

We have also, with the Advice of Our Privy Council, thought fit to annex the Islands of St. John's, and

Cape Breton or Isle Royale, with the lesser Islands adjacent thereto, to Our Government of Nova Scotia.

We have also, with the Advice of Our Privy Council aforesaid, annexed to Our Province of Georgia all the Lands lying between the Rivers Attamaha and St. Mary's.

And whereas it will greatly contribute to the speedy settling Our said new Governments, that Our loving Subjects should be informed of Our Paternal Care for the Security of the Liberties and Properties of those who are and shall become Inhabitants thereof; We have thought fit to publish and declare, by this Our Proclamation, that We have, in the Letters Patent under Our Great Seal of Great Britain, by which the said Governments are constituted, given express Power and Direction to Our Governors of Our said Colonies respectively, that so soon as the State and Circumstances of the said Colonies will admit thereof, they shall, with the Advice and Consent of the Members of Our Council, summon and call General Assemblies within the said Governments respectively, in such Manner and Form as is used and directed in those Colonies and Provinces in America, which are under Our immediate Government; and We have also given Power to the said Governors, with the Consent of Our said Councils, and the Representatives of the People, so to be summoned as aforesaid, to make, constitute, and ordain Laws, Statutes, and Ordinances for the Publick Peace, Welfare, and Good Government of Our said Colonies, and of the People and Inhabitants thereof, as near as may be agreeable to the Laws of England, and under such Regulations and Restrictions as are used in other Colonies: And in the mean Time, and until such Assemblies can be called as aforesaid, all Persons inhabiting in, or resorting to Our said Colonies, may confide in Our Royal Protection for the Enjoyment of the Benefit of the Laws of Our Realm of England; for which Purpose, We have given Power under Our Great Seal to the Governors of Our said Colonies respectively, to erect and constitute, with the Advice of Our said Councils respectively, Courts of Judicature and Publick Justice, within Our said Colonies, for the hearing and determining all Causes, as well Criminal as Civil, according to Law and Equity, and as near as may be agreeable to the Laws of England, with Liberty to all Persons who may think themselves aggrieved by the Sentences of such Courts, in all Civil Cases, to appeal, under the usual Limitations and Restrictions, to Us in Our Privy Council.

We have also thought fit, with the Advice of Our Privy Council as aforesaid, to give unto the Governors and Councils of Our said Three New Colonies upon the Continent, full Power and Authority to settle and agree with the Inhabitants of Our said New Colonies, or with any other Persons who shall resort thereto, for such Lands, Tenements, and Hereditaments, as are now, or hereafter shall be in Our Power to dispose of, and them to grant to any such Person or Persons, upon such Terms, and under such moderate Quit-Rents, Services, and Acknowledgements as have been appointed and settled in Our other Colonies, and under such other Conditions as shall appear to Us to be necessary and expedient for the Advantage of the Grantees, and the Improvement and Settlement of our said Colonies.

And whereas We are desirous, upon all Occasions, to testify Our Royal Sense and Approbation of the Conduct and Bravery of the Officers and Soldiers of Our Armies, and to reward the same, We do hereby command and impower Our Governors of Our said Three New Colonies, and all other Our Governors of Our several Provinces on the Continent of North America, to grant, without Fee or Reward, to such Reduced Officers as have served in North America during the late War, and to such Private Soldiers as have been or shall be disbanded in America, and are actually residing there, and shall personally apply for the same, the following Quantities of Lands, subject at the Expiration of Ten Years to the same Quit-Rents as other Lands are subject to in the Province within which they are granted, as also subject to the same Conditions of Cultivation and Improvement; viz.

To every Person having the Rank of a Field Officer, Five thousand Acres. — To every Captain, Three thousand Acres. — To every Subaltern or Staff Officer, Two thousand Acres. — To every Non-Commission Officer, Two hundred Acres. — To every Private Man, Fifty Acres.

We do likewise authorize and require the Governors and Commanders in Chief of all Our said Colonies upon the Continent of North America, to grant the like Quantities of Land, and upon the same

Conditions, to such Reduced Officers of Our Navy, of like Rank, as served on Board Our Ships of War in North America at the Times of the Reduction of Louisbourg and Quebec in the late War, and who shall personally apply to Our respective Governors for such Grants.

And whereas it is just and reasonable, and essential to Our Interest and the Security of Our Colonies, that the several Nations or Tribes of Indians, with whom We are connected, and who live under Our Protection, should not be molested or disturbed in the Possession of such Parts of Our Dominions and Territories as, not having been ceded to, or purchased by Us, are reserved to them, or any of them, as their Hunting Grounds; We do therefore, with the Advice of Our Privy Council, declare it to be Our Royal Will and Pleasure, that no Governor or Commander in Chief in any of Our Colonies of Quebec, East Florida, or West Florida, do presume, upon any Pretence whatever, to grant Warrants of Survey, or pass any Patents for Lands beyond the Bounds of their respective Governments, as described in their Commissions; as also, that no Governor or Commander in Chief in any of Our other Colonies or Plantations in America, do presume, for the present, and until Our further Pleasure be known, to grant Warrants of Survey, or pass Patents for any Lands beyond the Heads or Sources of any of the Rivers which fall into the Atlantick Ocean from the West and North-West, or upon any Lands whatever, which, not having been ceded to, or purchased by Us as aforesaid, are reserved to the said Indians, or any of them.

And We do further declare it to be Our Royal Will and Pleasure, for the present as aforesaid, to reserve under Our Sovereignty, Protection, and Dominion, for the Use of the said Indians, all the Lands and Territories not included within the Limits of Our said Three New Governments, or within the Limits of the Territory granted to the Hudson's Bay Company, as also all the Lands and Territories lying to the Westward of the Sources of the Rivers which fall into the Sea from the West and North West, as aforesaid; and We do hereby strictly forbid, on Pain of Our Displeasure, all Our loving Subjects from making any Purchases or Settlements whatever, or taking Possession of any of the Lands above reserved, without Our especial Leave and Licence for that Purpose first obtained.

And We do further strictly enjoin and require all Persons whatever, who have either wilfully or inadvertently seated themselves upon any Lands within the Countries above described, or upon any other Lands, which, not having been ceded to, or purchased by Us, are still reserved to the said Indians as aforesaid, forthwith to remove themselves from such Settlements.

And whereas great Frauds and Abuses have been committed in the purchasing Lands of the Indians, to the great Prejudice of Our Interests, and to the great Dissatisfaction of the said Indians; in order therefore to prevent such Irregularities for the future, and to the End that the Indians may be convinced of Our Justice, and determined Resolution to remove all reasonable Cause of Discontent, We do, with the Advice of Our Privy Council, strictly enjoin and require, that no private Person do presume to make any Purchase from the said Indians of any Lands reserved to the said Indians, within those Parts of Our Colonies where We have thought proper to allow Settlement; but that if, at any Time, any of the said Indians should be inclined to dispose of the said Lands, that same shall be purchased only for Us, in Our Name, at some publick Meeting or Assembly of the said Indians to be held for that Purpose by the Governor or Commander in Chief of Our Colonies respectively, within which they shall lie: and in case they shall lie within the Limits of any Proprietary Government, they shall be purchased only for the Use and in the Name of such Proprietaries, conformable to such Directions and Instructions as We or they shall think proper to give for that Purpose: And We do, by the Advice of Our Privy Council, declare and enjoin, that the Trade with the said Indians shall be free and open to all our Subjects whatever; provided that every Person, who may incline to trade with the said Indians, do take out a Licence for carrying on such Trade from the Governor or Commander in Chief of any of Our Colonies respectively, where such Person shall reside; and also give Security to observe such Regulations as We shall at any Time think fit, by Ourselves or by Our Commissaries to be appointed for this Purpose, to direct and appoint for the Benefit of the said Trade; And We do hereby authorize, enjoin, and require the Governors and Commanders in Chief of all Our Colonies respectively, as well Those under Our immediate Government as those under the

Government and Direction of Proprietaries, to grant such Licences without Fee or Reward, taking especial Care to insert therein a Condition, that such Licence shall be void, and the Security forfeited, in Case the Person, to whom the same is granted, shall refuse or neglect to observe such Regulations as We shall think proper to prescribe as aforesaid.

And We do further expressly enjoin and require all Officers whatever, as well Military as those employed in the Management and Direction of Indian Affairs within the Territories reserved as aforesaid for the Use of the said Indians, to seize and apprehend all Persons whatever, who, standing charged with Treasons, Misprisions of Treason, Murders, or other Felonies or Misdemeanours, shall fly from Justice, and take Refuge in the said Territory, and to send them under a proper Guard to the Colony where the Crime was committed of which they stand accused, in order to take their Tryal for the same.

Given at Our Court at St. James's, the Seventh Day of October, One thousand seven hundred and sixty three, in the Third Year of Our Reign.

God Save the King

QUESTIONS TO CONSIDER

1. What limits does King George impose on Anglo-American colonists' ability to make new settlements and interact with Native peoples?
2. What does King George demand that colonists who have settled on forbidden land do?

6.3 RESPONSE TO LORD DUNMORE'S PROCLAMATION IN *THE VIRGINIA GAZETTE* (1775)*

Lord Dunmore (1730–1809), governor of Virginia, issued a proclamation declaring martial law in the colony in November 1775 as some of the first fighting of what became the American War of Independence broke out. The proclamation also offered freedom to any enslaved person who agreed to fight for the Crown against the Americans. This sparked widespread fear in Virginia and throughout the Southern colonies that enslaved people across the region would revolt and attack their enslavers. Dunmore was widely portrayed as a villain who was resorting to bribes and treachery and endangering the homes of families of Southerners by motivating enslaved people to rebel. About three hundred enslaved people ultimately escaped and took up Dunmore's offer.

Most colonial newspapers were under control of revolutionaries, and the *Virginia Gazette* reflects the fear and hostility of patriot colonists toward Dunmore and his proclamation.

The second class of people, for whose sake a few remarks upon this proclamation seem necessary, is the *Negroes*. They have been flattered with their freedom, if they be able to bear arms, and will spedily join Lord *Dunmore*'s troops. To none then is freedom promised but to such as are able to do Lord

* *The Virginia Gazette* (Williamsburg, VA), November 25, 1775, https://research.colonialwilliamsburg.org/DigitalLibrary/va-gazettes/VGSinglePage.cfm?issueIDNo=75.DH.54&page=3&res=LO.

Dunmore service: The aged, the infirm, the women and children, are still to remain the property of their masters, masters who will be provoked to severity, should part of their slaves desert them. Lord *Dunmore's* declaration, therefore, is a cruel declaration to the Negroes. He does not even pretend to make it out of any tenderness to them, but solely on his own account; and should it meet with success, it leaves by far the greater number at the mercy of an enraged and injured people. But should there be any amongst the Negroes weak enough to believe that *Dunmore* intends to do them a kindness, and wicked enough to provoke the fury of the Americans against their defenceless fathers and mothers, their wives, their women and children, let them only consider the difficulty of effecting their escape, and what they must expect to suffer if they fall into the hands of the Americans. Let them farther consider what must be their fate, should the English prove conquerors in this dispute. If we can judge of the future from the past, it will not be much mended. Long have the Americans, moved by compassion, and actuated by sound policy, endeavoured to stop the progress of slavery. Our Assemblies have repeatedly passed acts laying heavy duties upon imported Negroes, by which they meant altogether to prevent the horrid traffick; but their humane intentions have been as often frustrated by the cruelty and covetousness of a set of English merchants, who prevailed upon the King to repeal our kind and merciful acts, little indeed to the credit of his humanity. Can it then be supposed that the Negroes will be better used by the English, who have always encouraged and upheld this slavery, than by their present masters, who pity their condition, who wish, in general, to make is as easy and comfortable as possible, and who would willingly, were it in their power, or were they permitted, not only prevent any more Negroes from losing their freedom, but restore it to such as have already unhappily lost it. No, the ends of Lord *Dunmore* and his party being answered, they will either give up the offending Negroes to the rigour of the laws they have broken, or sell them in the West Indies, where every year they sell many thousands of their miserable brethren, to perish either by the inclemency of the weather, or the cruelty of barbarous masters. Be not then, ye Negroes, tempted by this proclamation to ruin yourselves. I have given you a faithful view of what you are to expect; and I declare, before GOD, in doing it, I have considered your welfare, as well as that of the country. Whether you will profit by my advice I cannot tell; but this I know, that whether we suffer or not, if you desert us, you most certainly will.

QUESTIONS TO CONSIDER

1. Why does the *Gazette* call the proclamation "cruel"? What misfortune might happen to enslaved people who take up Dunmore's offer or their families?
2. How does the *Gazette* excuse the practice of slavery in the colonies?

6.4 MARY JEMISON, "REMEMBERING THE AMERICAN REVOLUTION IN INDIAN COUNTRY" (1775–1777)*

Mary Jemison (1743–1833) was a British colonist who was captured as a teenager in 1755 and lived the rest of her life among the Seneca of upstate New York. By the time the Revolutionary War broke out, she was an adult woman who had lived most of her life as a Seneca. In the 1820s she related much

---

* James E. Seaver, *A Narrative of the Life of Mrs. Mary Jemison* (Canadaigua, NY: J.D. Bemis, 1824), 71–84.

of her life story to a New York doctor who used her account to publish *A Narrative of the Life of Mrs. Mary Jemison* (1824).

Jemison describes the toll that the Revolutionary War took on the six Iroquois tribes who were divided among themselves over whose side to support in the conflict. While Jemison's Seneca ultimately chose to support the British, other nations like the Oneida supported the American cause. In the years following the American victory, Iroquois diplomatic and military influence precipitously declined, and Iroquois nations were repeatedly pressed into selling much of their traditional land in New York state.

Thus, at peace amongst themselves, and with the neighboring whites, though there were none at that time very near, our Indians lived quietly and peaceably at home, till a little before the breaking out of the revolutionary war, when they were sent for, together with the Chiefs and members of the Six Nations generally, by the people of the States, to go to the German Flats, and there hold a general council, in order that the people of the states might ascertain, in good season, who they should esteem and treat as enemies, and who as friends, in the great war which was then upon the point of breaking out between them and the King of England.

Our Indians obeyed the call, and the council was holden, at which the pipe of peace was smoked, and a treaty made, in which the Six Nations solemnly agreed that if a war should eventually break out, they would not take up arms on either side; but that they would observe a strict neutrality. With that the people of the states were satisfied, as they had not asked their assistance, nor did not wish it. The Indians returned to their homes well pleased that they could live on neutral ground, surrounded by the din of war, without being engaged in it.

About a year passed off, and we, as usual, were enjoying ourselves in the employments of peaceable times, when a messenger arrived from the British Commissioners, requesting all the Indians of our tribe to attend a general council which was soon to be held at Oswego. The council convened, and being opened, the British Commissioners informed the Chiefs that the object of calling a council of the Six Nations, was, to engage their assistance in subduing the rebels, the people of the states, who had risen up against the good King, their master, and were about to rob him of a great part of his possessions and wealth, and added that they would amply reward them for all their services.

The Chiefs then arose, and informed the Commissioners of the nature and extent of the treaty which they had entered into with the people of the states, the year before, and that they should not violate it by taking up the hatchet against them.

The Commissioners continued their entreaties without success, till they addressed their avarice, by telling our people that the people of the states were few in number, and easily subdued; and that on the account of their disobedience to the King, they justly merited all the punishment that it was possible for White men and Indians to inflict upon them; and added, that the King was rich and powerful, both in money and subjects: That his rum was as plenty as the water in lake Ontario: that his men were as numerous as the sands upon the lake shore:—and that the Indians, if they would assist in the war, and persevere in their friendship to the King, till it was closed, should never want for money or goods.

Upon this the Chiefs concluded a treaty with the British Commissioners, in which they agreed to take up arms against the rebels, and continue in the service of his Majesty till they were subdued, in consideration of certain conditions which were stipulated in the treaty to be performed by the British government and its agents.

As soon as the treaty was finished, the Commissioners made a present to each Indian of a suit of clothes, a brass kettle, a gun and tomahawk, a scalping knife, a quantity of powder and lead, a piece of gold, and promised a bounty on every scalp that should be brought in. Thus richly clad and equipped, they returned home, after an absence of about two weeks, full of the fire of war, and anxious to encounter their enemies. Many of the kettles which the Indians received at that time are now in use on the Genesee Flats.

Hired to commit depredations upon the whites, who had given them no offence, they waited impatiently to commence their labor, till sometime in the spring of 1776, when a convenient opportunity offered for them to make an attack. At that time, a party of our Indians were at Cau-te-ga, who shot a man that was looking after his horse, for the sole purpose, as I was informed by my Indian brother, who was present, of commencing hostilities.

In May following, our Indians were in their first battle with the Americans; but at what place I am unable to determine. . . .

Previous to the battle at Fort Stanwix, the British sent for the Indians to come and see them whip the rebels; and, at the same time stated that they did not wish to have them fight, but wanted to have them just sit down, smoke their pipes, and look on. Our Indians went, to a man; but contrary to their expectation, instead of smoking and looking on, they were obliged to fight for their lives, and in the end of the battle were completely beaten, with a great loss in killed and wounded. Our Indians alone had thirty-six killed, and a great number wounded. Our town exhibited a scene of real sorrow and distress, when our warriors returned and recounted their misfortunes, and stated the real loss they had sustained in the engagement. The mourning was excessive, and was expressed by the most doleful yells, shrieks, and bowlings, and by inimitable gesticulations.

During the revolution, my house was the home of Col's Butler and Brandt, whenever they chanced to come into our neighborhood as they passed to and from Fort Niagara, which was the seat of their military operations. Many and many a night I have pounded samp for them from sun-set till sun-rise, and furnished them with necessary provision and clean clothing for their journey.

For four or five years we sustained no loss in the war, except in the few who had been killed in distant battles; and our tribe, because of the remoteness of its situation from the enemy, felt secure from an attack. At length, in the fall of 1779, intelligence was received

that a large and powerful army of the rebels, under the command of General Sullivan, was making rapid progress towards our settlement, burning and destroying the huts and corn-fields; killing the cattle, hogs and horses, and cutting down the fruit trees belonging to the Indians throughout the country.

Our Indians immediately became alarmed, and suffered every thing but death from fear that they should be taken by surprize, and totally destroyed at a single blow. But in order to prevent so great a catastrophe, they sent out a few spies who were to keep themselves at a short distance in front of the invading army, in order to watch its operations, and give information of its advances and success.

Sullivan arrived at Canandaigua Lake, and had finished his work of destruction there, and it was ascertained that he was about to march to our flats, when our Indians resolved to give him battle on the way and prevent, if possible, the distresses to which they knew we should be subjected, if he should succeed in reaching our town. Accordingly they sent all their women and children into the woods a little west of Little Beard's Town, in order that we might make a good retreat if it should be necessary, and then, well armed, set out to face the conquering enemy. The place which they fixed upon for their battle ground lay between Honeoy Creek and the head of Connessius Lake.

At length a scouting party from Sullivan's army arrived at the spot selected, when the Indians arose from their ambush with all the fierceness and terror that it was possible for them to exercise, and directly put the party upon a retreat. Two Oneida Indians were all the prisoners that were taken in that skirmish. One of them was a pilot of Gen. Sullivan, and had been very active in the war, rendering to the people of the states essential services. At the commencement of the revolution he had a brother older than himself, who resolved to join the British service. . . . At this critical juncture they met, one in the capacity of a conqueror, the other in that of a prisoner . . . they recognized each other at sight. Envy and revenge glared in the features of the conquering savage, as he advanced to his brother (the prisoner) in all the haughtiness of Indian pride, heightened by a sense of power, and addressed him in the following manner:

"Brother, you have merited death! The hatchet or the war-club shall finish your career!—When I begged of you to follow me in the fortunes of war, you was deaf to my cries—you spurned my entreaties!

"Brother! you have merited death and shall have your deserts! When the rebels raised their hatchets to fight their good master, you sharpened your knife, you brightened your rifle and led on our foes to the fields of our fathers!—You have merited death and shall die by our hands! When those rebels had drove us from the fields of our fathers to seek out new homes, it was you who could dare to step forth as their pilot, and conduct them even to the doors of our wigwams, to butcher our children and put us to death! No crime can be greater!—But though you have merited death and shall die on this spot, my hands shall not be stained in the blood of a brother! Who will strike?"

Little Beard, who was standing by, as soon as the speech was ended, struck the prisoner on the head with his tomahawk, and despatched him at once!

Little Beard then informed the other Indian prisoner that as they were at war with the whites only, and not with the Indians, they would spare his life, and after a while give him his liberty in an honorable manner. The Oneida warrior, however, was jealous of Little Beard's fidelity; and suspecting that he should soon fall by his hands, watched for a favorable opportunity to make his escape; which he soon effected. Two Indians were leading him, one on each side, when he made a violent effort, threw them upon the ground, and run for his life towards where the main body of the American army was encamped. The Indians pursued him without success; but in their absence they fell in with a small detachment of Sullivan's men, with whom they had a short but severe skirmish, in which they killed a number of the enemy, took Capt. or Lieut. William Boyd and one private, prisoners, and brought them to Little Beard's Town, where they were soon after put to death in the most shocking and cruel manner. Little Beard, in this, as in all other scenes of cruelty that happened at his town, was master of ceremonies, and principal actor. Poor Boyd was stripped of his clothing, and then tied to a sapling, where the Indians menaced his life by throwing their tomahawks at the tree, directly over his head, brandishing their scalping knives around him in the most frightful manner, and

accompanying their ceremonies with terrific shouts of joy. Having punished him sufficiently in this way, they made a small opening in his abdomen, took out an intestine, which they tied to the sapling, and then unbound him from the tree, and drove him round it till he had drawn out the whole of his intestines. He was then beheaded, his head was stuck upon a pole, and his body left on the ground unburied. Thus ended the life of poor William Boyd, who, it was said, had every appearance of being an active and enterprizing officer, of the first talents. The other prisoner was (if I remember distinctly) only beheaded and left near Boyd.

This tragedy being finished, our Indians again held a short council on the expediency of giving Sullivan battle, if he should continue to advance, and finally came to the conclusion that they were not strong enough to drive him, nor to prevent his taking possession of their fields: but that if it was possible they would escape with their own lives, preserve their families, and leave their possessions to be overrun by the invading army.

The women and children were then sent on still further towards Buffalo, to a large creek that was called by the Indians Catawba, accompanied by a part of the Indians, while the remainder secreted themselves in the woods back of Beard's Town, to watch the movements of the army.

At that time I had three children who went with me on foot, one who rode on horse back, and one whom I carried on my back.

Our corn was good that year; a part of which we had gathered and secured for winter.

In one or two days after the skirmish at Connissius lake, Sullivan and his army arrived at Genesee river, where they destroyed every article of the food kind that they could lay their hands on. A part of our corn they burnt, and threw the remainder into the river. They burnt our houses, killed what few cattle and horses they could find, destroyed our fruit trees, and left nothing but the bare soil and timber. But the Indians had eloped and were not to be found.

Having crossed and recrossed the river, and finished the work of destruction, the army marched off to the east. Our Indians saw them move off, but suspecting that it was Sullivan's intention to watch our return, and then to take us by surprize, resolved that the main body of our tribe should hunt where we then were, till Sullivan had gone so far that there would be no danger of his returning to molest us.

This being agreed to, we hunted continually till the Indians concluded that there could be no risk in our once more taking possession of our lands. Accordingly we all returned; but what were our feelings when we found that there was not a mouthful of any kind of sustenance left, not even enough to keep a child one day from perishing with hunger.

The weather by this time had become cold and stormy; and as we were destitute of houses and food too, I immediately resolved to take my children and look out for myself, without delay. With this intention I took two of my little ones on my back, bade the other three follow, and the same night arrived on the Gardow flats, where I have ever since resided.

At that time, two negroes, who had run away from their masters sometime before, were the only X inhabitants of those flats. They lived in a small cabin and had planted and raised a large field of corn, which they had not yet harvested. As they were in want of help to secure their crop, I hired to them to husk corn till the whole was harvested.

I have laughed a thousand times to myself when I have thought of the good old negro, who hired me, who fearing that I should get taken or injured by the Indians, stood by me constantly when I was husking, with a loaded gun in his hand, in order to keep off the enemy, and thereby lost as much labor of his own as he received from me, by paying good wages. I, however, was not displeased with his attention; for I knew that I should need all the corn that I could earn, even if I should husk the whole. I husked enough for them, to gain for myself, at every tenth string, one hundred strings of ears, which were equal to twenty-five bushels of shelled corn. This seasonable supply made my family comfortable for samp and cakes through the succeeding winter, which was the most severe that I have witnessed since my remembrance. The snow fell about five feet deep, and remained so for a long time, and the weather was extremely cold; so much so indeed, that almost all the game upon which the Indians depended for subsistence, perished, and reduced them almost to a state of starvation through that and three or four succeeding years. When the snow melted in the spring, deer were found dead upon the ground in vast numbers; and other animals, of every description, perished from the cold also, and were found dead, in multitudes. Many of our people barely escaped with their lives, and some actually died of hunger and freezing.

QUESTIONS TO CONSIDER

1. According to Jemison, how did the Seneca reach decisions about how and whether to go to war?
2. What impact did the fighting have on Jemison and her village?

6.5 VISUAL SOURCE: BENJAMIN WEST, *THE DEATH OF GENERAL WOLFE* (1770)*

The Death of General Wolfe portrays the death of British commander James Wolfe (1727–1759) after leading his troops to victory at the Battle of Quebec in 1759. In what turned out to be one of the last major battles of the French and Indian War, the British secured control of the capital of New

---

* public domain/Wikipedia

France and would eventually gain control of all of French Canada in a negotiated peace. General Wolfe, the principal British commander, was shot multiple times near the end of the battle and died on the field.

Benjamin West's (1738–1820) painting of these events broke with contemporary convention, which called for subjects of historical paintings to be dressed like warriors from classical antiquity, not in modern uniforms. West portrayed Wolfe as a tragic martyr to the glory of the British Empire, felled in his moment of victory by a retreating enemy. The composition resembles medieval paintings of the crucified Jesus, in which the dying martyr is surrounded by a dutiful mourning entourage. The breaking clouds in the left side of the frame which give the painting its light (and show the steeple of Quebec in the distance) seem to invite Wolfe to heaven as he gazes at the sky.

QUESTIONS TO CONSIDER

1. What is the purpose of the Native warrior placed front and center in this painting? What is his attitude toward the death of Wolfe?
2. How is this painting composed to convey to the viewer that Wolfe is a dying hero? What about the way his companions are positioned and their expressions tells the viewer this?

6.6 VISUAL SOURCE: PAUL REVERE, *THE ABLE DOCTOR, OR AMERICA SWALLOWING THE BITTER DRAUGHT* (1774)*

This engraving by Boston silversmith Paul Revere (1735–1818) was a contemporary political cartoon, mocking the British government's Intolerable Acts as oppressive and tyrannical. The American colonies, symbolized by a Native woman, are held down by members of the British aristocracy, while Prime Minister Lord North force-feeds her tea. North carries a copy of the Boston Port Act in his pocket—a law which closed the port of Boston until the residents paid for the tea destroyed during the Boston Tea Party. While bystanders chuckle and one carries a sword proclaiming "military law," a woman personifying Britain hides her face in shame.

Revere used his skills as an engraver to create effective propaganda for the Patriot cause during the crisis that eventually became the American Revolution. Here he portrays the British response to the Boston Tea Party as harsh and unseemly, behavior that ought to shame Britons. Revere's illustrations, which were widely distributed throughout the colonies, were essential in convincing colonists who still understood themselves as British to view the government in London as an antagonistic foreign power.

QUESTIONS TO CONSIDER

1. What is the significance of the tea being force-fed to America in this image?
2. Why did Revere include an ashamed personification of the British Empire? How does it help his cause to show female Britannia disapproving of Lord North?

---

* Courtesy of the Library of Congress

CHAPTER 7

A POLITICAL REVOLUTION, 1776–1791

7.1 REV. MYLES COOPER, EXCERPTS FROM *THE PATRIOTS OF NORTH-AMERICA: A SKETCH* (1775)*

Myles Cooper (1735–1785) was an English clergyman who emigrated to New York in 1762 to work as a professor at King's College (now Columbia University). Cooper, like about one in three residents of the British colonies, opposed self-styled Patriots and their resistance to Parliament and King George. Cooper fled the colonies in 1775 under threat from mob violence and never returned to North America.

In this poem Cooper derides those who called themselves Patriots as foolish, authoritarian, and violent rogues. Cooper argues that the Patriots are not a popular movement but instead a gang of bullies who are misleading the public. He criticizes Patriots for acting as if they were better than they are, comparing them to "petulant and rash" children who will not heed the wisdom of those who know better—that is, Parliament and the king. Cooper warns that, regardless of whether the Patriots are intentionally malicious or simply fools, the result will be a destructive conflict that can only be avoided if they cease their agitation.

The Men deprav'd, who quit their Sphere,
Without Remorse, or Shame, or Fear,
And boldly rush, they know not where;
Seduc'd, alass! by fond Applause,
Of gaping Mobs, and loud Huzzas.
Unconscious all, of nobler Aim,
Than sordid Pelf, or vulgar Fame;
Men undefin'd, by any Rules,
Ambiguous Things, half Knaves, half Fools,
Whom God denied, the Talents great,

Requir'd, to make a Knave, complete;
Whom Nature form'd, vile Party-Tools,
Absurder much, than dowright Fools,
Who from their own dear Puppet-Show,
The World's great Stage, pretend to know.
In Politics, mere Punchinellos,
Yet pass for rare, for clever Fellows;
Like Punch, who struts, and swears, and roars,
And calls his Betters, Rogues and Whores;
Like Punch, who speak their Prompter's Sense,

---

* Myles Cooper, *The Patriots of North-America: A Sketch* (1775), Evans Early American Imprint Collection, https://quod.lib.umich.edu/e/evans/N11357.0001.001/1:3?rgn=div1;view=fulltext.

Like his, their pow'rful Eloquence,
Like his, their wond'ring Audience.
Poor, busy, factious, empty Things,
Who nothing know, of Courts or Kings;
Who Lords or Commons, ne'er have seen,
But think, they're like Committee-men;
By Rote, like clam'rous Parrots prate
Of Trade, Revenue, Church, and State.

. . .

Is there among them, who can read,
It serves to turn, the Ideots Head;
Is there among them, who can write,
It serves to wreak the Miscreant's Spite;
With Vipers leagu'd, in borrow'd Name,
They hiss and blast their Neighbour's Fame
Vipers like,
or Dolt.
Fair Truth, exclude, from many a Press,
On Pain, of every dread Distress:
As Priests, their Flocks to circumvent,
Forbid, to read Christ's Testament,
With senseless Jargon, stupid Lies,
Like Morpheus, close the People's Eyes,
Vile, false, pernicious Doctrines preach,
Rebellion rank, and Treason teach,
Malignant o'er the Land they crawl,
And wither, blast, and poison all.

. . .

Shall we applaud, this vagrant Crew,
Whose wretched Jargon, crude and new,
Whose Impudence, and Lies delude
The harmless, ign'rant Multitude:
To Varlets, weak, impure, unjust,
The Reins, of Government, entrust.
Will Raggamuffins bold like these,
Protect our Freedom, Peace, or Ease?
Ah! surely no, it cannot be,
These are false Sons of Liberty.

The Men, who form, their Hopes and Fears,
From Hand-Bills, Pamphlets, Gazetteers;
Swallow like Gudgeons, every Lie
Which Malice, Rage, and Guilt supply;
Whose Views reach, not an Inch, from Home,
Who think their little Mantua, Rome.
The dullest Ignorance betray,
In all they do, and write, and say.

Boldly affirm, each wild Position,
As if inspir'd, by Intuition;
Untaught, in Wisdom's modest School,
That Confidence, proclaims a Fool:
Their scanty Stock of useless Knowledge,
Taught them by Floggings sheer of College,
Or which, alass! in ten Times worse,
Deriv'd from some polluted Source.
From Clodius, Judge of Men, and Things,
Of Statesmen, Ministers and Kings;
Of Power supreme, of just Protection,
Of Order, Peace, and due Subjection;
Too fond, and credulous to see
Treason, in Mask of Liberty.
What false Conclusions, Knaves can draw
From Gospel Truths, from Statute Law;
How much like Fools, these Knaves can write,
From Hunger, or from Party Spite,
Of regal Power, of legal Right.
From Curio's frothy Declamation,
Decide on Trade, on Legislation,
On Charter Rights, and dread Taxation;

. . .

Alass! vain Men, how blind! how weak!
Give them the Liberty, they seek;
Grant all their vain, their fond Desires,
Grant all, that ev'ry Fool requires.
Let them convene, in vagrant Bands,
To play at Questions, and Commands,
In tatter'd Garb, with squallid Mein,
Like Children, play at King, and Queen.
Let them, round Freedom's sacred Pole,
Quaff Toddy, from the flowing Bowl.
The Tyler's, Cade's, and Straw's debate,
The dread Arcana's, of the State.
Issue their Mandates, near and far,
On Pain of Feathers, and of Tar . . .

Thus oft, a cocker'd, pamper'd Child,
By fond maternal Love, is spoil'd.
Froward, and petulant, and rash,
Neglects his Books, and feeds on Trash;
Flies in his aged Parent's Face,
For Whims, that Age, and Sense disgrace.
A weak, ungrateful, booby Son,
Sullen, controul'd; if pleas'd, undone:
Let him pursue, his idle Way,

'Twou'd be, one glorious Holiday;
Let the poor Thing, his Fancy please,
He'd perish soon by dire Disease.
Unconscious, of the Woes to come,
Unmindful of his future Doom,
How rough the World, compar'd with Home.
When left alone, on Life's sad Stag,
When anxious Cares, his Thoughts engage,
Of Parent's fost'ring Aid berest,
To the wide World, an Orphan left.
Too late, the fatal Truth, perceives,
Too late reflects, and vainly grieves,
His Parent, fondly was beguil'd,
Had spar'd the Rod, and spoil'd the Child.
Teach them, wise Patriot, t'obey,

. . .

Triumphant Crimes, pollute the Land,
Consign'd to ev'ry Butcher's Hand;
Spread Desolation, like a Flood,
And Brothers, shed, their Brother's Blood.
Rouse these dear Lands, from torpid Sleep,
Ah! rouse them, lest they 'wake to weep;
With Anguish weep, alass! in vain,
For thousands ruin'd, thousands slain.

Let not their fatal Rage, despise
The Orphans Tears, the Widows Sighs.
Kind aged Parents, left forlorn,
Their hapless, murder'd Sons, to mourn;
Dear, pious, Sons, whose frantic Eye,
Beholds their Sires, untimely die;

. . .

Warn them, of their impending Fate,
Lest sad Repentance comes too late.
Bid them survey the Realms above,
The blissful Seats, of Peace, and Love,
Yet there, even there, a rebel Crew,
That Peace, that Love, could joyless view;
See God, immortal Joys prepare,
Yet Joys, immortal, scorn to share.
Plac'd by the Side, of Pow'r divine,
Yet 'midst that Glory, could repine.
View Pow'r supreme, with envious Eye,
And God's Omnipotence defy:
To Envy, Rage, and Malice prone,
Invade th'indulgent Father's Throne,
Till by unjust Wrath, the Traitors fell,
Headlong from Heav'n, to endless Hell.

QUESTIONS TO CONSIDER

1. What misdeeds or bad behavior does Cooper accuse the Patriots of? Is this a fair assessment of Patriot conduct?
2. Does Cooper's position as an Anglican clergyman influence his perspective on the Patriot cause? If so, how?

7.2 THE SENTIMENTS OF AN AMERICAN WOMAN (1780)*

The Sentiments of an American Woman is an anonymous broadside or flyer, possibly authored by Esther de Berdt Reed (1746–1780), organizer of the Ladies Association of Philadelphia. The Ladies Association was a pioneering civilian aid group that organized relief efforts for the under-equipped

* *The Sentiments of an American Woman* (Philadelphia, 1780), Printed Ephemera Collection, Library of Congress, https://www. loc.gov/item/rbpe.14600300/.

Continental Army. At the time, it was unconventional and usually frowned upon for women to engage in fundraising and political organizing, but the Ladies Association provided much needed supplies for the chronically underfunded army.

The author argues that it is the duty of all American women to support the war effort in whatever way they can. Although she acknowledges that proposals for women's active involvement are unusual, she points to heroines from antiquity and the Bible as inspiration for women taking up their country's cause with zeal. The author references women's participation in boycotts of British goods as an example of the role American women had already taken on in the resistance to Britain. *Sentiments of an American Woman* stresses the need for sacrifice and unity of purpose among all Americans in order to win the war.

ON the commencement of actual war, the Women of America manifested a firm resolution to contribute as much as could depend on them, to the deliverance of their country. Animated by the purest patriotism, they are sensible of sorrow at this day, in not offering more than barren wishes for the success of so glorious a Revolution. They aspire to render themselves more really useful; and this sentiment is universal from the north to the south of the Thirteen United States. Our ambition is kindled by the same of those heroines of antiquity, who have rendered their sex illustrious, and have proved to the universe, that, if the weakness of our Constitution, if opinion and manners did not forbid us to march to glory by the same paths as the Men, we should at least equal, and sometimes surpass them in our love for the public good. I glory in all that which my sex has done great and commendable. I call to mind with enthusiasm and with admiration, all those acts of courage, of constancy and patriotism, which history has transmitted to us: The people favoured by Heaven, preserved from destruction by the virtues, the zeal and the resolution of Deborah, of Judith, of Esther! The fortitude of the mother of the Macchabees, in giving up her sons to die before her eyes: Rome saved from the fury of a victorious enemy by the efforts of Volumnia, and other Roman Ladies: So many famous sieges where the Women have been seen forgetting the weakness of their sex, building new walls, digging trenches with their feeble hands, furnishing arms to their defenders, they themselves darting the missile weapons on the enemy, resigning the ornaments of their apparel, and their fortune, to fill the public treasury, and to hasten the deliverance of their country; burying themselves under its ruins, throwing themselves into the flames rather than submit to the disgrace of humiliation before a proud enemy.

Born for liberty, disdaining to bear the irons of a tyrannic Government, we associate ourselves to the grandeur of those Sovereigns, cherished and revered, who have held with so much splendour the scepter of the greatest States, The Batildas, the Elizabeths, the Maries, the Catharines, who have extended the empire of liberty, and contented to reign by sweetness and justice, have broken the chains of slavery, forged by tryants in the times of ignorance and barbarity. The Spanish Women, do they not make, at this moment, the most patriotic sacrifices, to encrease the means of victory in the hands of their Sovereign. He is a friend to the French Nation. They are our allies. We call to mind, doubly interested, that it was a French Maid who kindled up amongst her fellow-citizens, the flame of patriotism buried under long misfortunes: It was the Maid of Orleans who drove from the kingdom of France the ancestors of those same British, whose odious yoke we have just shaken off; and whom it is necessary that we drive from this Continent.

But I must limit myself to the recollection of this small number of achievements. Who knows if persons disposed to censure, and sometimes too severely with regard to us, may not disapprove our appearing acquainted even with the actions of which our sex boasts? We are at least certain, that he cannot be a good citizen who will not applaud our efforts for the relief of the armies which defend our lives, our possessions, our liberty? The situation of our soldiery has been represented to me; the evils inseparable from war, and the firm and generous spirit which has enabled them to support these. But it has been said, that they may apprehend, that, in the course of a long war, the view of their distresses may be lost, and their services be forgotten. Forgotten! never; I can answer in the name of all my sex. Brave Americans, your disinterestedness, your courage, and your constancy will always be dear to America, as long as she shall preserve her virtue.

We know that at a distance from the theatre of war, if we enjoy any tranquility, it is the fruit of your watchings, your labours, your dangers. If I live happy in the midst of my family; if my husband cultivates his field, and reaps his harvest in peace; if, surrounded with my children, I myself nourish the youngest, and press it to my bosom, without being afraid of feeing myself separated from it, by a ferocious enemy; if the house in which we dwell; if our barns, our orchards are safe at the present time from the hands of those incendiaries, it is to you that we owe it. And shall we hesitate to evidence to you our gratitude? Shall we hesitate to wear a cloathing more simple; hair dressed less elegant, while at the price of this small privation, we shall deserve your benedictions. Who, amongst us, will not renounce with the highest pleasure, those vain ornaments, when-she shall consider that the valiant defenders of America will be able to draw some advantage from the money which she may have laid out in these; that they will be better defended from the rigours of the seasons, that after their painful toils, they will receive some extraordinary and unexpected relief; that these presents will perhaps be valued by them at a greater price, when they will have it in their power to say: This is the offering of the Ladies. The time is arrived to display the same sentiments which animated us at the beginning of the Revolution, when we renounced the use of teas, however agreeable to our taste, rather than receive them from our persecutors; when we made it appear to them that we placed former necessaries in the rank of superfluities, when our liberty was interested; when our republican and laborious hands spun the flax, prepared the linen intended for the use of our soldiers; when exiles and fugitives we supported with courage all the evils which are the concomitants of war. Let us not lose a moment; let us be engaged to offer the homage of our gratitude at the altar of military valour, and you, our brave deliverers, while mercenary slaves combat to cause you to share with them, the irons with which they are loaded, receive with a freehand our offering, the purest which can be presented to your virtue,

By An AMERICAN WOMAN.

QUESTIONS TO CONSIDER

1. What is the purpose of the author's allusions to women from ancient history? What are the examples of these heroines meant to prove?
2. What is an appropriate role for women to play in the struggle for independence, according to this author?

7.3 THE CHICKASAW SEND A MESSAGE OF CONCILIATION TO CONGRESS (1783)*

The Chickasaw are a Native people whose homeland is in what is now northern Mississippi. During the seventeenth and eighteenth centuries they often traded with the British, but their position along the Mississippi put them at a crossroads allowing them to regularly interact with Spanish

* William P. Palmer, ed., *Calendar of Virginia State Papers and Other Manuscripts from January 1, 1752 to December 31, 1784 Preserved in the Capitol at Richmond* (Richmond, VA, 1883), 3:515–17.

and sometimes French representatives as well. Their homeland was part of land ceded by the British Crown to the new United States following the 1783 Treaty of Paris.

With the British having left following the peace, the Chickasaw sought to establish relations with the new United States and better understand how diplomacy in North America had changed. They addressed their inquiry to the president of Congress as the United States under the Articles of Confederation had no chief executive. The Chickasaw sought to establish a trading relationship, specifically in order to acquire ammunition for firearms following the departure of their British suppliers.

July 28, 1783
TO HIS EXCELLENCY THE PRESIDENT OF THE HONORABLE CONGRESS OF THE UNITED AMERICAN STATES

Friend & Brother,
This is the first talk we ever sent you—we hope it will not be the last. We desire you to open your Ears to hear, and your heart to understand us, as we shall always be ready to do to your talks, which we expect will be good, as you are a great and wise man.

Brother,
When our great father the King of England called away his warriors, he told us to take your People by the hand as friends and brothers. Our hearts were always inclined to do so & as far as our circumstances permitted us, we evinced our good intentions as Brothers the Virginians can testify—It makes our hearts rejoice to find that our great father, and his children the Americans have at length made peace, which we wish may continue as long as the Sun and Moon, And to find that our Brothers the Americans are inclined to take us by the hand, and Smoke with us at the great Fire, which we hope will never be extinguished.

Brother,
Notwithstanding the Satisfaction all these things give us we are yet in confusion & uncertainty. The Spaniards are sending talks amongst us, and inviting our young Men to trade with them. We also receive talks from the Governor of Georgia to the same effect—We have had Speeches from the Illinois inviting us to a Trade and Intercourse with them—Our Brothers, the Virginians Call upon us to a Treaty, and want part of our land, and we expect our Neighbors who live on Cumberland

River, will in a Little time Demand, if not forcibly take part of it from us, also as we are informed they have been marking Lines through our hunting grounds: we are daily receiving Talks from one Place or other, and from People we Know nothing about. We Know not who to mind or who to neglect. We are told that the Americans have 13 Councils Compos'd of Chiefs and Warriors. We Know not which of them we are to Listen to, or if we are to hear some, and Reject others, we are at a loss to Distinguish those we are to hear. We are told that you are the head Chief of the Grand Council, which is above these 13 Councils: if so why have we not had Talks from you, —We are head men and Chiefs and Warriors also: and have always been accustomed to speak with great Chiefs & warriors—We are Likewise told that you and the Great men of your Council are Very Wise—we are glad to hear it, being assured that you will not do us any Wrong, and therefore we wish to Speak with you and your Council, or if you Do not approve of our so Doing, as you are wise, you will tell us who shall speak with us, in behalf of all our Brothers the Americans, and from whare and whome we are to be supplyed with necessarries in the manner our great father supplied us—we hope you will also put a stop to any encroachments on our lands, without our consent, and silence all those People who sends us Such Talks as inflame & exasperate our Young Men, as it is our earnest desire to remain in peace and friendship with our Br: the Americans for ever.

Brother,
The King our Common father always left one of his beloved Men among us, to whom we told anything we had to say, and he soon obtained an answer—and by him our great Father, his Chiefs & headmen spoke to us.

Our great father always gave him goods to cover the nakedness of our old men who could not hunt, our women and our children, and he was as one mouth, and one tongue between us, and was beloved of us all. Such a man living among us particularly at this time, would rescue us from the darkness and confusion we are in. By directing us to whom we should speak, and putting us in the right Path that we should not go wrong.

We have desired our Br. Mr. Donne, who brought talks from General Clark, and has been some time among us, to deliver this talk to you, and speak it in our behalf to your Grand Council, that you may know our want, and as you are wise, that you may direct us what to do for the best. He has Promised, at our desire to take it to your great council fire & to bring as your answer, that you may be no more in the dark—beleive what he tells you from us; we have told him all that is in our hearts.

Brothers, we are very poor for necessaries, for Amunition particularly. We can supply ourselves from the Spaniards but we are averse to hold any intercourse with them, as our hearts are always with our Brothers the Americans. We have advised our young men to wait with patience for the answer to this talk, when we rest assured of having supplies, and every thing so regulated that no further confusion may ensue. We wish that this land may never again be stained with the blood of either white or Red men, that piece may last forever and that both our women and children may sit down in safety under their own shade to enjoy without fear or apprehension the Blessing which the good Spirit enriches them with. Brother, we again desire you and your cheifs to Listen to what we say that we shall not have to Repeat it again, and as you are all Wise, you will know what to do.

Done at Chuck-ul-issah our Great Town the 28th Day of July, 1783.

> MINGHOMA, PYAMATHAHAW, KUSHTHAPU-SHASA, PYAMINGOE of Christhautra, PYAMINGO of Chuckaferah.

QUESTIONS TO CONSIDER

1. What questions do the Chickasaw have about the United States?
2. What is the Chickasaw relationship with the Spanish? How do the Chickasaw portray the Spanish in their letter?

7.4 JAMES MADISON, EXCERPTS FROM "VICES OF THE POLITICAL SYSTEM OF THE U. STATES" (1787)*

James Madison (1751–1836) was a delegate to the Congress of the Confederation, the national legislative body of the United States under the Articles of Confederation. Madison was also a vocal critic of the Articles, arguing that they were weak and ineffective. Due to the encouragement of Madison and others, the Constitutional Convention of 1787 assembled to amend the Articles. Instead, the convention started from scratch and replaced the Articles with the United States Constitution.

---

* James Madison, *Vices of the Political System of the U. States*, May 7, 1787, Manuscript/Mixed Material, Library of Congress, https://www.loc.gov/item/mjm012727/.

Madison's criticisms of the Articles concern their lack of coordination between the states and national Congress's inability to force states to comply with any law or regulation. In addition, Congress had little authority to enforce uniform regulations throughout the states so that conducting trade between multiple states could be challenging. Without any means to force states to comply with its edicts, Congress was left at the mercy of voluntary cooperation by the states. As Madison pointed out, some states were reticent to participate due to worries that other states were not paying their fair share. Madison argued in favor of a republican government with a stronger national authority over the individual states.

April, 1787.
Vices of the Political system of the U. States.

1. **Failure of the States to comply with the Constitutional requisitions.**

This evil has been so fully experienced both during the war and since the peace, results so naturally from the number and independent authority of the States and has been so uniformly exemplified in every similar Confederacy, that it may be considered as not less radically and permanently inherent in than it is fatal to the object of the present system.

2. **Encroachments by the States on the federal authority.**

Examples of this are numerous and repetitions may be foreseen in almost every case where any favorite object of a State shall present a temptation. Among these examples are the wars and treaties of Georgia with the Indians. The unlicensed compacts between Virginia and Maryland, and between Pena. & N. Jersey—the troops raised and to be kept up by Massts.

3. **Violations of the law of nations and of treaties.**

From the number of Legislatures, the sphere of life from which most of their members are taken, and the circumstances under which their legislative business is carried on, irregularities of this kind must frequently happen. Accordingly not a year has passed without instances of them in some one or other of the States. The Treaty of Peace—the treaty with France—the treaty with Holland have each been violated. [See the complaints to Congress on these subjects.] The causes of these irregularities must necessarily produce frequent violations of the law of nations in other respects. As yet foreign powers have not been rigorous in animadverting on us. This moderation, however cannot be mistaken for a permanent partiality to our faults, or a permanent security agst. those disputes with other

nations, which being among the greatest of public calamities, it ought to be least in the power of any part of the community to bring on the whole.

4. **Trespasses of the States on the rights of each other.**

These are alarming symptoms, and may be daily apprehended as we are admonished by daily experience. See the law of Virginia restricting foreign vessels to certain ports—of Maryland in favor of vessels belonging to her own citizens—of N. York in favor of the same—Paper money, instalments of debts, occlusion of Courts, making property a legal tender, may likewise be deemed aggressions on the rights of other States. As the Citizens of every State aggregately taken stand more or less in the relation of Creditors or debtors, to the Citizens of every other State, Acts of the debtor State in favor of debtors, affect the Creditor State, in the same manner as they do its own citizens who are relatively creditors towards other citizens. This remark may be extended to foreign nations. If the exclusive regulation of the value and alloy of coin was properly delegated to the federal authority, the policy of it equally requires a control on the States in the cases above mentioned. It must have been meant 1. to preserve uniformity in the circulating medium throughout the nation. 2. to prevent those frauds on the citizens of other States, and the subjects of foreign powers, which might disturb the tranquility at home, or involve the Union in foreign contests. The practice of many States in restricting the commercial intercourse with other States, and putting their productions and manufactures on the same footing with those of foreign nations, though not contrary to the federal articles, is certainly adverse to the spirit of the Union, and tends to beget retaliating regulations, not less expensive and vexatious in themselves than they are destructive of the general harmony.

5. **Want of concert in matters where common interest requires it.**

This defect is strongly illustrated in the state of our commercial affairs. How much has the national dignity, interest, and revenue, suffered from this cause? Instances of inferior moment are the want of uniformity in the laws concerning naturalization & literary property; of provision for national seminaries, for grants of incorporation for national purposes, for canals and other works of general utility, which may at present be defeated by the perverseness of particular States whose concurrence is necessary.

6. **Want of Guaranty to the States of their Constitutions & laws against internal violence.**

The confederation is silent on this point and therefore by the second article the hands of the federal authority are tied. According to Republican Theory, Right and power being both vested in the majority, are held to be synonymous. According to fact and experience a minority may in an appeal to force, be an overmatch for the majority. 1. if the minority happen to include all such as possess the skill and habits of military life, & such as possess the great pecuniary resources, one-third only may conquer the remaining two-thirds. 2. one-third of those who participate in the choice of the rulers, may be rendered a majority by the accession of those whose poverty excludes them from a right of suffrage, and who for obvious reasons will be more likely to join the standard of sedition than that of the established Government. 3. where slavery exists the republican Theory becomes still more fallacious.

7. **Want of sanction to the laws, and of coercion in the Government of the Confederacy.**

A sanction is essential to the idea of law, as coercion is to that of Government. The federal system being destitute of both, wants the great vital principles of a Political Constitution. Under the form of such a constitution, it is in fact nothing more than a treaty of amity of commerce and of alliance, between independent and Sovereign States. From what cause could

so fatal an omission have happened in the articles of Confederation? from a mistaken confidence that the justice, the good faith, the honor, the sound policy, of the several legislative assemblies would render superfluous any appeal to the ordinary motives by which the laws secure the obedience of individuals: a confidence which does honor to the enthusiastic virtue of the compilers, as much as the inexperience of the crisis apologizes for their errors. The time which has since elapsed has had the double effect, of increasing the light and tempering the warmth, with which the arduous work may be revised. It is no longer doubted that a unanimous and punctual obedience of 13 independent bodies, to the acts of the federal Government ought not to be calculated on. Even during the war, when external danger supplied in some degree the defect of legal &coercive sanctions, how imperfectly did the States fulfil their obligations to the Union? In time of peace, we see already what is to be expected. How indeed could it be otherwise? In the first place, Every general act of the Union must necessarily bear unequally hard on some particular member or members of it, secondly the partiality of the members to their own interests and rights, a partiality which will be fostered by the courtiers of popularity, will naturally exaggerate the inequality where it exists, and even suspect it where it has no existence, thirdly a distrust of the voluntary compliance of each other may prevent the compliance of any, although it should be the latent disposition of all. Here are causes & pretexts which will never fail to render federal measures abortive. If the laws of the States were merely recommendatory to their citizens, or if they were to be rejudged by County authorities, what security, what probability would exist, that they would be carried into execution? Is the security or probability greater in favor of the acts of Congs. Which depending for their execution on the will of the State legislatures, wch. are tho' nominally authoritative, in fact recommendatory only?

. . .

QUESTIONS TO CONSIDER

1. Why have the individual states not been able to work effectively together, according to Madison?
2. Why does Madison think it will be a good idea to make laws and policies more uniform throughout the United States?

7.5 VISUAL SOURCE: JEAN-BAPTISTE-ANTOINE DEVERGER, *AMERICAN SOLDIERS AT THE SIEGE OF YORKTOWN (1781)**

French lieutenant Jean-Baptiste-Antoine DeVerger (1762–1851) made this sketch in his personal notebook while serving in the French army at the siege of Yorktown near the end of the American War for Independence. He captures the diversity of the Continental Army in terms of both its personnel and accessories. Three of the soldiers are pictured wearing standard military uniforms, but all are of different colors. One appears to be a frontiersman, clothed in a fringed shirt, armed with a hatchet, and missing the military bayonet that his comrades carry. One of the soldiers is African American and part of a Rhode Island regiment of Black soldiers made up of volunteer enslaved people who were freed once they entered service. Estimates for how many Black Americans served with Patriot armed forces vary, but they numbered in the thousands and there may have been as many as eight thousand in total.

QUESTIONS TO CONSIDER

1. In what ways is the Black soldier in DeVerger's sketch similar to his comrades? Are there any noticeable differences?
2. What does this sketch say about the people who served in the Continental Army? What does the lack of consistent uniforms and arms suggest?

---

* public domain/Wikipedia

7.6 VISUAL SOURCE: EDWARD SAVAGE, *THE WASHINGTON FAMILY* (1789–1796)*

Edward Savage (1761–1817), an American painter and engraver, composed this portrait of the Washington family in the early 1790s during Washington's presidency. George Washington (1732–1799) appears with his wife Martha, her grandchildren George Washington Parke Custis (left) and Eleanor Parke Custis (center), and one of the men they enslaved. This man's identity has not been conclusively established. Some suggest it may be Christopher Sheels, who acted as George Washington's personal valet during this time, but this is only one possibility.

The family is pictured at their home at Mount Vernon plantation, along the Potomac River, with the plans for the new Washington city on the table before them. According to Savage's notes, Martha is tracing "the grand avenue," which could be either Pennsylvania Avenue or the National Mall. Washington's military uniform and the papers in his left hand were intended to allude to his authority in both military and civil matters.

---

* public domain/Wikipedia

QUESTIONS TO CONSIDER

1. Why might Savage have placed the plans for Washington city so prominently in the composition? What meaning did that city have for the future of the United States?
2. How does the inclusion of the enslaved man to the far right change the composition?

CHAPTER 8

SECURING A REPUBLIC, IMAGINING AN EMPIRE, 1789–1815

8.1 JAMES MADISON, *FEDERALIST NO. 10* (1787)*

Following the Constitutional Convention several supporters of the new constitution, including James Madison (1751–1836) and Alexander Hamilton (c. 1757–1804), published essays encouraging its ratification by the states. Known as the *Federalist* papers, these essays remain important sources for understanding how the architects of the Constitution believed the political system they had created would work. *Federalist No. 10*, in which Madison argues that the new constitution will be able to prevent "factions" or concerted interests from abusing the government, is commonly regarded as one of the most important of these.

Madison and other statesmen of his generation hoped that government policy would be determined by enlightened men who would pursue only the public good. The idea that politicians would form alliances based on common interest, form a majority, and then use that majority to enact legislation in support of those interests was seen as a potential threat to the republic. Such a majority, Madison feared, would have no respect for anyone who was not part of the majority and would abuse their rights. Only a large republic, Madison argued, with many diverse interests and passions, could guard against such a majority.

. . . AMONG the numerous advantages promised by a well-constructed Union, none deserves to be more accurately developed than its tendency to break and control the violence of faction. The friend of popular governments never finds himself so much alarmed for their character and fate, as when he contemplates their propensity to this dangerous vice. He will not fail, therefore, to set a due value on any plan which, without violating the principles to which he is attached, provides a proper cure for it. The instability, injustice, and confusion introduced into the public councils, have, in truth, been the mortal diseases under which popular governments have everywhere perished; as they continue to be the favorite and fruitful topics

---

* James Madison, *Federalist No. 10*: "The Union as a Safeguard Against Domestic Faction and Insurrection," *New York Packet*, November 23, 1787, https://guides.loc.gov/federalist-papers/text-1-10#s-lg-box-wrapper-25493273.

from which the adversaries to liberty derive their most specious declamations. The valuable improvements made by the American constitutions on the popular models, both ancient and modern, cannot certainly be too much admired; but it would be an unwarrantable partiality, to contend that they have as effectually obviated the danger on this side, as was wished and expected. Complaints are everywhere heard from our most considerate and virtuous citizens, equally the friends of public and private faith, and of public and personal liberty, that our governments are too unstable, that the public good is disregarded in the conflicts of rival parties, and that measures are too often decided, not according to the rules of justice and the rights of the minor party, but by the superior force of an interested and overbearing majority. However anxiously we may wish that these complaints had no foundation, the evidence, of known facts will not permit us to deny that they are in some degree true. It will be found, indeed, on a candid review of our situation, that some of the distresses under which we labor have been erroneously charged on the operation of our governments; but it will be found, at the same time, that other causes will not alone account for many of our heaviest misfortunes; and, particularly, for that prevailing and increasing distrust of public engagements, and alarm for private rights, which are echoed from one end of the continent to the other. These must be chiefly, if not wholly, effects of the unsteadiness and injustice with which a factious spirit has tainted our public administrations.

By a faction, I understand a number of citizens, whether amounting to a majority or a minority of the whole, who are united and actuated by some common impulse of passion, or of interest, adversed to the rights of other citizens, or to the permanent and aggregate interests of the community.

There are two methods of curing the mischiefs of faction: the one, by removing its causes; the other, by controlling its effects.

There are again two methods of removing the causes of faction: the one, by destroying the liberty which is essential to its existence; the other, by giving to every citizen the same opinions, the same passions, and the same interests.

It could never be more truly said than of the first remedy, that it was worse than the disease. Liberty is to faction what air is to fire, an aliment without which it instantly expires. But it could not be less folly to abolish liberty, which is essential to political life, because it nourishes faction, than it would be to wish the annihilation of air, which is essential to animal life, because it imparts to fire its destructive agency.

The second expedient is as impracticable as the first would be unwise. As long as the reason of man continues fallible, and he is at liberty to exercise it, different opinions will be formed. As long as the connection subsists between his reason and his self-love, his opinions and his passions will have a reciprocal influence on each other; and the former will be objects to which the latter will attach themselves. The diversity in the faculties of men, from which the rights of property originate, is not less an insuperable obstacle to a uniformity of interests. The protection of these faculties is the first object of government. From the protection of different and unequal faculties of acquiring property, the possession of different degrees and kinds of property immediately results; and from the influence of these on the sentiments and views of the respective proprietors, ensues a division of the society into different interests and parties.

The latent causes of faction are thus sown in the nature of man; and we see them everywhere brought into different degrees of activity, according to the different circumstances of civil society. A zeal for different opinions concerning religion, concerning government, and many other points, as well of speculation as of practice; an attachment to different leaders ambitiously contending for pre-eminence and power; or to persons of other descriptions whose fortunes have been interesting to the human passions, have, in turn, divided mankind into parties, inflamed them with mutual animosity, and rendered them much more disposed to vex and oppress each other than to co-operate for their common good. So strong is this propensity of mankind to fall into mutual animosities, that where no substantial occasion presents itself, the most frivolous and fanciful distinctions have been sufficient to kindle their unfriendly passions and excite their most violent conflicts. But the most common and durable source of factions has been the various and unequal distribution of property. Those who hold and those who are without property have ever formed distinct interests in society. Those who are creditors, and those who are debtors, fall under a like discrimination. A landed interest, a manufacturing interest, a mercantile interest, a moneyed interest, with many lesser interests, grow up of necessity in civilized nations, and divide them into different classes, actuated by different sentiments and views. The regulation of these various and interfering interests forms the principal task of modern legislation, and involves the spirit of party and faction in the necessary and ordinary operations of the government.

. . . It is in vain to say that enlightened statesmen will be able to adjust these clashing interests, and render them all subservient to the public good. Enlightened statesmen will not always be at the helm. Nor, in many cases, can such an adjustment be made at all without taking into view indirect and remote considerations, which will rarely prevail over the immediate interest which one party may find in disregarding the rights of another or the good of the whole.

The inference to which we are brought is, that the CAUSES of faction cannot be removed, and that relief is only to be sought in the means of controlling its EFFECTS.

If a faction consists of less than a majority, relief is supplied by the republican principle, which enables the majority to defeat its sinister views by regular vote. It may clog the administration, it may convulse the society; but it will be unable to execute and mask its violence under the forms of the Constitution. When a majority is included in a faction, the form of popular government, on the other hand, enables it to sacrifice to its ruling passion or interest both the public good and the rights of other citizens. To secure the public good and private rights against the danger of such a faction, and at the same time to preserve the spirit and the form of popular government, is then the great object to which our inquiries are directed. Let me add that it is the great desideratum by which this form of government can be rescued from the opprobrium under which it has so long labored, and be recommended to the esteem and adoption of mankind.

By what means is this object attainable? Evidently by one of two only. Either the existence of the same passion or interest in a majority at the same time must be prevented, or the majority, having such coexistent passion or interest, must be rendered, by their number and local situation, unable to concert and carry into effect schemes of oppression. If the impulse and the

opportunity be suffered to coincide, we well know that neither moral nor religious motives can be relied on as an adequate control. They are not found to be such on the injustice and violence of individuals, and lose their efficacy in proportion to the number combined together, that is, in proportion as their efficacy becomes needful.

From this view of the subject it may be concluded that a pure democracy, by which I mean a society consisting of a small number of citizens, who assemble and administer the government in person, can admit of no cure for the mischiefs of faction. A common passion or interest will, in almost every case, be felt by a majority of the whole; a communication and concert result from the form of government itself; and there is nothing to check the inducements to sacrifice the weaker party or an obnoxious individual. Hence it is that such democracies have ever been spectacles of turbulence and contention; have ever been found incompatible with personal security or the rights of property; and have in general been as short in their lives as they have been violent in their deaths. Theoretic politicians, who have patronized this species of government, have erroneously supposed that by reducing mankind to a perfect equality in their political rights, they would, at the same time, be perfectly equalized and assimilated in their possessions, their opinions, and their passions.

A republic, by which I mean a government in which the scheme of representation takes place, opens a different prospect, and promises the cure for which we are seeking. Let us examine the points in which it varies from pure democracy, and we shall comprehend both the nature of the cure and the efficacy which it must derive from the Union.

The two great points of difference between a democracy and a republic are: first, the delegation of the government, in the latter, to a small number of citizens elected by the rest; secondly, the greater number of citizens, and greater sphere of country, over which the latter may be extended.

The effect of the first difference is, on the one hand, to refine and enlarge the public views, by passing them through the medium of a chosen body of citizens, whose wisdom may best discern the true interest of their country, and whose patriotism and love of justice will be least likely to sacrifice it to temporary or partial considerations. Under such a regulation, it may well happen that the public voice, pronounced by the representatives of the people, will be more consonant to the public good than if pronounced by the people themselves, convened for the purpose. On the other hand, the effect may be inverted. Men of factious tempers, of local prejudices, or of sinister designs, may, by intrigue, by corruption, or by other means, first obtain the suffrages, and then betray the interests, of the people. The question resulting is, whether small or extensive republics are more favorable to the election of proper guardians of the public weal; and it is clearly decided in favor of the latter by two obvious considerations:

In the first place, it is to be remarked that, however small the republic may be, the representatives must be raised to a certain number, in order to guard against the cabals of a few; and that, however large it may be, they must be limited to a certain number, in order to guard against the confusion of a multitude. Hence, the number of representatives in the two cases not being in proportion to that of the two constituents, and being proportionally greater in the small republic, it follows that, if the proportion of fit characters be not less in the large than in the small republic, the former will present a greater option, and consequently a greater probability of a fit choice.

In the next place, as each representative will be chosen by a greater number of citizens in the large than in the small republic, it will be more difficult for unworthy candidates to practice with success the vicious arts by which elections are too often carried; and the suffrages of the people being more free, will be more likely to centre in men who possess the most attractive merit and the most diffusive and established characters.

It must be confessed that in this, as in most other cases, there is a mean, on both sides of which inconveniences will be found to lie. By enlarging too much the number of electors, you render the representatives too little acquainted with all their local circumstances and lesser interests; as by reducing it too much, you render him unduly attached to these, and too little fit to comprehend and pursue great and national objects. The federal Constitution forms a happy combination in this respect; the great and aggregate interests being referred to the national, the local and particular to the State legislatures.

The other point of difference is, the greater number of citizens and extent of territory which may be brought within the compass of republican than of democratic government; and it is this circumstance principally which renders factious combinations less to be dreaded in the former than in the latter. The smaller the society, the fewer probably will be the distinct parties and interests composing it; the fewer the distinct parties and interests, the more frequently will a majority be found of the same party; and the smaller the number of individuals composing a majority, and the smaller the compass within which they are placed, the more easily will they concert and execute their plans of oppression. Extend the sphere, and you take in a greater variety of parties and interests; you make it less probable that a majority of the whole will have a common motive to invade the rights of other citizens.

Hence, it clearly appears, that the same advantage which a republic has over a democracy, in controlling the effects of faction, is enjoyed by a large over a small republic,—is enjoyed by the Union over the States composing it. Does the advantage consist in the substitution of representatives whose enlightened views and virtuous sentiments render them superior to local prejudices and schemes of injustice? It will not be denied that the representation of the Union will be most likely to possess these requisite endowments. Does it consist in the greater security afforded by a greater variety of parties, against the event of any one party being able to outnumber and oppress the rest? In an equal degree does the increased variety of parties comprised within the Union, increase this security. Does it, in fine, consist in the greater obstacles opposed to the concert and accomplishment of the secret wishes of an unjust and interested majority? Here, again, the extent of the Union gives it the most palpable advantage.

The influence of factious leaders may kindle a flame within their particular States, but will be unable to spread a general conflagration through the other States. A religious sect may degenerate into a political faction in a part of the Confederacy; but the variety of sects dispersed over the entire face of it must secure the national councils against any danger from that source. A rage for paper money, for an abolition of debts, for an equal division of property, or for any other improper or wicked project, will be less apt to pervade the whole body of the Union than a particular member of it; in the same proportion as such a malady is more likely to taint a particular county or district, than an entire State.

In the extent and proper structure of the Union, therefore, we behold a republican remedy for the diseases most incident to republican government.

QUESTIONS TO CONSIDER

1. What does Madison mean by "faction"? Why is he so worried about avoiding or minimizing factions?
2. Does Madison's description of politics in a large republic resemble the modern United States? Why or why not?

8.2 BENJAMIN RUSH, "OF THE MODE OF EDUCATION PROPER IN A REPUBLIC" (1798)*

Benjamin Rush (1746–1813) was a physician, educator, and a leader of the American independence movement. He was also an advocate of the importance of education for women, although he deemed some subjects (mostly mathematics and science) unnecessary for them to learn. In this essay Rush lays out the importance of education as he sees it, especially for Americans. Rush, like many elite Republicans of the time, was well-versed in classical history and believed that republics in ancient times had failed due to a lack of civic virtue among their people. Therefore, Rush felt that education was important from a young age to help Americans grow up into capable citizens who could participate in representative government. He believed women should be educated as well because "the first impressions upon the minds of children are generally derived from women" and American women should have a role in inculcating republican principles in the future generations.

The business of education has acquired a new complexion by the independence of our country. The form of government we have assumed, has created a new class of duties to every American. It becomes us, therefore, to examine our former habits upon this subject, and in laying the foundations for nurseries of wise and good men, to adapt our modes of teaching to the peculiar form of our government.

The first remark that I shall make upon this subject is, that an education in our own, is to be preferred to an education in a foreign country. The principle of patriotism stands in need of the reinforcement of prejudice, and it is well known that our strongest prejudices in favour of our country are formed in the first one and twenty years of our lives. The policy of the Lacedemonians is well worthy of our imitation. When Antipater

---

* Benjamin Rush, "Of the Mode of Education Proper in a Republic" (1798), in *The Selected Writings of Benjamin Rush*, ed. Dagobert D. Runes (New York: Philosophical Library, 1947), 87–89, 92, 94–96.

demanded fifty of their children as hostages for the ful-fillment of a distant engagement, those wise republicans refused to comply with his demand, but readily offered him double the number of their adult citizens, whose habits and prejudices could not be shaken by residing in a foreign country. Passing by, in this place, the ad-vantages to the community from the early attachment of youth to the laws and constitution of their country, I shall only remark, that young men who have trodden the paths of science together, or have joined in the same sports, whether of swimming, skating, fishing, or hunt-ing, generally feel, thro' life, such ties to each other, as add greatly to the obligations of mutual benevolence.

I conceive the education of our youth in this coun-try to be peculiarly necessary in Pennsylvania, while our citizens are composed of the natives of so many different kingdoms in Europe. Our schools of learn-ing, by producing one general, and uniform system of education, will render the mass of the people more homogeneous, and thereby fit them more easily for uniform and peaceable government.

I proceed in the next place, to enquire, what mode of education we shall adopt so as to secure to the state all the advantages that are to be derived from the proper instruction of youth; and here I beg leave to remark, that the only foundation for a useful educa-tion in a republic is to be laid in Religion. Without this there can be no virtue, and without virtue there can be no liberty, and liberty is the object and life of all republican governments.

Such is my veneration for every religion that reveals the attributes of the Deity, or a future state of rewards and punishments, that I had rather see the opinions of Confucius or Mahomed inculcated upon our youth, than see them grow up wholly devoid of a system of religious principles. But the religion I mean to recom-mend in this place, is that of the New Testament.

It is foreign to my purpose to hint at the arguments which establish the truth of the Christian revelation. My only business is to declare, that all its doctrines and precepts are calculated to promote the happiness of society, and the safety and well being of civil govern-ment. A Christian cannot fail of being a republican. The history of the creation of man, and of the relation of our species to each other by birth, which is recorded in the Old Testament, is the best refutation that can be given to the divine right of kings, and the stron-gest argument that can be used in favor of the original

and natural equality of all mankind. A Christian, I say again, cannot fail of being a republican, for every pre-cept of the Gospel inculcates those degrees of humility, self-denial, and brotherly kindness, which are directly opposed to the pride of monarchy and the pageantry of a court. A Christian cannot fail of being useful to the republic, for his religion teacheth him, that no man "liveth to himself." And lastly, a Christian cannot fail of being wholly inoffensive, for his religion teacheth him, in all things to do to others what he would wish, in like circumstances, they should do to him.

. . . I beg pardon for having delayed so long to say any thing of the separate and peculiar mode of edu-cation proper for women in a republic. I am sensible that they must concur in all our plans of education for young men, or no laws will ever render them effectual. To qualify our women for this purpose, they should not only be instructed in the usual branches of female education, but they should be taught the principles of liberty and government; and the obligations of pa-triotism should be inculcated upon them. The opin-ions and conduct of men are often regulated by the women in the most arduous enterprizes of life; and their approbation is frequently the principal reward of the hero's dangers, and the patriot's toils. Besides, the first impressions upon the minds of children are generally derived from the women. Of how much consequence, therefore, is it in a republic, that they should think justly upon the great subject of liberty and government!

The complaints that have been made against reli-gion, liberty and learning, have been, against each of them in a separate state. Perhaps like certain liquors, they should only be used in a state of mixture. They mutually assist in correcting the abuses, and in im-proving the good effects of each other. From the com-bined and reciprocal influence of religion, liberty and learning upon the morals, manners and knowledge of individuals, of these, upon government, and of gov-ernment, upon individuals, it is impossible to measure the degrees of happiness and perfection to which man-kind may be raised. For my part, I can form no ideas of the golden age, so much celebrated by the poets, more delightful, than the contemplation of that happiness which it is now in the power of the legislature of Penn-sylvania to confer upon her citizens, by establishing proper modes and places of education in every part of the state.

1. What is the relationship between religion and education according to Rush?
2. What is Rush's view on the role of women in American society?

8.3 REBEL'S STATEMENT FROM GABRIEL'S CONSPIRACY (1800)*

Gabriel's Conspiracy or Gabriel's Rebellion was a planned rebellion of enslaved people in the Richmond, Virginia, area in 1800 that never happened. Gabriel Prosser (1776–1800), a literate enslaved blacksmith in Richmond, organized enslaved people in the surrounding area to revolt, seize weapons, and end slavery in Virginia. On August 30, 1800, the supposed day the revolt was to take place, Gabriel's plans were betrayed by another enslaved person, and the Virginia planters called out the militia. Gabriel was captured along with dozens of other enslaved people, but he refused to reveal anything. Gabriel, his two brothers, and twenty-three other enslaved people were eventually executed by the state of Virginia.

Having lived through the American Revolution themselves, Gabriel and his fellow rebels may have drawn deliberate parallels between their efforts to fight slavery and the American war against Britain. The supposed words of Gabriel's co-conspirator highlight the hypocrisy of Virginians for exulting one Virginian freedom fighter (Washington) and executing another (Gabriel).

9th Month, 25th. I pursued my way to Richmond in the mail stage, through a beautiful country, but clouded and debased by Negro slavery. At the house here I breakfasted, which is called the Bowling-green, I was told that the owner had in his passession [sic] 200 slaves. In one field near the house, planted with tobacco, I counted nearly 20 women and children, employed in picking grubs from the plant. In the afternoon I passed by a field in which several poor slaves had lately been executed, on the charge of having an intention to rise against their masters. A lawyer who was present at their trials at Richmond, informed me that on one of them being asked, what he had to say to the court on his defence, he replied, in a manly tone of voice: "I have nothing more to offer than what General Washington would have had to offer, had he been taken by the British and put to trial by them. I have adventured my life in endeavouring to obtain the liberty of my countrymen, and am a willing sacrifice in their cause: and I beg, as a favour, that I may be immediately led to execution. I know that you have pre-determined to shed my blood, why then all this mockery of a trial?"

1. What is Gabriel's co-conspirator saying about Virginians by comparing them to the British?
2. What similarities or differences were there in the causes that Washington and Gabriel fought for?

* Robert Sutcliff, *Travels in Some Parts of North America in the Years 1804, 1805, & 1806* (Philadelphia: B. & T. Kite, 1812), 50, https://www.google.com/books/edition/Travels_in_Some_Parts_of_North_America_i/6xcCAAAAYAAJ?hl=en.

8.4 TECUMSEH, SPEECH TO GOVERNOR HARRISON AT VINCENNES (1810)*

Tecumseh (1768–1813) was a notable Shawnee leader who formed an intertribal Native alliance in the Great Lakes region. A magnificent orator, Tecumseh articulated the common interest of all Indigenous peoples in opposing land sales to agents of the United States and encroachment on Native land by white settlers. Along with Tecumseh's message of unified political opposition, his brother Tenskwatawa advocated a spiritual mission to reject European influences and return to more traditional Native ways of life. The two brothers founded a village, Prophetstown, in what is now Indiana, where their followers from a variety of tribes gathered.

Tecumseh opposed the sale of land to the United States and led a band of warriors to the Vincennes, the capital of the Indiana Territory, to demand that the territorial governor, William Harrison, rescind a recent sale. He argued that while Native Americans were not one people, no single group of Natives could sell land on behalf of any other group. A year after this unsuccessful meeting, Harrison led American troops in a surprise attack on Prophetstown, burning the settlement. Tecumseh and his allies fought the United States for the next two years until Tecumseh was killed during fighting in Canada in 1813.

Governor Harrison, who dispatched a messenger to him, to state "that any claims he might have to the lands which had been ceded, were not affected by the treaty; that he might come to Vincennes and exhibit his pretensions, and if they were found to be solid, that the land would either be given up, or an ample compensation made for it." This, it must be confessed, was not in a strain calculated to soothe a mighty mind, when once justly irritated, as was that of *Tecumseh*, at least as he conceived. However, upon the 12 August, 1810 (a day which cannot fail to remind the reader of the fate of his great archetype, *Philip of Pokanoket*), he met the governor in council at Vincennes, with many of his warriors; at which time he spoke to him as follows:

"It is true I am a Shawnee. My forefathers were warriors. Their son is a warrior. From them I take only my existence; from my tribe I take nothing. I am the maker of my own fortune; and oh! that I could make that of my red people, and of my country, as great as the conceptions of my mind, when I think of the Spirit that rules the universe. I would not then come to Governor Harrison to ask him to tear the treaty, and to obliterate the landmark; but I would say to him: Sir, you have liberty to return to your own country. The being within, communing with past ages, tells me that once, nor until lately, there was no white man on this continent; that it then all belonged to red men, children of the same parents, placed on it by the Great Spirit that made them, to keep it, to traverse it, to enjoy its productions, and to fill it with the same race, once a happy race, since made miserable by the white people who are never contented but always encroaching. The way, and the only way, to check and to stop this evil, is for all the red men to unite in claiming a common and equal right in the land, as it was at first, and should be yet; for it never was divided, but belongs to all, for the use of each. That no part has a right to sell, even to each other, much less to strangers; those who want all, and will not do with less. The white people have no right to take the land from the

* Samuel G. Drake, *Biography and History of the Indians of North America* (1835), 100–101, https://www.google.com/books/edition/Biography_and_History_of_the_Indians_of/wPsoAAAAYAAJ?hl=en&gbpv=0.

Indians, because they had it first; it is theirs. They may sell, but all must join. Any sale not made by all is not valid. The late sale is bad. It was made by a part only. Part do not know how to sell. It requires all to make a bargain for all. All red men have equal rights to the unoccupied land. The right of occupancy is as good in one place as in another. There cannot be two occupations in the same place. The first excludes all others. It is not so in hunting or traveling; for there the same ground will serve many, as they may follow each other all day; but the camp is stationary, and that is occupancy. It belongs to the first who sits down on his blanket or skins which he has thrown upon the ground; and till he leaves it no other has a right."

QUESTIONS TO CONSIDER

1. What is Tecumseh's position on land ownership? What Native people can buy and sell land, according to him?
2. What is Tecumseh's view of the history between Native Americans and white settlers? What might have led him to these conclusions?

8.5 VISUAL SOURCE: MONTICELLO'S ENTRANCE HALL (COMPLETED IN 1809)*

Monticello was the personal residence of Thomas Jefferson (1743–1826) at his plantation in central Virginia. Designed by Jefferson himself, it was originally built in 1772, but Jefferson continued to augment the building and its décor for decades. Jefferson envisioned the entrance hall as a museum displaying various works of American culture and natural history. Remains of American wildlife such as bighorn sheep and moose are mounted on the wall, and various bones including the jaw of a mastodon are also displayed. A Mandan buffalo robe depicting a battle scene adorns a balcony. Maps of Virginia, South America, and the United States are prominently displayed on the walls. Busts of Enlightenment thinkers such as Anne-Robert-Jacques Turgot and Voltaire can also be seen. At a time when many artifacts and antiquities were in private hands, Jefferson's entrance hall was uncommon in both the variety of objects on display and their placement in the relatively public opening to the home.

---

* ©Thomas Jefferson Foundation at Monticello

QUESTIONS TO CONSIDER

1. Why might Jefferson have wanted to publicly display so many artifacts from throughout America? What might visitors have thought upon seeing such a varied collection?
2. Jefferson's entrance hall was large and could sit as many as twenty people at a time. Why might Jefferson have displayed these artifacts in such a large, relatively public room?

8.6 VISUAL SOURCE: A SCENE ON THE FRONTIERS AS PRACTICED BY THE "HUMANE" BRITISH AND THEIR "WORTHY" ALLIES (1812)*

Following the American Revolution, white Americans began to settle in the Ohio River valley and Great Lakes region. There they came into conflict with the Indigenous peoples whose lands they encroached on. Native peoples began to follow two Shawnee brothers, Tenskwatawa and Tecumseh, who called for a pan-Indian alliance to oppose white settlement. They launched raids against white settler towns and villages, which led to consternation among white residents of Ohio and the Indiana Territory.

White Americans directed their anger at the British in Canada who were supplying Native peoples with weapons in order to build alliances and trading relationships. Some accused the British of deliberately provoking Native groups to attack Americans and paying bounties for those they killed. In this illustration a British officer is shown promising Native Americans money for the scalps of dead Americans. While a Native man mutilates an American soldier, British soldiers and Native people dance around a fire together in the background. An accompanying song encourages Americans to avenge the wrongs done against them and condemns Indians as cowardly pawns of the British.

---

* Courtesy of the Library of Congress

QUESTIONS TO CONSIDER

1. How does this illustration explain the violence on the Ohio Valley frontier? In what ways is that explanation incomplete?
2. Why might Americans have fixated on British culpability for Native attacks? How would British instigation have changed Americans' understanding of violence on the frontier?

CHAPTER 9

EXPANSION AND ITS DISCONTENTS, 1815–1840

9.1 HENRY CLAY, EXCERPTS FROM "ON AMERICAN INDUSTRY" (1824)*

Henry Clay (1777–1852) was a prominent senator from Kentucky and proponent of American industry and infrastructure. He delivered this address to the House of Representatives in support of what became the Tariff of 1824, a tax on imports of certain manufactured goods designed to protect American industry from foreign competition. Clay was a lifetime advocate for what he called his "American System"—trade protections and infrastructure improvements that would make the US economy prosperous and competitive.

Clay argued that trade protections were important because the United States needed to be able to supply its own citizens and that the recent war with Britain had shown how dependent it still was on British goods. Some Southern delegates opposed Clay's plan, however, as those states had fewer existing manufacturing industries and thus did not stand to benefit as much from Clay's proposal. Clay insisted that Southern states were welcome to develop their own industry, and that it was better to support American businesses, wherever they may be, than foreign ones.

Two classes of politicians divide the people of the United States. According to the system of one, the produce of foreign industry should be subjected to no other impost than such as may be necessary to provide a public revenue; and the produce of American industry should be left to sustain itself, if it can, with no other than that incidental protection, in its competition, at home as well as abroad, with rival foreign articles. According to the system of the other class, whilst they agree that the imposts should be mainly, and may under any modification be safely, relied on as a fit and convenient source of public revenue, they would so adjust and arrange the duties on foreign fabrics as to afford a gradual but adequate

---

* F. W. Tausigg, ed., *State Papers and Speeches on the Tariff* (Cambridge, MA: Harvard University, 1892), https://oll.libertyfund .org/title/taussig-state-papers-and-speeches-on-the-tariff.

protection to American industry, and lessen our dependence on foreign nations, by securing a certain and ultimately a cheaper and better supply of our own wants from our own abundant resources. . . .

In casting our eyes around us, the most prominent circumstance which fixes our attention and challenges our deepest regret is the general distress which pervades the whole country. It is forced upon us by numerous facts of the most incontestable character. It is indicated by the diminished exports of native produce; by the depressed and reduced state of our foreign navigation; by our diminished commerce; by successive unthrashed crops of grain, perishing in our barns and barn-yards for the want of a market; by the alarming diminution of the circulating medium; by the numerous bankruptcies, not limited to the trading classes, but extending to all orders of society; by a universal complaint of the want of employment, and a consequent reduction of the wages of labor; by the ravenous pursuit after public situations, not for the sake of their honors and the performance of their public duties, but as a means of private subsistence; by the reluctant resort to the perilous use of paper money; by the intervention of legislation in the delicate relation between debtor and creditor; and, above all, by the low and depressed state of the value of almost every description of the whole mass of the property of the nation, which has, on an average, sunk not less than about fifty per centum within a few years. This distress pervades every part of the Union, every class of society; all feel it. . . .

What, again I would ask, is the cause of the unhappy condition of our country, which I have faintly depicted? It is to be found in the fact that, during almost the whole existence of this government, we have shaped our industry, our navigation, and our commerce, in reference to an extraordinary war in Europe, and to foreign markets which no longer exist; in the fact that we have depended too much upon foreign sources of supply, and excited too little the native; in the fact that, whilst we have cultivated, with assiduous care, our foreign resources, we have suffered those at home to wither in a state of neglect and abandonment. . . .

Is there no remedy within the reach of the government? Are we doomed to behold our industry languish and decay, yet more and more? But there is a remedy, and that remedy consists in modifying our

foreign policy, and in adopting a genuine American system. We must naturalize the arts in our country; and we must naturalize them by the only means which the wisdom of nations has yet discovered to be effectual,—by adequate protection against the otherwise overwhelming influence of foreigners. This is only to be accomplished by the establishment of a tariff, to the consideration of which I am now brought.

And what is this tariff? It seems to have been regarded as a sort of monster, huge and deformed,—a wild beast, endowed with tremendous powers of destruction, about to be let loose among our people, if not to devour them, at least to consume their substance. But let us calm our passions, and deliberately survey this alarming, this terrific being. The sole object of the tariff is to tax the produce of foreign industry, with the view of promoting American industry. The tax is exclusively leveled at foreign industry. That is the avowed and the direct purpose of the tariff. If it subjects any part of American industry to burdens, that is an effect not intended, but is altogether incidental, and perfectly voluntary.

It has been treated as an imposition of burdens upon one part of the community by design, for the benefit of another; as if, in fact, money were taken from the pockets of one portion of the people and put into the pockets of another. But is that a fair representation of it? No man pays the duty assessed on the foreign article by compulsion, but voluntarily; and this voluntary duty, if paid, goes into the common exchequer, for the common benefit of all. Consumption has four objects of choice. First, it may abstain from the use of the foreign article, and thus avoid the payment of the tax. Second, it may employ the rival American fabric. Third, it may engage in the business of manufacturing, which this bill is designed to foster. Fourth, or it may supply itself from the household manufactures. But it is said, by the honorable gentleman from Virginia, that the South, owing to the character of a certain portion of its population, cannot engage in the business of manufacturing. Now, I do not agree in that opinion, to the extent in which it is asserted. . . .

. . . we perceive that the proposed measure, instead of sacrificing the South to the other parts of the Union, seeks only to preserve them from being absolutely sacrificed under the operation of the tacit compact which

I have described. Supposing the South to be actually incompetent, or disinclined, to embark at all in the business of manufacturing, is not its interest, nevertheless, likely to be promoted by creating a new and an American source of supply for its consumption? Now foreign powers, and Great Britain principally, have the monopoly of the supply of Southern consumption. If this bill should pass, an American competitor, in the supply of the South, would be raised up, and ultimately I cannot doubt that it will be supplied more cheaply and better. . . .

Mr. Chairman, our confederacy comprehends within its vast limits great diversity of interests: agricultural, planting, farming, commercial, navigating, fishing, manufacturing. No one of these interests is felt in the same degree and cherished with the same solicitude throughout all parts of the Union. Some of them are peculiar to particular sections of our common country. But all these great interests are confided to the protection of one Government,—to the fate of one ship; and a most gallant ship it is, with a noble crew. If we prosper and are happy, protection must be extended to all; it is due to all. It is the great principle on which obedience is demanded from all. If our essential interests cannot find protection from our own Government against the policy of foreign powers, where are they to get it? We did not unite for sacrifice, but for preservation. . . . This is the only mode by which we can preserve, in full vigor, the harmony of the whole Union. The South entertains one opinion, and imagines that a modification of the existing policy of the country for the protection of American industry involves the ruin of the South. The North, the East, the West hold the opposite opinion, and feel and contemplate, in a longer adherence to the foreign policy as it now exists, their utter destruction. Is it true that the interests of these great sections of our country are irreconcilable with each other? Are we reduced to the sad and afflicting dilemma of determining which shall fall a victim to the prosperity of the other? Happily, I think, there is no such distressing alternative. If the North, the West, and the East formed an independent State, unassociated with the South, can there be a doubt that the restrictive system would be carried to the point of prohibition of every foreign fabric of which they produce the raw material, and which they could manufacture? Such would

be their policy, if they stood alone; but they are fortunately connected with the South, which believes its interests to require a free admission of foreign manufactures. Here, then, is a case for mutual concession, for fair compromise.

The bill under consideration presents this compromise. It is a medium between the absolute exclusion and the unrestricted admission of the produce of foreign industry. It sacrifices the interest of neither section to that of the other; neither, it is true, gets all that it wants, nor is subject to all that it fears. But it has been said that the South obtains nothing in this compromise. Does it lose anything? is the first question. I have endeavored to prove that it does not, by showing that a mere transfer is effected in the source of the supply of its consumption from Europe to America; and that the loss, whatever it may be, of the sale of its great staple in Europe is compensated by the new market created in America. But does the South really gain nothing in this compromise? The consumption of the other sections, though somewhat restricted, is still left open by this bill, to foreign fabrics purchased by Southern staples. So far its operation is beneficial to the South, and prejudicial to the industry of the other sections, and that is the point of mutual concession. The South will also gain by the extended consumption of its great staple, produced by an increased capacity to consume it in consequence of the establishment of the home market. But the South cannot exert its industry and enterprise in the business of manufactures! Why not? The difficulties, if not exaggerated, are artificial, and may therefore be surmounted. But can the other sections embark in the planting occupations of the South? The obstructions which forbid them are natural, created by the immutable laws of God, and therefore unconquerable.

Other and animating considerations invite us to adopt the policy of this system. Its importance, in connection with the general defense in time of war, cannot fail to be duly estimated. Indeed I recall to our painful recollection the sufferings, for the want of an adequate supply of absolute necessaries, to which the defenders of their country's rights and our entire population were subjected during the late war? Or to remind the Committee of the great advantage of a steady and unfailing source of supply, unaffected alike in war and in peace? Its importance, in reference to the stability of our Union, that paramount and greatest of all our interests, cannot fail warmly to recommend it. . . .

Even if the benefits of the policy were limited to certain sections of our country, would it not be satisfactory to behold American industry, wherever situated, active, animated, and thrifty, rather than persevere in a course which renders us subservient to foreign industry? . . .

. . . the cause is the cause of the country, and it must and will prevail. It is founded in the interests and affections of the people. It is as native as the granite deeply imbosomed in our mountains. And, in conclusion, I would pray God, in his infinite mercy, to avert from our country the evils which are impending over it, and, by enlightening our councils, to conduct us into that path which leads to riches, to greatness, to glory.

QUESTIONS TO CONSIDER

1. What impact has the recent wartime experience had on Clay's beliefs?
2. Why do some of Clay's opponents view his proposed legislation as unfair?

9.2 *THE LIBERATOR,* EXCERPTS FROM "A VOICE FROM NEW-YORK!" AND "A VOICE FROM PROVIDENCE!" (1831)*

The Liberator was an abolitionist newspaper that frequently printed the opinions and writing of Black Americans, an unusual practice for American newspapers in the nineteenth century. Its editor, William Lloyd Garrison (1805–1879), and many of his readers opposed colonization, plans for ending slavery by gradually freeing enslaved people on the condition that they be re-settled outside the United States in West Africa or the Caribbean. Garrison and Black abolitionists instead advocated for the immediate abolition of slavery in the US and for the legal equality of Black Americans.

Here *The Liberator* reprints resolutions agreed to by various meetings of Black Americans who opposed colonization efforts. Updates like these were quite common as part of the purpose of a newspaper like *The Liberator* was to help establish connections between disparate abolitionist groups that held similar views. Colonization was a popular idea among a number of reformist elites, and abolitionist groups had to work to convince reformers that colonization was not a solution to slavery that Black Americans welcomed.

* William Lloyd Garrison, "Sentiments of the People of Color," in *Thoughts on African Colonization Or an Impartial Exhibition of the Doctrines, Principles and Purposes of the American Colonization Society. Together with the Resolutions, Addresses and Remonstrances of the Free People of Color,* part 1 (Boston: Garrison & Knapp, 1832), https://www.google.com/books/edition/Thoughts_on_African_Colonization/nKFrsO-yBjEC?hl=en&gbpv=0.

A VOICE FROM NEW-YORK

New-York, January 1831
An Address to the Citizens of New York

In protesting against the sentiments and declarations to our prejudice with which the above noticed "address" and "resolutions" abound, we are well aware of the power and influence we have attempted to resist. The gentlemen named as officers of the "Colonization Society" are men of high standing, their dictum is law in morals with our community; but we who feel the effect of their proscription, indulge the hope of an impartial hearing.

We believe many of those gentlemen are our friends, and we hope they all mean well; we care not how many Colonization Societies they form to send slaves from the south to a place where they may enjoy freedom; and if they can "drain the ocean with a bucket," may send *with their own consent,*" the increasing free colored population: but we solemnly protest against that Christian philanthropy which in acknowledging our wrongs commits a greater by vilifying us. The conscientious man would not kill the animal, but cried "mad dog," and the rabble dispatched him. These gentlemen acknowledge the anomaly of those political ethics which make a distinction between man and man, when their foundation is, "that all men are born equal," and possess in common "unalienable rights;" and to justify the withholding of these "rights" would proclaim to foreigners that we are "a distinct and inferior race," without religion or morals, and implying that our condition cannot be improved here because there exists an unconquerable prejudice in the whites towards us. We absolutely deny these positions, and we call upon the learned author of the "address" for the indications of distinction between us and other men. There are different *colors* among all species of animated creation. A difference of color is not a difference of species. Our structure and organization are the same, and not distinct from other men; and in what respects are we inferior? Our political condition we admit renders us less respectable, but does it prove us an inferior part of the human family? Inferior indeed we are as to the means which we possess of becoming wealthy and learned men; and it would argue well for the cause of justice, humanity and true religion, if the reverend gentlemen whose names are found at the bottom of President Duer's address, instead of showing their benevolence by laboring to move us some four thousand miles off, were to engage actively in the furtherance of plans for the improvement of our moral and political condition in the country of our birth. It is too late now to brand with inferiority any one of the races of mankind. We ask for proof. Time was when it was thought impossible to civilize the red man. Yet our own country presents a practical refutation of the vain assertion in the flourishing condition of the Cherokees, among whom intelligence and refinement are seen in somewhat fairer proportions than are exhibited by some of their white neighbors. In the language of a writer of expanded views and truly noble sentiments, "the blacks must be regarded as the real authors of most of the arts and sciences which give the whites at present the advantage over them. While Greece and Rome were yet barbarous, we find the light of learning and improvement emanating from this, by supposition, degraded and accursed continent of Africa, out of the midst of this very woolly-haired, flat-nosed, thick lipped, and coal black race, which some persons are tempted to station at a pretty low intermediate point between men and monkeys." It is needless to dwell on this topic; and we say with the same writer, the blacks had a long and glorious day: and after what they have been and done, it argues not so much a mistaken theory, as sheer ignorance of the most notorious historical facts, to pretend that they are naturally inferior to the whites.

A VOICE FROM PROVIDENCE

Providence, November 1, 1831

Whereas our brethren, in different parts of the United States, have thought proper to call meetings to express their disapprobation of the American Colonization Society; we, concurring fully with them in opinion, have assembled ourselves together for the purpose of uniting with them, in declaring that we believe the operations of the Society have been unchristian and anti-republican, and at variance with our best interests as a people. Therefore,

Resolved, That we will use every fair and honorable means in our power, to oppose the operations of the above mentioned Society.

Resolved, That we are truly sensible that we are in this country a degraded and ignorant people; but that our ignorance and degradation are not to be attributed to the inferiority of our natural abilities, but to the oppressive treatment we have experienced from the whites in general, and to the prejudice excited against us by the members of the Colonization Society, their aiders and abettors.

Resolved, That we view, we unfeigned astonishment, the anti-christian and inconsistent conduct of those who so strenuously advocate our removal from this our native country to the burning shores of Liberia, and who with the same breath contend against the cruelty and injustice of Georgia in her attempt to remove the Cherokee Indians west of the Mississippi.

QUESTION TO CONSIDER

1. What objections do these groups raise to the idea of colonization?
2. What arguments do they advance to prove the equality of Black Americans?

9.3 GEORGE W. HARKINS, "FAREWELL TO THE AMERICAN PEOPLE" (1832)*

The Choctaw were one of five Native peoples from the Southern United States (along with the Cherokee, Choctaw, Seminole, and Chickasaw) who were forced by the US government to abandon their ancestral lands and relocate to a reservation in modern Oklahoma. Between 1830 and 1833 the US War Department moved about seventeen thousand of around twenty-two thousand Mississippi Choctaws to a reservation in a process of ethnic cleansing that resulted in thousands of deaths. This forced relocation, often referred to as the "Trail of Tears," allowed white Americans to seize land that constituted much of the modern states of Georgia, Florida, Alabama, and Mississippi.

George W. Harkins (1810–1861) was a Mississippi Choctaw who attended college in Kentucky and was elected chief of the Choctaw in his early twenties after the previous chief was deposed for consenting to removal. He wrote the "Farewell Letter to the American People," which was widely reprinted, shortly thereafter.

To the American People:

It is with considerable diffidence that I attempt to address the American people, knowing and feeling sensibly my incompetency; and believing that your highly and well improved minds would not be well entertained by the address of a Choctaw. But having determined to emigrate west of the Mississippi river this fall, I have thought proper in bidding you farewell to make a few remarks expressive of my views, and the feelings that actuate me on the subject of our removal.

Believing that our all is at stake and knowing that you readily sympathize with the distressed of every

* George W. Harkins, "Farewell Letter to the American People" (1832), *The American Indian*, December 1926. Reprinted in *Great Documents in American Indian History*, ed. Wayne Moquin with Charles Van Doren (New York: DaCapo Press, 1995), 151.

country, I confidently throw myself upon your indulgence and ask you to listen patiently. I do not arrogate to myself the prerogative of deciding upon the expediency of the late treaty, yet I feel bound as a Choctaw, to give a distinct expression of my feelings on that interesting, (and to the Choctaws), all important subject.

We were hedged in by two evils, and we chose that which we thought the least. Yet we could not recognize the right that the state of Mississippi had assumed, to legislate for us.—Although the legislature of the state were qualified to make laws for their own citizens, that did not qualify them to become law makers to a people that were so dissimilar in manners and customs as the Choctaws are to the Mississippians. Admitting that they understood the people, could they remove that mountain of prejudice that has ever obstructed the streams of justice, and prevent their salutary influence from reaching my devoted countrymen. We as Choctaws rather chose to suffer and be free, than live under the degrading influence of laws, which our voice could not be heard in their formation.

Much as the state of Mississippi has wronged us, I cannot find in my heart any other sentiment than an ardent wish for her prosperity and happiness.

I could cheerfully hope, that those of another age and generation may not feel the effects of those oppressive measures that have been so illiberally dealt out to us; and that peace and happiness may be their reward. Amid the gloom and horrors of the present separation, we are cheered with a hope that ere long we shall reach our destined land, and that nothing short of the basest acts of treachery will ever be able to wrest it from us, and that we may live free. Although your ancestors won freedom on the field of danger and glory, our ancestors owned it as their birthright, and we have had to purchase it from you as the vilest slaves buy their freedom.

Yet it is said that our present movements are our own voluntary acts—such is not the case. We found ourselves like a benighted stranger, following false guides, until he was surrounded on every side, with fire and water. The fire was certain destruction, and a feeble hope was left him of escaping by water. A distant view of the opposite shore encourages the hope; to remain would be inevitable annihilation. Who would hesitate, or who would say that his plunging into the water was

his own voluntary act? Painful in the extreme is the mandate of our expulsion. We regret that it should proceed from the mouth of our professed friend, for whom our blood was co-mingled with that of his bravest warriors, on the field of danger and death.

But such is the instability of professions. The man who said that he would plant a stake and draw a line around us, that never should be passed, was the first to say he could not guard the lines, and drew up the stake and wiped out all traces of the line. I will not conceal from you my fears, that the present grounds may be removed. I have my foreboding; who of us can tell after witnessing what has already been done, what the next force may be.

I ask you in the name of justice, for repose for myself and for my injured people. Let us alone—we will not harm you, we want rest. We hope, in the name of justice, that another outrage may never be committed against us, and that we may for the future be cared for as children, and not driven about as beasts, which are benefited by a change of pasture.

Taking an example from the American government, and knowing the happiness which its citizens enjoy under the influence of mild republican institutions, it is the intention of our countrymen to form a government assimilated to that of our white brethren in the United States, as nearly as their condition will permit.

We know that in order to protect the rights and secure the liberties of the people, no government approximates so nearly to perfection as the one to which we have alluded. As east of the Mississippi we have been friends, so west we will cherish the same feelings with additional fervour; and although we may be removed to the desert, still we shall look with fond regard, upon those who have promised us their protection. Let that feeling be reciprocated.

Friends, my attachment to my native land was strong—that cord is now broken; and we must go forth as wanderers in a strange land! I must go—let me entreat you to regard us with feelings of kindness, and when the hand of oppression is stretched against us, let me hope that every part of the United States, filling the mountains and valleys, will echo and say stop, you have no power, we are the sovereign people, and our friends shall no more be disturbed. We ask you for nothing that is incompatible with your other duties.

We go forth sorrowful, knowing that wrong has been done. Will you extend to us your sympathizing regards until all traces of disagreeable oppositions are obliterated, and we again shall have confidence in the professions of our white brethren.

Here is the land of our progenitors, and here are their bones; they left them as a sacred deposit, and we have been compelled to venerate its trust; it is dear to us, yet we cannot stay, my people are dear to me, with them I must go. Could I stay and forget them and leave them to struggle alone, unaided, unfriended, and forgotten by our great father? I should then be unworthy the name of a Choctaw, and be a disgrace to my blood. I must go with them; my destiny is cast among the Choctaw people. If they suffer, so will I; if they prosper, then I will rejoice. Let me again ask you to regard us with feelings of kindness.

QUESTIONS TO CONSIDER

1. What emotions does Harkins express toward white Mississippians?
2. Why are the Choctaw going along with removal according to Harkins?

9.4 HARRIET HANSON ROBINSON, EXCERPT FROM A DESCRIPTION OF THE 1836 STRIKE IN *LOOM AND SPINDLE, OR, LIFE AMONG THE EARLY MILL GIRLS* (1898)*

Some of the first industrial factories in the United States were the New England textile mills, such as those in Lowell, Massachusetts. These factories operated much like company towns, employing large workforces of young women for extraordinarily long hours and requiring them to sleep in dormitories with their coworkers. Workers were required to abide by a rigid code of conduct and to attend church services and educational classes in their little time off. Despite the strict conditions, this was seen as an improvement by many who deplored the use of child labor in British manufacturing.

After a period of success in the 1810s and 1820s, financial difficulties in the 1830s led the Lowell mills to impose significant cuts in pay, which provoked a unionization campaign and a series of strikes in 1834 and 1836. As this account of the strike by Harriet Hanson Robinson (1825–1911) describes, the wage issues were never resolved and much of the workforce eventually left and was replaced in the 1840s by Irish immigrants who, desperate to escape famine in their homeland, would accept a lower wage.

* Harriet Jane Hanson Robinson, *Loom and Spindle, or, Life among the Early Mill Girls* (New York: T.Y. Crowell, 1898), 83–86, https://id.lib.harvard.edu/curiosity/women-working-1800-1930/45-990022084580203941.

One of the first strikes of cotton-factory operatives that ever took place in this country was that in Lowell, in October, 1836. When it was announced that the wages were to be cut down, great indignation was felt, and it was decided to strike, *en masse*. This was done. The mills were shut down, and the girls went in procession from their several corporations to the "grove" on Chapel Hill, and listened to "incendiary" speeches from early labor reformers.

One of the girls stood on a pump, and gave vent to the feelings of her companions in a neat speech, declaring that it was their duty to resist all attempts at cutting down the wages. This was the first time a woman had spoken in public in Lowell, and the event caused surprise and consternation among her audience.

Cutting down the wages was not their only grievance, nor the only cause of this strike. Hitherto the corporations had paid twenty-five cents a week towards the board of each operative, and now it was their purpose to have the girls pay the sum; and this, in addition to the cut in the wages, would make a difference of at least one dollar a week. It was estimated that as many as twelve or fifteen hundred girls turned out, and walked in procession through the streets. They had neither flags nor music, but sang songs, a favorite (but rather inappropriate) one being a parody on "I won't be a nun."

"Oh! Isn't it a pity, such a pretty girl as I—
Should be sent to the factory to pine away and
       die?
Oh! I cannot be a slave,
I will not be a slave,
For I'm so fond of liberty
That I cannot be a slave."

My own recollection of this first strike (or "turn out" as it was called) is very vivid. I worked in a lower room, where I had heard the proposed strike fully, if not vehemently, discussed; I had been an ardent listener to what was said against this attempt at "oppression" on the part of the corporation, and naturally I took sides with the strikers. When the day came on which the girls were to turn out, those in the upper rooms started first, and so many of them left that our mill was at once shut down. Then, when the girls in my room stood irresolute, uncertain what to do, asking each other, "Would you?" or "Shall we turn out?" and not one of them having the courage to lead off, I, who began to think they would not go out, after all their talk, became impatient, and started on ahead, saying, with childish bravado, "I don't care what you do, *I* am going to turn out, whether any one else does or not;" and I marched out, and was followed by the others.

As I looked back at the long line that followed me, I was more proud than I have ever been since at any success I may have achieved, and more proud than I shall ever be again until my own beloved State gives to its women citizens the right of suffrage.

The agent of the corporation where I then worked took some small revenges on the supposed ringleaders; on the principle of sending the weaker to the wall, my mother was turned away from her boarding-house, that functionary saying, "Mrs. Hanson, you could not prevent the older girls from turning out, but your daughter is a child, and her you could control."

It is hardly necessary to say that so far as results were concerned this strike did no good. The dissatisfaction of the operatives subsided, or burned itself out, and though the authorities did not accede to their demands, the majority returned to their work, and the corporation went on cutting down the wages.

And after a time, as the wages became more and more reduced, the best portion of the girls left and went to their homes, or to the other employments that were fast opening to women, until there were very few of the old guard left; and thus the status of the factory population of New England gradually became what we know it to be today.

QUESTIONS TO CONSIDER

1. What grievances did the Lowell workers have with the corporation?
2. Why did this worker feel pride in her actions during the strike?

9.5 VISUAL SOURCE: JOHN SARTAIN AFTER GEORGE CALEB BINGHAM, *THE COUNTY ELECTION* (1854)*

Election days in the early republic were major events in which people from throughout the town or county would gather to vote, discuss, eat, and drink. This engraving by John Sartain (1808–1897) of a painting by George Caleb Bingham (1811–1879) shows this day in the political process. In keeping with contemporary gendered assumptions that electoral politics was a male activity, the subjects of this painting are almost uniformly men. All classes gather to cast their votes—businessmen in top hats, farmers and laborers in shirtsleeves. A new citizen must take an oath before he can vote, and an older man who likely voted many times before descends from the platform having just cast his ballot. In a time before blank ballots issued by local authorities, representatives of political parties encourage prospective voters to take and cast a ticket listing their party's candidates. Alcohol was consumed liberally by Americans in this time; one man enjoys a fresh glass of whiskey or cider, while another, too inebriated to stand, is nevertheless dragged to cast a vote. The large crowd continues beyond the frame of the painting as more wait in line to vote and others gleefully ride horses through the street. Bingham captures the hubbub and energy of democracy in an American county during the early republic.

* Gift of Gaillard F. Ravenel and Frances P. Smyth-Ravenel

QUESTIONS TO CONSIDER

1. How were Americans' voting practices different in the early to mid-1800s? What influence might those differences have had on electoral outcomes?
2. Many pairs and groups of men are shown discussing or debating. What does their presence in this painting say about the practice of democracy?

9.6 VISUAL SOURCE: POSTER OPPOSING A NEW RAILROAD BETWEEN PHILADELPHIA AND NEW YORK (1839)*

Although transport by rail could be significantly faster than travel by stagecoach or boat, some Americans opposed the expansion of what they perceived to be dangerous machines. The steam-powered engine was a novel invention and only began to see use for public transport in the 1830s. The noise that came with a locomotive, along with the smoke that billowed from the engines, could be a nuisance to anybody in its vicinity. The combination of higher travel speeds with heavy machinery that had few safety mechanisms produced numerous injuries among railway employees and sometimes passengers as well.

The Camden and Amboy Railroad which this poster opposes was one of the first railway lines established in the United States. Designed to connect New York and Philadelphia, then the country's largest cities, some feared that the railroad would not only pose a danger to Philadelphians but would turn their city into a mere satellite of New York. Although the fear that Philadelphia would become a "suburb of New York" never came to pass, the physical dangers this poster warned of were real.

* Poster circulated in Philadelphia in 1839 to discourage the coming of the railroad; 1839; Records of the Bureau of Public Roads, Record Group 30. [Online Version, https://www.docsteach.org/documents/document/poster-circulated-in-philadelphia-in-1839-to-discourage-the-coming-of-the-railroad, January 29, 2023]

QUESTIONS TO CONSIDER

1. What appeals does this poster make to Philadelphia residents? On what grounds does it encourage them to oppose the railroad?
2. What dangers does the poster's illustration portray? Do these seem like reasonable fears for contemporary Philadelphians?

CHAPTER 10

SOCIAL REFORM AND THE NEW POLITICS OF SLAVERY, 1820–1840

10.1 JOHN C. CALHOUN, EXCERPTS FROM *SOUTH CAROLINA EXPOSITION AND PROTEST* (1828)*

John C. Calhoun (1782–1850) was an influential statesman from South Carolina who was a vocal proponent of enslavement. In 1828 he proposed a novel constitutional theory called "nullification" that would allow individual states to declare a federal law unconstitutional and refuse to enforce it.

Calhoun expressed these views in the *South Carolina Exposition and Protest* as part of a protest against a recent national tariff, or tax on imported goods. Calhoun believed that the tariff was unconstitutional because while Congress had the ability to impose tariffs for revenue, part of the goal of this tariff was to support American manufacturers by making foreign goods more expensive. Calhoun believed that this was unfair to states in the South because they had to pay the tariff even though the region had few manufacturing centers and so would not receive much benefit. With Calhoun's encouragement, South Carolina passed a nullification ordinance in 1832, but the crisis was defused in 1833 with the adoption of a new, lower tariff.

The committee have bestowed on the subjects referred to them the deliberate attention which their importance demands; and the result, on full investigation, is a unanimous opinion that the act of Congress of the last session, with the whole system of legislation imposing duties on imports—not for revenue, but the protection of one branch of industry at the expense of others—is unconstitutional, unequal, and oppressive, and calculated to corrupt the public virtue and destroy the liberty of the country; which propositions they propose to consider in the order stated, and then to conclude their report with the consideration of the important question of the remedy.

The committee do not propose to enter into an elaborate or refined argument on the question of the constitutionality of the Tariff system. The General

* *Exposition and Protest, Reported By the Special Committee of the House of Representatives, on the Tariff,* December 19, 1828 (Columbia, SC: South Carolina State Library, 1829), https://dc.statelibrary.sc.gov/bitstream/handle/10827/21911/HOUSE_CR_Exposition_and_Protest_1828-12-19.pdf.

Government is one of specific powers, and it can rightfully exercise only the powers expressly granted, and those that may be necessary and proper to carry them into effect, all others being reserved expressly to the States or the people. It results, necessarily, that those who claim to exercise power under the Constitution, are bound to show that it is expressly granted, or that it is necessary and proper as a means to some of the granted powers. The advocates of the Tariff have offered no such proof. It is true that the third section of the first article of the Constitution authorizes Congress to lay and collect an impost duty, but it is granted as a tax power for the sole purpose of revenue—a power in its nature essentially different from that of imposing protective or prohibitory duties. . . . The facts are few and simple. The Constitution grants to Congress the power of imposing a duty on imports for revenue, which power is abused by being converted into an instrument of rearing up the industry of one section of the country on the ruins of another. The violation, then, consists in using a power granted for one object to advance another, and that by the sacrifice of the original object. It is, in a word, a violation by perversion—the most dangerous of all, because the most insidious, and difficult to resist. . . .

. . . On the great and vital point, the industry of the country, which comprehends nearly all the other interests, two great sections of the Union are opposed. We want free trade; they, restrictions. We want moderate taxes, frugality in the government, economy, accountability, and a rigid application of the public money, to the payment of the public debt, and the objects authorized by the constitution; in all these particulars, if we may judge by experience, their views of their interest are the opposite.—They act and feel on all questions connected with the American System, as sovereigns; as those always do who impose burdens on others for their own benefit; and we, on the contrary, like those on whom such burdens are imposed. In a word; to the extent stated, the country is divided and organized into two great opposing parties, one sovereign and the other subject; marked by all the characteristics which must ever accompany that relation, under whatever form it may exist.

. . . In order to have a full and clear conception of our institutions, it will be proper to remark, that there is in our system a striking distinction between the government and the sovereign power. Whatever may be the true doctrine in regard to the sovereignty of the states individually, it is unquestionably clear that while the government of the union is vested in its legislative, executive and political departments, the actual sovereign power, resides in the several states, who created it, in their separate and distinct political character. But by an express provision of the constitution it may be amended or changed, by three fourths of the states; and each state by assen[t]ing to the constitution with this provision, has surrendered its original rights as a sovereign, which made its individual consent necessary to any change in its political condition, and has placed this important power in the hands of three fourths of the states; in which the sovereignty of the union under the constitution does now actually reside. Not the least portion of this high sovereign authority, resides in Congress or any of the departments of the general government. They are but the creatures of the constitution, appointed, but to execute its provisions, and therefore, any attempt in all or any of the departments to exercise any power definitely, which in its consequences may alter the nature of the instrument or change the condition of the parties to it, would be an act of the highest political usurpation. It is thus, that our political system, recognizing the opposition of geographical interests in the community, has provided the most efficient check against its dangers. Looking to facts and not mere hypothesis, the constitution has made us a community only to the extent of our common interest, leaving the states distinct and independent, as to their peculiar interests, and has drawn the line of separation with consummate skill. . . .

With these views the committee are solemnly of impression if the system be persevered in, after due forbearance on the part of the state, that it will be her sacred duty to interpose her veto; a duty to herself, to the Union, to present, and to future generations, and to the cause of liberty over the world, to arrest the progress of a power, which, if not arrested, must in its consequences, corrupt the public morals, and destroy the liberty of the country.

QUESTIONS TO CONSIDER

1. What differences does Calhoun see between separate regions of the United States?
2. Why does Calhoun believe that South Carolina and other Southern states have been wronged by the federal government?

10.2 HARRIET JACOBS, WHITE RESIDENTS OF EDENTON, NORTH CAROLINA, RESPOND TO NEWS OF NAT TURNER'S REBELLION (1831, PUBLISHED 1861)*

Harriet Jacobs (1813–1897) was an abolitionist who lived in slavery in North Carolina until her escape in 1842. In 1861 she published an autobiography detailing her life as an enslaved woman. In this narrative, she also describes the events in her town that followed from Nat Turner's Rebellion, a revolt that occurred in 1831, when Jacobs was in her late teens. Nat Turner (1800–1831) was an enslaved preacher who led a group of enslaved people in a revolt in southern Virginia. The rebellion lasted several days and resulted in the deaths of more than sixty white Virginians, before the Virginia militia arrested most of the rebels. Turner evaded capture for two months but was eventually discovered, arrested, and executed.

Jacobs describes the aftermath of the rebellion in which white Southerners embarked on a reign of terror as they feared a more widespread plot, or that enslaved people would take inspiration from Turner. White people throughout the South engaged in retaliation for the rebellion, targeting free and enslaved Black people with no connection to Turner or the revolt. Hundreds of enslaved people were killed throughout the South in this outbreak of violence.

Not far from this time Nat Turner's insurrection broke out; and the news threw our town into great commotion. Strange that they should be alarmed when their slaves were so "contented and happy"! But so it was.

It was always the custom to have a muster every year. On that occasion every white man shouldered his musket. The citizens and the so-called country gentlemen wore military uniforms. The poor whites took their places in the ranks in every-day dress, some without shoes, some without hats. This grand occasion had already passed; and when the slaves were told there was to be another muster, they were surprised and

rejoiced. Poor creatures! They thought it was going to be a holiday. I was informed of the true state of affairs, and imparted it to the few I could trust. Most gladly would I have proclaimed it to every slave; but I dared not. All could not be relied on. Mighty is the power of the torturing lash. By sunrise, people were pouring in from every quarter within twenty miles of the town. I knew the houses were to be searched; and I expected it would be done by country bullies and the poor whites. I knew nothing annoyed them so much as to see colored people living in comfort and respectability; so I made arrangements for them with especial care. I arranged every thing in my grandmother's house

---

* Harriet Ann Jacobs, *Incidents in the Life of a Slave Girl. Written by Herself* (Boston, 1861), 97–104.

as neatly as possible. I put white quilts on the beds, and decorated some of the rooms with flowers. When all was arranged, I sat down at the window to watch. Far as my eye could reach, it rested on a motley crowd of soldiers. Drums and fifes were discoursing martial music. The men were divided into companies of sixteen, each headed by a captain. Orders were given, and the wild scouts rushed in every direction, wherever a colored face was to be found.

It was a grand opportunity for the low whites, who had no negroes of their own to scourge. They exulted in such a chance to exercise a little brief authority, and show their subserviency to the slaveholders; not reflecting that the power which trampled on the colored people also kept themselves in poverty, ignorance, and moral degradation. Those who never witnessed such scenes can hardly believe what I know was inflicted at this time on innocent men, women, and children, against whom there was not the slightest ground for suspicion. Colored people and slaves who lived in remote parts of the town suffered in an especial manner. In some cases the searchers scattered powder and shot among their clothes, and then sent other parties to find them, and bring them forward as proof that they were plotting insurrection. Every where men, women, and children were whipped till the blood stood in puddles at their feet. Some received five hundred lashes; others were tied hands and feet, and tortured with a bucking paddle, which blisters the skin terribly. The dwellings of the colored people, unless they happened to be protected by some influential white person, who was nigh at hand, were robbed of clothing and every thing else the marauders thought worth carrying away. All day long these unfeeling wretches went round, like a troop of demons, terrifying and tormenting the helpless. At night, they formed themselves into patrol bands, and went wherever they chose among the colored people, acting out their brutal will. Many women hid themselves in woods and swamps, to keep out of their way. If any of the husbands or fathers told of these outrages, they were tied up to the public whipping post, and cruelly scourged for telling lies about white men. The consternation was universal. No two people that had the slightest tinge of color in their faces dared to be seen talking together.

I entertained no positive fears about our household, because we were in the midst of white families

who would protect us. We were ready to receive the soldiers whenever they came. It was not long before we heard the tramp of feet and the sound of voices. The door was rudely pushed open; and in they tumbled, like a pack of hungry wolves. They snatched at every thing within their reach. Every box, trunk, closet, and corner underwent a thorough examination. A box in one of the drawers containing some silver change was eagerly pounced upon. When I stepped forward to take it from them, one of the soldiers turned and said angrily, "What d'ye foller us fur? D'ye s'pose white folks is come to steal?"

I replied, "You have come to search; but you have searched that box, and I will take it, if you please."

At that moment I saw a white gentleman who was friendly to us; and I called to him, and asked him to have the goodness to come in and stay till the search was over. He readily complied. His entrance into the house brought in the captain of the company, whose business it was to guard the outside of the house, and see that none of the inmates left it. This officer was Mr. Litch, the wealthy slaveholder whom I mentioned, in the account of neighboring planters, as being notorious for his cruelty. He felt above soiling his hands with the search. He merely gave orders; and, if a bit of writing was discovered, it was carried to him by his ignorant followers, who were unable to read.

My grandmother had a large trunk of bedding and table cloths. When that was opened, there was a great shout of surprise; and one exclaimed, "Where'd the damned niggers git all dis sheet an' table clarf?"

My grandmother, emboldened by the presence of our white protector, said, "You may be sure we didn't pilfer 'em from your houses."

"Look here, mammy," said a grim-looking fellow without any coat, "you seem to feel mighty gran' 'cause you got all them 'ere fixens. White folks oughter have 'em all."

His remarks were interrupted by a chorus of voices shouting, "We's got 'em! We's got 'em! Dis 'ere yaller gal's got letters!"

There was a general rush for the supposed letter, which, upon examination, proved to be some verses written to me by a friend. In packing away my things, I had overlooked them. When their captain informed them of their contents, they seemed much disappointed.

He inquired of me who wrote them. I told him it was one of my friends. "Can you read them?" he asked. When I told him I could, he swore, and raved, and tore the paper into bits. "Bring me all your letters!" said he, in a commanding tone. I told him I had none. "Don't be afraid," he continued, in an insinuating way. "Bring them all to me. Nobody shall do you any harm." Seeing I did not move to obey him, his pleasant tone changed to oaths and threats. "Who writes to you? half free niggers?" inquired he. I replied, "O, no; most of my letters are from white people. Some request me to burn them after they are read, and some I destroy without reading."

An exclamation of surprise from some of the company put a stop to our conversation. Some silver spoons which ornamented an old-fashioned buffet had just been discovered. My grandmother was in the habit of preserving fruit for many ladies in the town, and of preparing suppers for parties; consequently she had many jars of preserves. The closet that contained these was next invaded, and the contents tasted. One of them, who was helping himself freely, tapped his neighbor on the shoulder, and said, "Wal done! Don't wonder de niggers want to kill all de white folks, when dey live on 'sarves" [meaning preserves]. I stretched out my hand to take the jar, saying, "You were not sent here to search for sweetmeats."

"And what were we sent for?" said the captain, bristling up to me. I evaded the question.

The search of the house was completed, and nothing found to condemn us. They next proceeded to the garden, and knocked about every bush and vine with no better success. The captain called his men together, and, after a short consultation, the order to march was given. As they passed out of the gate, the captain turned back, and pronounced a malediction on the house. He said it ought to be burned to the ground, and each of its inmates receive thirty-nine lashes. We came out of this affair very fortunately; not losing any thing except some wearing apparel.

Towards evening the turbulence increased. The soldiers, stimulated by drink, committed still greater cruelties. Shrieks and shouts continually rent the air. Not daring to go to the door, I peeped under the window curtain. I saw a mob dragging along a number of colored people, each white man, with his musket upraised, threatening instant death if they did not stop their shrieks. Among the prisoners was a respectable old colored minister. They had found a few parcels of shot in his house, which his wife had for years used to balance her scales. For this they were going to shoot him on Court House Green. What a spectacle was that for a civilized country! A rabble, staggering under intoxication, assuming to be the administrators of justice!

The better class of the community exerted their influence to save the innocent, persecuted people; and in several instances they succeeded, by keeping them shut up in jail till the excitement abated. At last the white citizens found that their own property was not safe from the lawless rabble they had summoned to protect them. They rallied the drunken swarm, drove them back into the country, and set a guard over the town.

The next day, the town patrols were commissioned to search colored people that lived out of the city; and the most shocking outrages were committed with perfect impunity. Every day for a fortnight, if I looked out, I saw horsemen with some poor panting negro tied to their saddles, and compelled by the lash to keep up with their speed, till they arrived at the jail yard. Those who had been whipped too unmercifully to walk were washed with brine, tossed into a cart, and carried to jail. One black man, who had not fortitude to endure scourging, promised to give information about the conspiracy. But it turned out that he knew nothing at all. He had not even heard the name of Nat Turner. The poor fellow had, however, made up a story, which augmented his own sufferings and those of the colored people.

The day patrol continued for some weeks, and at sundown a night guard was substituted. Nothing at all was proved against the colored people, bond or free. The wrath of the slaveholders was somewhat appeased by the capture of Nat Turner. The imprisoned were released. The slaves were sent to their masters, and the free were permitted to return to their ravaged homes. Visiting was strictly forbidden on the plantations. The slaves begged the privilege of again meeting at their little church in the woods, with their burying ground around it. It was built by the colored people, and they had no higher happiness than to meet there and sing hymns together, and pour out their hearts in spontaneous prayer. Their request was denied, and the church was demolished. They were permitted to attend the white churches, a certain portion of the galleries being appropriated to their use. There, when every body else had partaken of the communion, and the benediction had been pronounced, the minister said, "Come down, now, my colored friends." They obeyed the summons, and partook of the bread and wine, in commemoration of the meek and lowly Jesus, who said, "God is your Father, and all ye are brethren."

QUESTIONS TO CONSIDER

1. Why did the militia companies search the homes of enslaved people? What objects attracted their interest and why?
2. What does Jacobs think about the poorer white people of Edenton? According to her, what is their relationship to slavery?

10.3 NEW-YORK FEMALE MORAL REFORM SOCIETY, EXCERPTS FROM "APPEAL TO WOMEN TO TAKE PART IN MORAL REFORM" (1836)*

Throughout the first half of the nineteenth century, many Americans, especially women, converted to new forms of evangelical Christianity that emphasized improving the world around them. As a result, many women, especially in the North and in towns and cities, joined moral reform societies. These were groups of activist women who sought to spread the gospel and prevent or end behavior that was contrary to their Christian standards of morality. Moral reform societies engaged in campaigns to end work on Sundays, ban or limit alcohol sales, abolish slavery, outlaw dueling, and end prostitution (licentiousness).

Moral reform societies subscribed to a common conception of gender in which women were believed to be innately virtuous and moral. It was their responsibility, therefore, to use their influence to convince the men in their lives, who lacked this innate morality, to make better choices. This extended to other women, such as those who worked as prostitutes, who did not live up to these moral standards and who, these activists believed, had to be redeemed. Highly motivated and well organized, moral reform societies succeeded in changing laws in numerous states.

---

* New-York Female Moral Reform Society, *An Appeal to the Wives, Mothers and Daughters of Our Land* (New York: Female Moral Reform Society, 1836).

Beloved Sisters:—

We come before you now, not to ask your assistance in an untried experiment, but to give you the high privilege of becoming fellow-laborers with us, in a cause which is already triumphing, and is *destined* to triumph, until the floods of pollution are stayed, and the whole earth purified by the spirit of the Lord.

In our efforts hitherto, we have had to contend not *only*, or *mainly*, with ignorance and vice.—They are our natural foes, and we had counted the cost of their opposition, and made up our minds accordingly. But we had a right to expect the cooperation of the virtuous and intelligent, of all who are seeking to effect the removal of sin and suffering, and the universal prevalence of purity and holiness. Our Society has these great objects expressly in view. It seeks to correct public sentiment by the dissemination of light and truth; to awaken in mothers a sense of their duties and responsibilities, and to save the young and inexperienced by warning them of the snares and artifices of the destroyer. . . .

Now, if God is the fountain of purity and honor, then his Word must be the perfect standard of both. And how full and explicit is the language of the Bible, with regard to the sin of licentiousness! It is mentioned so frequently, and in terms of such unmeasured abhorrence, that we could not be ignorant of its estimation in the eyes of a holy God, even if he had not stamped it with the seal of his special displeasure. Shall we, then, "be wise above what is written?" Shall we charge God with folly, by pronouncing it "*improper*" or "*inexpedient*" to insist on the keeping of *all* his commandments?

THE DUTY OF MOTHERS TO THEIR CHILDREN.

MOTHER! while you are hesitating about your duty in reference to this matter, or it may be, totally *regardless* of it, think not that the future destiny of the children you so tenderly love will be uninfluenced by your decision. You may consider them safe beneath your sheltering wing, and guarded by your vigilant eye; but *facts* have taught us the contrary. They are exposed to corrupting influences where you least suspect it, and their minds may be fearfully contaminated, in very early childhood. If our limits permitted, we could lay before you instances of deep and thrilling interest, which show the dangers to which even infant purity is constantly

exposed. To *you* as Mothers, is committed in a special manner the formation of the character of your children; you are their best and safest friend, and to you they look for counsel and example. We ask you, then, in the name of Him to whom you are responsible for this interesting charge, is it not a *paramount* duty to fortify their minds, against the temptations to which they will inevitably be exposed? Ought you not in the *nursery* to sow the seeds of chastity and virtue, and to build up a wall of principle around these little ones, which shall stand in coming years, to beat back the surges of corruption? Say not, "The subject is so delicate we dare not meddle with it, lest we should do more harm than good in the attempt." You are not at *liberty* to keep back any part of the counsel of God against this sin. He has spoken plainly, and if you refuse to repeat his instructions, it is as palpable an act of disobedience as the transgression of the command, "Thou shalt not kill." How many have been ruined by disease, and covered with infamy, who might now have been ornaments to society, had their minds been early strengthened against temptations by the prayerful instructions of a tender and judicious mother! The unhappy young man whose case has caused so much excitement in the community, and who, though legally acquitted, must wear through life the brand of suspected guilt, was once an innocent boy, the pride and hope of the parents whose hearts his conduct has wrung with anguish. So appalling have been the developments of this trial, with regard to the state of morals among a portion of the young men of this city, that men who care for nothing but the temporal interests of society, have expressed the most fearful forebodings. When habits and sentiments of such shameless profligacy are openly avowed by beardless boys, the Christian and the patriot may well tremble for the future destinies of his country. Mother! what shall secure your child from the snares into which so many have fallen?

DANGERS OF NEGLECTING THIS DUTY.

Follow in imagination your darling son from the country, into this great city. He is the child perhaps, of many prayers and tears; but you have failed, from a mistaken sense of delicacy, to caution him against the evils to which he is here particularly exposed. He would shrink from the thought of theft, drunkenness, or profanity, but *licentiousness*, the sin which kills both soul and body, is passed by in silence. His first step in the downward road is taken with hesitancy and dread; but this barrier passed, his departure from the habits and principles of his father's house, is fearfully rapid. The broken Sabbath, the midnight revel, the crowded theatre, all say, "The glory is departing." From the theatre to the brothel, the transition is easy and natural; and now the voice of conscience is silenced, the last restraints of virtue are withdrawn, and riot and murder close the dreadful scene. But the ruin he has brought upon himself ends not here. "Sin kills *beyond the tomb*." There is a day of retribution coming—a day that shall bring to light all the hidden things of darkness; and then you will meet your child again. The Son of Man is seated on the great white throne, the books are opened, and the dead, both small and great, are standing before God. See that trembling sinner, as he comes up from his premature and dishonored grave, to meet Him who hath said, "Whoremongers and adulterers God will judge." The withering frown of an angry God is upon him, and he seeks in vain to escape the searching glance which reads the inmost recesses of the soul. Can you endure the thought of hearing the plea of parental neglect and unfaithfulness urged by your lost child, and urged in *vain*? Dear sister, you must stand before the judgment seat of Christ, with the children God hath given you; and as you hope for a happy meeting with them there, fail not *now* to train them up in the "way they should go," and labor diligently for their early conversion, as the only safeguard of honor and happiness. . . .

DUTY OF UNMARRIED FEMALES.

Upon your regard and attention, dear young friends, we feel that this cause has great and special charms. You belong to the class particularly exposed to the artifices of the destroyer, and in your hands are the principal weapons of defence. While you smile on the fashionable libertine—while you admit him to your presence, and receive his proffered attentions—our efforts to effect a reformation in public sentiment, will be comparatively in vain. Would you associate familiarly with one whom you knew to be a thief, or a murderer? You turn away with disgust from the mere supposition; and is it then in your estimation a crime of less magnitude to steal from the trusting female, the priceless gem of

honor and virtue, and expose her immortal soul to all the horrors of the second death?

Away with that sickly sentimentalism, which spends all its energies in weeping over fictitious woes, while it looks with utter indifference on the sin and suffering by which it is surrounded. Let us call things by their right names, and shun vice in its alluring, as well as in its most disgusting forms. Much is now depending on the stand taken by young ladies, individually and collectively, upon the question of Moral Reform. If you come boldly out on the side of purity and virtue, your influence will be felt to the remotest corners of our country. Fear not the reproach and ridicule of the world. Depend upon it, he who scoffs at what he calls your "prudish severity," is secretly trembling for fear of the consequences of your firmness. Satan knows, and his children know, that their only hope lies in the disunion and timeserving timidity of the friends of goodness. Could they now see us united heart and hand, moving on with a firm step to the accomplishment of our purpose, all hell would at once anticipate the result.

Do you ask, what there is for you to do? Suffer us to remind you of your duty in a few particulars, and urge you to a conscientious performance of it.

SHUN ASSOCIATION WITH THE PROFLIGATE OF EITHER SEX.

Two objections are often urged against this course, which have some weight with the truly conscientious. The first, assumes that "young ladies, are not supposed to *know* any thing of the profligate habits of those with whom they associate." This objection supposes a degree of ignorance which we believe very rarely exists, and its fallacy is clearly evident from the fact that it is only applicable to the case of the licentious *man*. Why not admit the guilty *woman*, to the same degree of intimacy, sheltered under the same plea? a knowledge of the criminality of the one, involves of necessity, that of the other why then this invidious distinction? no mother would hesitate to warn her daughter against association with the abandoned woman, or to give her reasons for such prohibition, and this warning, to be efficacious or consistent must extend alike to both sexes. The other objection is this, that the course in question, "will be calculated to drive the libertine to desperation and thus prevent all hope of his being reformed and saved." We say to the *objector*, that we believe such treatment would have a directly contrary effect on all who were not entirely given up to the dominion of sin, by rendering their situation so intolerable, as to force them to reflection, and perhaps repentance. But even should not this be the result, is it not better that the *few* should be sacrificed to the welfare of the many? If those now in the way to death, will press on to destruction, shall we not endeavor to save the innocent and unwary from the same awful doom? Let our principles be thoroughly examined and established, and then let us *act* upon them, whatever may be the result.

"Can one take fire in his bosom and his clothes not be burned?" Association with the vicious, of whatever rank or station, degrades the mind and lowers the standard of morality.

"We are all," says Locke, "a kind of camelions, that take a tincture from the objects that surround us." A still wiser man has told us, that, "the companion of fools shall be destroyed." The example of an associate will exert a powerful influence in the formation of our own character, especially if it is a sinful one, because a bad model, finds in the depravity of our nature, something that prepares it to receive the impression. One evil companion will undo in a month all that parents and teachers have been laboring for years to accomplish. Remember, that the character of your associates, will in all probability be your own. If you do not *carry* to them a similarity of taste, you will be sure to *acquire* it, "for how can two walk together except they are agreed?" The more external accomplishments any one possesses, without religious principle, the greater is his power to do mischief, for attracting qualities are like the fair speech, and lovely form, and glowing colors, which the serpent assumed when he attacked and destroyed the innocence of Eve. When you have listened to his wiles, and felt his sharp tooth and the deadly poison of his venom, will it be a consolation that you have looked on his brilliant colors, and been ruined by the fascination of his charms? Shun then, all intercourse with the abandoned of *either* sex, as you value honor and happiness here, or hope hereafter.

SEEK TO ACQUIRE AND DIFFUSE INFORMATION ON THE SUBJECT.

When the ignorance and prejudice of the community are enlightened and subdued, and the overwhelming *facts* which daily come to our knowledge, are laid before them, we can safely leave the cause to make its own way to their hearts and consciences. For this purpose we commend to your attention the "ADVOCATE OF MORAL REFORM," and request you not only to take it yourselves, but to assist us in extending its circulation. We do this, believing it to be the most efficient way in which your assistance can at present be given, and one which falls peculiarly within your province. . . . There are hundreds of females in the factory villages that are springing up over our land, who are peculiarly exposed, by their youth and inexperience, to the arts of those wretches who visit the country to obtain supplies for the haunts of infamy in the large towns. It is ascertained that a majority of the abandoned females in this city are from the country, and who can say they might not have been saved, by the timely warnings of the Advocate? If the streams of pollution that flow from other sources can be dried up, we may then hope that in process of time these deadly waves will be stayed, but this can only be effected by light and knowledge. We can never intelligently combat an evil, until we know something of its *extent* and characteristics, and it is to supply this information as well as to awaken the public to feeling and action that the advocate is published. Every day brings fresh testimony from all quarters, to the value and usefulness of this paper; and by making it known still more widely, you may do much to reclaim and bless mankind. . . .

QUESTIONS TO CONSIDER

1. What is the role of women according to this essay? How does that role change depending on a woman's age or station in life?
2. What societal issues is this essay interested in addressing? Why do you think moral reformers focused on these problems in particular?

10.4 FREDERICK DOUGLASS, "COLONIZATION" (1849)*

Colonization was a movement that encompassed a variety of plans to end slavery in the United States by emancipating enslaved people on the condition that they leave the country. The American Colonization Society (ACS) was a group founded in 1816 to establish a colony, Liberia, in West Africa where free and enslaved Black Americans could be sent. Although the ACS had numerous wealthy members, including some significant slaveholders, it never adequately addressed the enormous costs their plan entailed or overcame the suspicion and hostility with which free Black Americans viewed the plan.

The overwhelming majority of Black Americans opposed colonization. Most had lived their entire lives in the United States and did not want to uproot themselves and their families just to suit the whims of the wealthy supporters of the ACS. To leave the US while millions of Black people were still enslaved in the South also felt to many like a betrayal. Some Black Americans did emigrate, but the difficulties and disease they often experienced in Africa further convinced Black Americans to oppose colonization.

In order to divert the hounds from the pursuit of the fox, a *"red herring"* is sometimes drawn across the trail, and the hounds mistaking it for the real scent, the game is often lost. We look upon the recent debate in the Senate of the United States, over this wrinkled old "red herring" of colonization as a *ruse* to divert the attention of the people from the foul abomination which is sought to be forced upon the free soil of California and New Mexico, and which is now struggling for existence in Kentucky, Virginia and the District of Columbia. The slaveholders are evidently at a stand to know what trick they shall try next to turn the scorching rays of anti-slavery light and truth from the bloodshot eyes of the monster slavery. The discussion of it is most painful and agonizing; and if it continues, the very life of this foul, unnatural and adulterous beast will be put in imminent peril; so the slaveholding *charmers* have conjured up their old *familiar spirits* of colonization, making the old *essence* of abomination to flounder about in its grave clothes before the eyes of Northern men, to their utter confusion and bewilderment.

A drowning man will catch at a straw. Slavery is sinking in public estimation. It is going down. It wants help, and asks through Mr. Underwood, of Kentucky, how much of the public money (made by the honest toil of Northern men) will be at its service in the event of emancipation, "as some are in favor of emancipation, provided that the Negroes can be sent to Liberia, or beyond the limits of the United States."

Here we have the old colonization spirit revived, and the impudent proposition entertained by the Senate of the United States of expelling the free colored people from the United States, their native land, to Liberia.

In view of this proposition, we would respectfully suggest to the assembled wisdom of the nation, that it might be well to ascertain the number of free colored people who will be likely to need the assistance of government to help them out of this country to Liberia, or elsewhere, beyond the limits of these United States—since this course might save any embarrassment which would result from an appropriation

* Frederick Douglass, "Colonization," *The North Star* (Rochester), January 26, 1849.

more than commensurate to the numbers who might be disposed to leave this, our own country, for one we know not of. We are of the opinion that the *free* colored people generally mean to live in America, and not in Africa; and to appropriate a large sum for our removal, would merely be a waste of the public money. We do not mean to go to Liberia. Our minds are made up to live here if we can, or die here if we must; so every attempt to remove us will be, as it ought to be, labor lost. Here we are, and here we shall remain. While our brethren are in bondage on these shores, it is idle to think of inducing any considerable number of the free colored people to quit this for a foreign land.

For two hundred and twenty-eight years has the colored man toiled over the soil of America, under a burning sun and a driver's lash—plowing, planting, reaping, that white men might roll in ease, their hands unhardened by labor, and their brows unmoistened by the waters of genial toil; and now that the moral sense of mankind is beginning to revolt at this system of foul treachery and cruel wrong, and is demanding its overthrow, the mean and cowardly oppressor is meditating plans to expel the colored man entirely from the country. Shame upon the guilty wretches that dare propose, and all that countenance such a proposition. We live here—have lived here—have a right to live here, and mean to live here.—F.D.

QUESTIONS TO CONSIDER

1. Why does Douglass say it is unfair to suggest that Black Americans emigrate to Liberia?
2. Why are Black Americans determined to stay in the United States, according to Douglass?

10.5 VISUAL SOURCE: CHILDS & INMAN, *INTEMPERANCE AND TEMPERANCE (1831)**

Alcohol consumption was a serious social problem and public health concern in the early republic. Alcohol consumption rose throughout the first decades of the 1800s, and by 1830 the average American consumed 7.1 gallons per year—more than triple what the average American consumed in 2014. Ready access to alcoholic spirits and cider was part of the problem, as was a culture that encouraged alcohol consumption throughout the day for men. In response, reformers began advocating temperance—that is, the limiting or abstaining from drinking alcoholic beverages. This movement was particularly popular among Christian women of the Second Great Awakening, who stressed that alcoholism was a moral problem that required national attention.

This illustration was meant to support temperance campaigns by presenting a stark contrast between the negative consequences of drinking and the pleasant life that could be lived without alcohol. It exemplifies many of the criticisms of temperance advocates, highlighting the harm alcohol posed to families, health, and productive labor.

* Courtesy, American Antiquarian Society

QUESTIONS TO CONSIDER

1. What role does nature play in this illustration? How is the variation in vegetation used to make a point about alcohol and temperance?
2. How does this illustration use ideals of gender and family to encourage the viewer to abstain from alcohol?

10.6 VISUAL SOURCE: ENDICOTT & SWETT, *NULLIFICATION . . . DESPOTISM* (1833)*

During the Nullification Crisis of 1832, John C. Calhoun (1782–1850), pictured at center here, led his home state of South Carolina to declare a federal tax law unconstitutional. Many South Carolinians subscribed to Calhoun's theory of nullification and interposition, according to which individual

---

* From The New York Public Library

states had the power to determine the constitutionality of laws as well as the power to secede from the United States rather than be forced to follow laws they believed were unconstitutional. Calhoun believed that the individual states had formed the United States like a contract, and that if that contract were breeched—for instance, when unconstitutional laws were passed—a state had the right to leave.

To many other Americans, this sounded like treason. Calhoun and South Carolina were asserting powers not granted by the Constitution and were threatening to break up the country if they did not get their way. In this illustration, Calhoun ascends steps that lay out all the ill effects of his leadership to grasp the crown of despotism, a concept anathema to the republican self-government that Americans valued.

QUESTIONS TO CONSIDER

1. Two murdered men labelled "Constitution" and "*E Pluribus Unum*" lie at the foot of the stairs Calhoun ascends. What is the artist saying by including these figures and positioning them front and center?

2. At the peak of the stairs, partially obscured by Calhoun, is an explosion labelled "Anarchy." Why might contemporary Americans have seen anarchy as the natural conclusion of nullification?

CHAPTER 11

WARRING FOR THE PACIFIC, 1836–1848

11.1 JOHN L. O'SULLIVAN, EXCERPT FROM "THE GREAT NATION OF FUTURITY" (1839)*

John L. O'Sullivan (1813–1895) was an American editor and writer famous for espousing the principles of the Jacksonian Democratic Party and American exceptionalism. He wrote and edited *The Democratic Review*, where he published essays celebrating American culture and the working-class base of the Democratic Party ("the mechanical and agricultural population"). A proponent of aggressive American expansion, O'Sullivan is now most famous for declaring that it was the "manifest destiny" (i.e., the clear or obvious future) of the United States to reach to the Pacific Ocean.

O'Sullivan touches on many of his common themes in "The Great Nation of Futurity." He advances the idea that the United States is a nation out of time, unbound and uninfluenced by the past history of the world. He supports the development of a uniquely American culture, including through literature and law, and believes that American craftsmen and farmers best represent the ideal American spirit. These ideas, in which the exceptional and splendid nature of the United States was connected to the working class, were common within the antebellum Democratic Party.

The American people having derived their origin from many other nations, and the Declaration of National Independence being entirely based on the great principle of human equality, these facts demonstrate at once our disconnected position as regards any other nation; that we have, in reality, but little connection with the past history of any of them, and still less with all antiquity, its glories, or its crimes. On the contrary, our national birth was the beginning of a new history, the formation and progress of an untried political system, which separates us from the past and connects us with the future only; and so far as regards

---

* John L. O'Sullivan, "The Great Nation of Futurity," in *The United States Democratic Review*, 1839 (Washington, DC: Langtree and O'Sullivan, 1837–40), 6:426–30, https://babel.hathitrust.org/cgi/pt?id=coo.31924085376634&view=1up&seq=350&skin=2021.

the entire development of the natural rights of man, in moral, political, and national life, we may confidently assume that our country is destined to be *the great nation* of futurity.

It is so destined, because the principle upon which a nation is organized fixes its destiny, and that of equality is perfect, is universal. It presides in all the operations of the physical world, and it is also the conscious law of the soul—the self-evident dictate of morality, which accurately defines the duty of man to man, and consequently man's rights as man. Besides, the truthful annals of any nation furnish abundant evidence, that its happiness, its greatness, its duration, were always proportionate to the democratic equality in its system of government.

How many nations have had their decline and fall, because the equal rights of the minority were trampled on by the despotism of the majority; or the interests of the many sacrificed to the aristocracy of the few; or the rights and interests of all given up to the monarchy of one? These three kinds of government have figured so frequently and so largely in the ages that have passed away, that their history, through all time to come, can only furnish a resemblance. Like causes produce like effects, and the true philosopher of history will easily discern the principle of equality, or of privilege, working out its inevitable result. The first is regenerative, because it is natural and right; the latter is destructive to society, because it is unnatural and wrong.

What friend of human liberty, civilization, and refinement, can cast his view over the past history of the monarchies and aristocracies of antiquity, and not deplore that they ever existed? What philanthropist can contemplate the oppressions, the cruelties, and injustice inflicted by them on the masses of mankind, and not turn with moral horror from the retrospect?

America is destined for better deeds. It is our unparalleled glory that we have no reminiscences of battle fields, but in defence of humanity, of the oppressed of all nations, of the rights of conscience, the rights of personal enfranchisement. Our annals describe no scenes of horrid carnage, where men were led on by hundreds of thousands to slay one another, dupes and victims to emperors, kings, nobles, demons in the human form called heroes. We have had patriots to defend our homes, our liberties, but no aspirants to crowns or thrones; nor have the American people ever suffered themselves to be led on by wicked ambition to depopulate the land, to spread desolation far and wide, that a human being might be placed on a seat of supremacy.

We have no interest in the scenes of antiquity, only as lessons of avoidance of nearly all their examples. The expansive future is our arena, and for our history. We are entering on its untrodden space, with the truths of God in our minds, beneficent objects in our hearts, and with a clear conscience unsullied by the past. We are the nation of human progress, and who will, what can, set limits to our onward march? Providence is with us, and no earthly power can. We point to the everlasting truth on the first page of our national declaration, and we proclaim to the millions of other lands, that "the gates of hell"—the powers of aristocracy and monarchy—"shall not prevail against it."

The far-reaching, the boundless future will be the era of American greatness. In its magnificent domain of space and time, the nation of many nations is destined to manifest to mankind the excellence of divine principles; to establish on earth the noblest temple ever dedicated to the worship of the Most High—the Sacred and the True. Its floor shall be a hemisphere—its roof the firmament of the star-studded heavens, and its congregation an Union of many Republics, comprising hundreds of happy millions, calling, owning no man master, but governed by God's natural and moral law of equality, the law of brotherhood—of "peace and good will amongst men."

But although the mighty constituent truth upon which our social and political system is founded will assuredly work out the glorious destiny herein shadowed forth, yet there are many untoward circumstances to retard our progress, to procrastinate the entire fruition of the greatest good to the human race. There is a tendency to imitativeness, prevailing amongst our professional and literary men, subversive of originality of thought, and wholly unfavorable to progress. Being in early life devoted to the study of the laws, institutions, and antiquities of other nations, they are far behind the mind and movement of the age in which they live: so much so, that the spirit of improvement, as well as of enfranchisement, exists, chiefly in the great masses—the agricultural and mechanical population.

This propensity to imitate foreign nations is absurd and injurious. It is absurd, for we have never yet drawn on our mental resources that we have not found them ample and of unsurpassed excellence; witness our constitutions of government, where we had no foreign ones to imitate. It is injurious, for never have we followed foreign examples in legislation; witness our laws, our charters of monopoly, that we did not inflict evil on ourselves, subverting common right, in violation of common sense and common justice. The halls of legislation and the courts of law in a Republic are necessarily the public schools of the adult population. If, in these institutions, foreign precedents are legislated, and foreign decisions adjudged over again, is it to be wondered at that an imitative propensity predominates amongst professional and business men. Taught to look abroad for the highest standards of law, judicial wisdom, and literary excellence, the native sense is subjugated to a most obsequious idolatry of the tastes, sentiments, and prejudices of Europe. Hence our legislation, jurisprudence, literature, are more reflective of foreign aristocracy than of American democracy.

European governments have plunged themselves in debt, designating burthens on the people "national blessings." Our State Legislatures, humbly imitating their pernicious example, have pawned, bonded the property, labor, and credit of their constituents to the subjects of monarchy. It is by our own labor, and with our own materials, that our internal improvements are constructed, but our British-law-trained legislators have enacted that we shall be in debt for them, paying interest, but never to become owners. With various climates, soils, natural resources, and products, beyond any other country, and producing more real capital annually than any other sixteen millions of people on earth, we are, nevertheless, borrowers, paying tribute to the money powers of Europe.

Our business men have also conned the lesson of example, and devoted themselves body and mind to the promotion of foreign interests. If States can steep themselves in debt, with any propriety in times of peace, why may not merchants import merchandise on credit? If the one can bond the labor and property of generations yet unborn, why may not the other contract debts against the yearly crops and daily labor of their contemporary fellow citizens?

And our literature!—Oh, when will it breathe the spirit of our republican institutions? When will it be imbued with the God-like aspiration of intellectual freedom—the elevating principle of equality? When will it assert its national independence, and speak the soul—the heart of the American people? Why cannot our literati comprehend the matchless sublimity of our position amongst the nations of the world—our high destiny—and cease bending the knee to foreign idolatry, false tastes, false doctrines, false principles? When will they be inspired by the magnificent scenery of our own world, imbibe the fresh enthusiasm of a new heaven and a new earth, and soar upon the expanded wings of truth and liberty? Is not nature as original—her truths as captivating—her aspects as various, as lovely, as grand—her Promethean fire as glowing in this, our Western hemisphere, as in that of the East? And above all, is not our private life as morally beautiful and good—is not our public life as politically right, as indicative of the brightest prospects of humanity, and therefore as inspiring of the highest conceptions? Why, then, do our authors aim at no higher degree of merit, than a successful imitation of English writers of celebrity?

But with all the retrograde tendencies of our laws, our judicature, our colleges, our literature, still they are compelled to follow the mighty impulse of the age; they are carried onward by the increasing tide of progress; and though they cast many a longing look behind, they cannot stay the glorious movement of the masses, nor induce them to venerate the rubbish, the prejudices, the superstitions of other times and other lands, the theocracy of priests, the divine right of kings, the aristocracy of blood, the metaphysics of colleges, the irrational stuff of law libraries. Already the brightest hopes of philanthropy, the most enlarged speculations of true philosophy, are inspired by the indications perceptible amongst the mechanical and agricultural population. There, with predominating influence, beats the vigorous national heart of America, propelling the onward march of the multitude, propagating and extending, through the present and the future, the powerful purpose of soul, which, in the seventeenth century, sought a refuge among savages, and reared in the wilderness the sacred altars of intellectual freedom. This was the seed that produced individual equality, and political liberty, as its natural fruit; and this is our true nationality. American patriotism is not of soil; we are not aborigines, nor of ancestry, for we are of all nations; but it is essentially personal enfranchisement, for "where liberty dwells," said Franklin, the sage of the Revolution, "there is my country."

Such is our distinguishing characteristic, our popular instinct, and never yet has any public functionary stood forth for the rights of conscience against any, or all, sects desirous of predominating over such right, that he was not sustained by the people. And when a venerated patriot of the Revolution appealed to his fellow-citizens against the overshadowing power of a monarch institution, they came in their strength, and the moneyed despot was brought low. Corporate powers and privileges shrink to nothing when brought in conflict against the rights of individuals. Hence it is that our professional, literary, or commercial aristocracy, have no faith in the virtue, intelligence or capability of the people. The latter have never responded to their exotic sentiments, nor promoted their views of a strong government irresponsible to the popular majority, to the will of the masses.

Yes, we are the nation of progress, of individual freedom, of universal enfranchisement. Equality of rights is the cynosure of our union of States, the grand exemplar of the correlative equality of individuals; and while truth sheds its effulgence, we cannot retrograde, without dis- solving the one and subverting the other. We must onward to the fulfilment of our mission—to the entire development of the principle of our organization—freedom of conscience, freedom of person, freedom of trade and business pursuits, universality of freedom and equality. This is our high destiny, and in nature's eternal, inevitable decree of cause and effect we must accomplish it. All this will be our future history, to establish on earth the moral dignity and salvation of man—the immutable truth and beneficence of God. For this blessed mission to the nations of the world, which are shut out from the life-giving light of truth, has America been chosen; and her high example shall smite unto death the tyranny of kings, hierarchs, and oligarchs, and carry the glad tidings of peace and good will where myriads now endure an existence scarcely more enviable than that of beasts of the field. Who, then, can doubt that our country is destined to be *the great nation* of futurity?

QUESTIONS TO CONSIDER

1. Why is O'Sullivan so confident about the future of the United States?
2. What makes the United States different from other countries according to O'Sullivan? Is this difference a good thing?

11.2 *TELEGRAPH AND TEXAS REGISTER,* "UNTITLED" (1836)*

Texas was a sparsely populated northern state of Mexico, which suffered considerable instability over the course of the 1820s. Far from the capital at Mexico City, and with few reliable roads in between, Texas suffered frequent raids from the Comanche, who controlled a large region of the southern

---

* "Untitled," *Telegraph and Texas Register*, November 2, 1836, p. 3, http://www.texasslaveryproject.org/sources/TTR/display .php?f=TSP0120.xml.

Great Plains. In the late 1820s, Mexico began to invite immigrants to Texas to stabilize their frontier. Thousands emigrated from the Southern United States to Texas in the following years, many of them bringing enslaved people with them, contrary to Mexican law.

In 1835 tensions between slaveholding American Texans and the Mexican federal government led to violence, and the Texans declared themselves an independent country. Most Texans hoped to convince US Congress to annex Texas and incorporate it into the American union, thereby adding another slave state to the United States. This article from the London *Sun* was reprinted in a Texas newspaper to show readers that some foreigners supported Texan independence and eventual annexation by the United States.

The following extract from the London Sun, we feel much pleasure in presenting to our readers, not only because it is avowedly the organ of the present Government of England, and therefore may be considered a transcript in its editorial articles of the prevalent opinions of the Administration; but the sound policy of its views—the accurate antithesis it proclaims to the world between the "freemen of Texas," and "the usurper Santa Anna," and the hope it indulges amounting to certainty of our annexation to the States, indicating a strong presumption that England too only awaits the request to proclaim Texas free and independent, would tender it an unpardonable omission on our part to suppress a document of so much importance.

FROM THE LONDON SUN.

The war whoop has been raised in another quarter by a Mr. Hoy and a Mr. Ward. We are now to go to war—God save the mark—with the United States of America. Of all the moon-calf Quixotisms projected by the pugnacious statesmen of Britain for the last hundred years, this would be the most absurd. Our league with the despots of Europe against France was not a greater dereliction of principle: our appearance at New-Orleans was less degrading. We have our national feelings—prejudices as warm and powerful as many who talk more about them; but if our pugnacious praters in the Senate succeed in innoculating ministers with their folly, we shall not break our hearts even tho[*sic*] the "ould General" gives the expedition fitted out such another drubbing as he gave the last.

What is the case of these talking heroes who speak not "daggers," like Hamlet, but great guns, regular forty pounders! General Santa Anna has usurped the supreme power of Mexico. The rights of the confederate States of the Mexican Union have been grossly outraged. Texas has asserted its independence. We are told that we are bound to support Mexico. The speakers mean to say that we are bound to support the usurper, Santa Anna, against the freemen of Texas. To interfere between the Mexicans and Texians would be either to interfere in a family squabble between two districts of the same [illegible word] it would be to take part with one of two belligerent powers to subdue the other to its dominion. Either the one or the other [illegible word] be contrary to every sound principle of international law, and to the interests of Britain.

But, say our wiseacres, the United States are taking part in the war between Texas and Mexico, (always meaning between the Texians and Gen. Santa Anna.) In the first place, this is not true. America has taken no part in the war. Volunteers have been raised in America, and have marched into Texas, just in the same way as volunteers have been raised in England and transported into Spain; that is all. If there be any difference it has been here, that the mass of the American auxiliary troops, in so far as individual character is concerned, seems to be of a more respectable "caste," than the British. With what face could Britain take upon it to forbid America to do in Texas what Britain is doing in Spain?

If Texas succeed in vindicating its independence; if independent Texas seeks to strengthen itself against Mexico by getting itself incorporated into the American

Union; if the American Union listen to the petition of Texas and stamp another star on its banner, WHAT IS THAT TO US? WHAT RIGHT HAVE WE TO SAY "NO" TO FORBID THE BANS?

We have just as much right as America would have had to forbid the union of England and Ireland. But we are told that this union between Texas and the United States will favor the slave trade. Every new State, say these wise men, retains its internal laws on being admitted into the Union; slaveholding States retain their slaves. Texas, which is a slave-trading State, will continue to trade in slaves. They overlook an important distinction. Every State admitted into the Union retains its internal arrangements, the municipal laws, as far as they are consistent with democratic republicanism. But every State admitted into the Union conform to its public law, by which it is guided in its dealings with external nations. The possession of slaves is a matter of local municipal law; the carrying on of the slave trade is a matter of international law. We believe one of the surest means to check the slave trade in the Gulf of Mexico would be to incorporate Texas into the N. American Union. Again, we are told that Britain ought not to allow the United States to extend their territory. Why? Will the extension do Britain any harm? Let the Union extend as it will while its present constitution endures, it never can be an aggressive warlike nation.—And for other considerations, the better regulated policy which would be introduced into Texas (we will be reminded of Lynch law, but all things are good or bad by comparison) would be in favor of trade. Of one thing we may be sure, that the Texian deputies in Congress will be strong anti-tariff men, and that is in our favor.

We regret to see Lord Palmerston seeking to conciliate the "sons of thunder," by affecting a coincidence of sentiment. He ought to have assumed the manlier and more Christian tone assumed by Lord Glenelg towards Sir Benjamin D'Urban and the Cape Colonists, who are whining and wincing, like hounds held in the leash, praying to be let slip upon the Caffres. He should have advised the dreamers of hot dreams, that it was sometime expedient for those whose hot blood made them over valiant at times, to lose a few ounces in the dog days by leeching or the lancet.

To speak seriously: we know that war, horrible though it be, is at times unavoidable. But it is not an undertaking to be asked in the light dare-devil fashion with which we enter upon a Christmas frolic—nor are those who would run upon it with their eyes shut, the persons most likely to carry it on with sagacity and foresight to a successful termination. We will tell the lovers of war two things upon which they would do well to reflect: Situated as this country at present is, the first serious war in which Britain is engaged will blow up the national debt. The blowing up of the national debt will be followed in a week by a national convention. All who approve of the end, and think that the end sanctifies the means, cannot do better than persist in urging the nation to go to war.

QUESTIONS TO CONSIDER

1. According to the article, why should Great Britain refrain from interfering in the conflict between Texas and Mexico?
2. Why does the author believe that Texas joining the United States might ultimately be good for the British?

11.3 JOSÉ MARÍA FLORES, ADDRESS TO THE MEXICAN ARMY, ANGELES SECTION OF OPERATIONS (1846)*

José María Flores (1818–1866) was the Mexican governor of California when the United States invaded in 1846. Following the annexation of Texas by the US in 1846, President James Polk dispatched General Zachary Taylor to the disputed frontier between Texas and Mexico to provoke conflict. Polk used the skirmishing that broke out between Taylor's army and Mexican forces as a pretext to declare war, and the United States proceeded to invade Mexico.

While much of the fighting occurred near Texas and Mexico City, many expansionist Americans hoped to secure California as well. Mexican authorities in California dealt with revolts by American settlers as well as coastal invasions by the US Navy. With the help of Mexican civilians, Flores was able to expel an American outpost from Los Angeles in September 1846. Following the capture of Mexico City by the US a year later, however, the Mexican government decided to sue for peace. In the treaty that followed, Mexico ceded a huge portion of its northern territory, including California north to the modern border with Oregon, to the United States.

MEXICAN ARMY, SECTION OF OPERATIONS.

ANGELES, October 1, 1846.

FELLOW CITIZENS: It is a month and a half that, by lamentable fatality, fruit of cowardice and inability of the first authorities of the department, we behold ourselves subjugated and oppressed by an insignificant force of adventurers of the United States of America, and placing us in a worse condition than that of slaves.

They are dictating to us despotic and arbitrary laws, and loading us with contributions and onerous burdens which have for an object the ruin of our industry and agriculture, and to force us to abandon our property, to be possessed and divided among themselves.

And shall we be capable to allow ourselves to be subjugated and to accept, by our silence, the weighty chains of slavery? Shall we permit to be lost the soil inherited from our fathers, which cost them so much blood and so many sacrifices? Shall we make our families victims of the most barbarous slavery? Shall we wait to see our wives violated; our innocent children punished by the American whips; our property sacked our temples profaned; and, lastly, to drag through an existence full of insult and shame? No! a thousand times no! Countrymen, first death!

Who of you does not feel his heart beat with violence; who does not feel his blood boil, to contemplate our situation? And who will be the Mexican who will not feel indignant, and who will not rise to take up arms to destroy our oppressors? We believe there is not one so vile and cowardly. With such a motive the majority of the inhabitants of the districts, justly indignant against our tyrants, raise the cry of war, with arms in their hands, and of one accord swear to sustain the following articles:

1st. We, the inhabitants of the department of California as, members of the great Mexican nation, declare that it is, and has been, our wish to belong to her alone, free and independent.

2nd. Consequently, the authorities intended and named by the invading forces of the United States are held null and void.

* Harry Laurenz Wells, Frank T. Gilbert, and W. L. Chambers, *History of Butte County, California* (1882), 1–2:71, https://books .google.ca/books?id=9BYVAAAAYAAJ&printsec=frontcover&source=gbs_ge_summary_r&cad=0#v=onepage&q&f=false.

3rd. All the North American, being enemies of Mexico, we swear not to lay down our arms, till they are expelled from the Mexican territory.

4th. All Mexican citizens, from the age of fifteen to 60 sixty, who do not take up arms to forward the present plan, are declared traitors and under pain of death.

5th. Every Mexican or foreigner, who may directly, or indirectly, aid the enemies of Mexico will be punished in the same manner.

6th. The property of the North Americans in the department, who may have directly or indirectly taken part with, or aided, the enemies, shall be confiscated and used for the expenses of war, and their persons shall be taken to the interior of the republic.

7th. All those who may oppose the present plan will be punished with arms.

8th. All the inhabitants of Santa Barbara, and the district of the north, will be invited immediately to adhere to the present plan.

JOSE MA. FLORES
CAMP IN ANGELES, September 24, 1846.
[Signed by more than 300 persons.]

QUESTIONS TO CONSIDER

1. How does Flores describe the American invasion? What does he argue is at stake in this fight?
2. Why did Flores believe Mexicans were "justly indignant" toward the United States? Why did they see the US as the aggressor in this war?

11.4 WILLIAM ELSEY CONNELLEY, EXCERPT FROM *DONIPHAN'S EXPEDITION AND THE CONQUEST OF NEW MEXICO AND CALIFORNIA* (1847)*

Alexander William Doniphan (1808–1887) was an American lawyer and soldier who led an invasion of Mexico during the Mexican–American War. While he attempted to coordinate with other US forces to capture the Mexican city of Chihuahua, he also came into contact and conflict with Indigenous peoples of northern Mexico, including the Apache, Navajo, and Ute. While both Mexico and now the United States claimed sovereignty over what is now Texas, New Mexico, and Arizona, in practice there were few Mexicans or Americans there and the land was still the *de facto* domain of the Native groups there. The Navajo chief who rebukes Doniphan in this excerpt says as much when explaining that the Navajo had existing conflicts and relationships with the Mexicans that Doniphan and his fellow Americans did not understand.

On the 22nd, Captain Waldo having come in with one hundred and fifty men, swelling the aggregate number of the Americans present to three hundred and thirty, the treaty was recommenced. Colonel Doniphan now explained to the chiefs, "that the United States had taken military possession of

---

* William Elsey Connelley, John Taylor Hughes, and Charles R. Morehead, *Doniphan's Expedition and the Conquest of New Mexico and California* (Topeka, KS, 1907), 305–6, https://archive.org/details/doniphansexpeditooconn/page/n5/mode/2up.

New Mexico; that her laws were now extended over that territory, that the New Mexicans would be protected against violence and invasion; and that their rights would be amply preserved to them; that the United States was also anxious to enter into a treaty of peace and lasting friendship with her red children, the Navajos; that the same protection would be given them against encroachments, and usurpation of their rights, as had been guaranteed the New Mexicans; that the United States claimed all the country by the right of conquest and both they and the New Mexicans were now become equally her children; that he had come with ample powers to negotiate a permanent peace between the Navajos, the Americans, and New Mexicans; and that if they refused to treat on terms honorable to both parties, he was instructed to prosecute a war against them." He also admonished them, "to enter into no treaty stipulations unless they meant to observe them strictly, and in good faith; that the United States made no second treaty with the same people; that she first offered the olive branch, and if that were rejected, then powder, bullet, and the steel."

Then the same young chief, of great sagacity and boldness, stood up and replied to the American commander thus: "Americans! You have a strange cause of war against the Navajos. We have waged war against the New Mexicans for several years. We have plundered their villages and killed many of their people, and made many prisoners. We had just cause for all this. *You* have lately commenced a war against the same people. You are powerful. You have great guns and many brave soldiers. You have therefore conquered them, the very thing we have been attempting to do for so many years. You now turn upon us for attempting to do what you have done yourselves. We cannot see why you have cause of quarrel with us for fighting the New Mexicans on the west, while you do the same thing on the east. Look how matters stand. This is *our war.* We have more right to complain of you for interfering in our war, than you have to quarrel with us for continuing a war we had begun long before you got here. If you will act justly, you will allow us to settle our own differences."

QUESTIONS TO CONSIDER

1. What is Doniphan's message to the Navajo?
2. Why does the Navajo chief rebuke Doniphan? What does he want Doniphan and his men to do?

11.5 VISUAL SOURCE: H. BUCHOLZER, *MATTY MEETING THE TEXAS QUESTION* (1844)*

Under the leadership of slaveholding American emigrants, a portion of the Mexican state of Coahuila y Tejas declared independence in 1836. This sparked a military conflict between allegedly independent Texas and Mexico, as well as a political conflict in the United States over whether to annex Texas (which American Texans desired). Martin Van Buren (1782–1862; second from the left in the illustration below) ascended to the presidency in 1837 and refused to proceed with annexation despite pressure from politicians like John Calhoun and Thomas H. Benton (shown in the center). Southern Democrats like Benton and Calhoun supported adding a new slave state in Texas, but Van Buren feared that annexation would unnecessarily agitate Northerners who had opposed adding additional slave states in the past. Texas appears as a figure of chaos, bearing a dagger, whips, and chains, and Medusa-like serpentine hair. She is supported by Benton and Calhoun, while an elderly Jackson prods a reluctant Van Buren toward her. In the background, presidential hopefuls George Dallas and James Polk remark that Texas is ugly but that if they were in Van Buren's place, they would accept her anyway.

QUESTIONS TO CONSIDER

1. Why is Texas depicted as an ugly caricature bearing weapons and implements of slavery?
2. Who is this cartoon making light of? What does the artist believe should be done about Texas?

11.6 VISUAL SOURCE: EMANUEL GOTTLIEB LEUTZE, *WESTWARD THE COURSE OF EMPIRE TAKES ITS WAY* (1862)*

Emmanuel Leutze (1816–1868) was a German-American painter known for his detailed compositions on patriotic subjects. In 1860 the US Congress commissioned him to paint a stairway in the Capitol building, and Leutze produced this piece celebrating the westward expansion of the United States. The painting evokes many themes consistent with "manifest destiny," the idea that it was the clear and natural fate of the United States to expand and span the entire width of North America. White American settlers appear as dogged, industrious, cheerful pioneers. Families are prominently featured with children, symbolizing how Americans will quickly populate the new lands they inhabit. The wilderness around them is largely empty, and while smoke far in the distance signals some sparse human habitation, the overwhelming impression is of virgin land just waiting to be discovered and settled. The margins of the painting pay homage to the icons and heroes of the American frontier. Explorer William Clark and frontiersman Daniel Boone appear in portraits. Icons of guns, hatchets, and plows—the tools used to tame the wilderness—decorate the corners.

* public domain/Wikipedia

QUESTIONS TO CONSIDER

1. Who is absent from this painting? How would the inclusion of more people besides the predominantly white settlers change the story this painting tells?
2. Why does Leutze take care to portray multiple children and infants? Why are families important to the message of this painting?

CHAPTER 12

COMING APART, 1848–1857

12.1 MARY E. BLANCHARD, LETTER TO BENJAMIN SEAVER DESCRIBING THE TUMULTUOUS SCENE IN BOSTON DURING THE TRIAL AND RETURN TO SLAVERY OF ANTHONY BURNS (1854)*

Anthony Burns (1834–1862) was a man who escaped slavery in 1854, only to be captured and remanded to slavery under the Fugitive Slave Act of 1850. The Fugitive Slave Act was a controversial law that gave slaveholders new opportunities to recapture people who had escaped slavery. An alleged escaped enslaved person could be arrested and brought before a special judge for a hearing. The alleged fugitive was not allowed to testify in the hearing, and the judge's fee would be twice as large if they found the alleged fugitive to be an enslaved person than if they declared them free. Many Northerners felt that the law was unjust because it provided no protection against free Black people living in free states being arrested and enslaved by unscrupulous slave catchers.

Anthony Burns escaped slavery but was recaptured in Boston several months later. President Franklin Pierce ordered US Marines to ensure Burns was returned to slavery and was not rescued by the antislavery residents of Boston. The case quickly became famous as many Northerners saw it as evidence that slavery was being enforced even in "free" states. The following letter was written by Mary E. Blanchard to her father Benjamin Seaver, who was previously mayor of Boston and travelling in Europe at the time these events unfolded.

---

* "Letter from Mary E. Blanchard to Benjamin Seaver, 4 June 1854," *Letters to Benjamin Seaver*, Massachusetts Historical Society, Collections Online, https://www.masshist.org/database/viewer.php?item_id=1999&pid=3.

Roxbury June 4th 1854
My very dear Father,

I have so much to tell you I hardly know where to begin. I duly received your kind letter of the 15th & 17th May, and am much obliged for it. . . . The last week will long be remembered as a sad one by the citizens of Boston, for as the account which I commenced of the fugitive slave affair in last Sunday's letter, was only the beginning of difficulties. Many times have we rejoiced that you were not in Boston, in the capacity of Mayor. The trial was continued on Monday and Tuesday & Wednesday, and each day the excitement increased, and crowds collected around the Court House, and soldiers & Marines were inside the building to protect it. Judge Loring then said, that his decision would be given on Friday. The slave's council endeavored to prove that he was in Boston the 1st of March, on the other hand the Master and his witness, swore to his running away on the 27th inst, and also to his identity. On Friday at ten o'clock the judge gave his decision in favor of the claimant, and immediately preparations were begun for taking him away. A steamer was in readiness at L wharf, and the Mayor ordered out all the <u>State</u> military and police force, and gave General Edmands discretionary powers to keep the peace of the city. From ten o'clock till three, the streets from the wharf to the Court House were lined with military, and State street during all that time was impassable, so that <u>business</u> <u>there</u> <u>was</u> <u>necessarily</u> <u>suspended</u>. In the centre of a hollow square formed of volunteers, about 200, all the worst blacklegs and pimps of the city, walked the slave, a good looking fellow. Each one of these men had a drawn sword, or knife. Several companies of soldiers marched before and behind, and the Artillery had a six pound cannon all loaded.

This procession was witnessed by thousands of spectators, and was every where greeted with hisses and shouts. Many of the buildings were draped with black, and the Commonwealth building put out a black coffin with the word Liberty upon it. An effort was made during the week to purchase the slave, and the money 1200 dolls raised, but when it was offered Capt Suttle refused it. One of the police officers Mr J K Hayes resigned his office, on receiving orders to be one of that procession. Much blame is put upon the Mayor for blockading the streets, and putting the City under military law. I see that five of the Aldermen have published a letter saying that they did not advise, but on the contrary discouraged it. But Mr Otis thinks that unless all that precaution had been taken, the public feeling is such, that the slave would have been rescued. I do not know the time when there has been so much excitement, almost all are unanimous in feelings of indignation, and mortification, and humiliation. It is a very hard struggle to keep faith with those, who have just broken faith with us. I suppose the South will consider it a great victory. Some of the abolitionists were on the watch, all the time to get hold of Capt Suttle and his friend, and tar and feather them, but they were too shrewd for them. Theodore Parker of course preached a made some very severe remarks last Sunday, and was to preach today on the subject. He last Sunday denounced Judge Loring, and wound up his remarks, by charging him with the murder of the police man, and the risk of the lives of the twelve men, who were arrested as ringleaders in the riot. Today Dr Putnam gave us a some remarks on the subject, and spoke most eloquently. He said it was the darkest week in our history, and we needed more than ever the Sunday's rest and quiet. He said that now is no time, while there are so many revengeful and excited feelings in the breast, to view the matter in its proper light, and decide upon our duty in the future, but prayed most earnestly, that we might be strengthened for the duties or trials which are before us. He also prayed that our rulers might repent of their sins, and have a change of heart. Mr P then said he did not dare to trust himself to preach on the subject, and could not write on any other the past week so he made some very fine remarks upon the Sabbath rest and influence.

One of the lessons of today was, that we must remember that when our earthly rulers prove faithless, we have an Eternal one who never faileth, and many other similar appropriate remarks.

[*Written from bottom to top in the left-hand margin of the page:*] The papers say that this slave affair will cost over 30,000 dollars.

[*The following lines continue the text on the main part of the page:*] There is a petition now in the Merchants Exchange for a repeal of the Fugitive Slave law, which has been signed by very many of the leading merchants of Boston. Strange to say the weather during the past week has been pleasant every day and I believe the Anniversary meetings went off very harmoniously.

Frank of course is in a great state of excitement about the slave affair.

. . .

With a great deal of love from William and myself, I am Ever Yr Affect daughter

Mary E Blanchard

QUESTIONS TO CONSIDER

1. How does Mary Blanchard describe the attitude of Bostonians? What is the common public opinion about Burns and his trial?
2. How does Blanchard feel about the presence of soldiers and martial law?

12.2 EXAMINER'S QUESTIONS FOR ADMITTANCE TO THE AMERICAN (OR KNOW-NOTHING) PARTY (1854)*

The American Party was a secretive political party that achieved a rapid rise in popularity during the mid-1850s. Members of the party were instructed to tell anyone who asked that they knew nothing of the party's membership or activities, and consequently the party was often known as the "Know Nothings." Know Nothings opposed immigration and were suspicious of Catholic immigrants in particular. They supported quadrupling the years of residency required to become a citizen (from five to twenty-one) and proposed restricting public offices to American-born citizens.

During the 1840s the United States had experienced three times as much immigration as it had in the 1830s. Many of these immigrants were Irish Catholics who settled in eastern cities like New York, Boston, and Philadelphia, and Germans (some of whom were also Catholic) who mostly made their homes in the Midwest. Americans, especially eastern Protestants, had long harbored suspicion and anxiety about immigrants and Catholics, but it was the dramatic increase in immigration that made these fears politically salient. The Know-Nothing Party quickly gained traction as Protestants tried to prevent recent immigrants from gaining the right to vote, hold office, and help determine the course of the United States.

---

* *Examiner's Questions for Admittance to the American (or Know-Nothing) Party. July, 1854*, Manuscript/Mixed Material, Library of Congress, https://www.loc.gov/item/mcc.062/.

Examiner to Candidate: Are you a candidate for membership to our order?

(I am)

You will place your right hand on this holy emblem.

Obligation:

You do solemnly promise declare and swear upon that sacred and holy emblem before Almighty God, and these witnesses, that you will not divulge or make known to any person *whatever*, the nature of the questions I may ask you here, the names of the persons you may see here or that you know that such an organization is going on *as such*, whether you become a member of our organization or not?

Will you promise me this?

(I will)

And that you will true and faithful answers give to all the questions I may ask you,

(So help you God)

Are you by religious faith a Roman Catholic?

(I am not)

Were you born in this country?

(I was)

Were either of your parents? Heritage of your grand-parents? Were any of your ancestors in this country during the Revolutionary War?

If so then:

Are you willing to use your influence to elect to all offices of *Honor*, *Profit*, or *Trust* now but nature born citizens of *America*, of this *Country* to the exclusion of *all* foreigners, and to all Roman Catholics, *whether* they be of nature or foreign birth, regardless of all party predilections *whatever*?

(Answer I am)

QUESTIONS TO CONSIDER

1. What is disqualifying for a prospective member of the Know Nothings? What would help their candidacy?
2. What do the Know Nothings hope to accomplish? What do they ask of their members?

12.3 W. F. BRANNIN, "NICARAGUA NATIONAL SONG" (1856)*

William Walker (1824–1860) was an American physician, soldier, and supporter of slavery who led an American invasion of Nicaragua in 1855. In the 1840s and 1850s he was one of a number of Americans who supported aggressively expanding the borders of the United States in order to also extend slavery. After the US annexed much of northern Mexico in 1848, some Southerners dreamed of further expansion throughout the Caribbean. Cuba and Central America were popular targets of these plans as Americans believed that their climate would support plantation-grown cash crops and that these places would be easy to conquer.

In 1855 Walker landed in Nicaragua with sixty men and succeeded in taking advantage of the civil war there to make himself president. As president of Nicaragua, Walker re-legalized slavery and attempted to encourage immigration from the United States. Walker was soon expelled by a coalition

* "Grey-Eyed Man of Destiny. The Great Filibuster: William Walker," Tennessee State Library and Archives, https://sharetngov.tnsosfiles.com/tsla/exhibits/walker/index.htm.

of other Latin American countries, and he was later executed by the Honduran government during another coup attempt. Walker's reputation was divisive in the United States. Southerners viewed him as a heroic statesman and general while Northerners saw him as little more than a bandit.

VERSE 1

The Puritans fled from oppression,
    And after resolv'd to be free,
They voted a final secession,
    Back'd up by a strong cup of tea.
They had but a foretaste of Freedom,
    But such was their love for the same,
They call'd a Commander to lead them,
    And who but George Washington came.
Thus the spark which liberty kindled,
    Has grown to a glorious flame.

CHORUS
Then shout for Liberty,
    Freedoms battle cry,
Let all the nations see,
    We can do or die;
And here after Sages
    will record each name,
So that future ages,
    Loudly will proclaim;
That we fought and bled,
    For Liberty and fame.

VERSE 2

The oppress'd and downtrodden all over,
    The wide world will soon follow suit,
For Freedoms becoming a rover,
    Whose prowess none dare to dispute,
Then let the old Monarchies tremble,
    As now petty Tyrannies must,
For Liberty's sons will soon humble

Their overblown pride in the dust
And poets and sages will tell you
    'Twas right for their cause was but just.
CHORUS. Then shout for Liberty &c.

VERSE 3

That era is swiftly approaching,
    Then Tyrants no longer will reign;
The day will arrive when encroaching,
    Will lose even Cuba to Spain.
It needs not a Prophet or talker
    To tell you in prose or in verse,
The exploits of Patriot Walker,
    Whom Tyrants will long deem a curse—
A brave son of Freedom is Walker
    And Nations his fame will rehearse.
CHORUS. Then shout for Liberty &c.

VERSE 4

Then join in our ranks all ye freemen,
    Who feel for a people enthralled—
For tis time that each Tyranic demon
    By Freemen should be overhauled.
Kentucky has sent forth her legion
    To aid on the glorious cause,
In the Central American region
    Where President Walker makes laws—
There all who are brave sons of Freedom
    Will gain everlasting applause.
CHORUS. Then shout for Liberty &c.

QUESTIONS TO CONSIDER

1. What values does William Walker represent to the composer of this song?
2. Why does the composer of the song make reference to events from American history? What connection are they drawing between that history and Walker?

12.4 MAHALA DOYLE, LETTER TO JOHN BROWN (1859)*

John Brown (1800–1859) was an abolitionist who established a home in Kansas in 1855 to help secure the territory as a free state. Following the destruction of the antislavery town of Lawrence, Kansas, by a proslavery mob in 1856, Brown sought vengeance. Brown targeted the homes of proslavery Kansas settlers (although they owned no slaves and had not participated in the Lawrence attack) and attacked at night with a band of men, executing a man called James Doyle and two of his sons, along with two other men.

In October 1859, Brown led a raid on the federal arsenal in Harper's Ferry, Virginia. He hoped to capture weapons that could be used to help establish and defend settlements of escaped enslaved people in the Appalachian Mountains. The raid was a failure. Several of Brown's party, including two of his sons, were killed, while Brown was captured and sentenced to death for treason against Virginia. While in prison awaiting execution, Brown received this letter from Mahala Doyle, wife and mother of the three Doyles Brown had helped murder three years earlier.

Chattanooga Tennessee
20th November 1859.
JOHN BROWN—Sir:

Altho vengence [sic] is not mine, I confess, that I do feel gratified to hear that you ware stopt in your fiendish career at Harper's Ferry, with the loss of your two sons, you can now appreciate my distress, in Kansas, when you then and there entered my house at midnight and arrested my husband and two boys and took them out of the yard and in cold blood shot them dead in my hearing, you cant say you done it to free our slaves, we had none and never expected to own one, but has only made me a poor disconsolate widow with helpless children while I feel for your folly. I do hope & trust that you will meet your just reward. O how it pained my Heart to hear the dying groans of my Husband and children if this scrawl give you any consolation you are welcome to it

Mahala Doyle
N.B. My son John Doyle whose life I begged of (you) is now grown up and is very desirous to
be at Charleston on the day of your execution would certainly be there if his means would permit it, that he might adjust the rope around your neck if gov: wise would permit it
M. D.

QUESTIONS TO CONSIDER

1. What is the purpose of Mahala Doyle's letter? What does she want Brown to know?
2. Were either of John Brown's attacks justifiable? What are some important differences between them?

* "Doyle, Mahala (fl. 1859) to John Brown. (The Gilder Lehrman Institute of American History, GLC07590)."

12.5 VISUAL SOURCE: WILLIAM C. REYNOLDS, POLITICAL MAP OF THE UNITED STATES, DESIGNED TO EXHIBIT THE COMPARATIVE AREA OF THE FREE AND SLAVE STATES (1856)*

The Missouri Compromise of 1820 had guaranteed much of the western US territories as free territory where slavery would not be permitted. Many Northerners from free states were therefore angry when the 1854 Kansas–Nebraska Act rescinded that rule, opening the entirety of the US territories to the possibility of slavery. Northerners, many of whom had lived their entire lives believing those territories were guaranteed free territory, were outraged at what they perceived as Southern duplicity.

This map is intended to outline the advantages that the slave states enjoy by highlighting the current free states (light gray), slave states (dark gray), and western territories open to free or slave settlement (gray). The accompanying statistics highlight that despite the Northern states being more populous, the slave states get disproportionate representation in the national government due to constitutional provisions, like the three-fifths clause, that grant states representatives based on how many people are enslaved there. The Senate, which grants each state two seats regardless of the size of its population, takes no account of how many more people live in the free states than the slave states. The Republican Party used arguments like these to contend that slaveholders had too much power in the federal government and that slavery should be curtailed.

* Courtesy of the Library of Congress

QUESTIONS TO CONSIDER

1. What stands out about the size of the different regions? Who is not included in this map?
2. Why is slavery a problem according to this map? What other objections did Americans raise about slavery?

12.6 VISUAL SOURCE: JOHN MAGEE, *FORCING SLAVERY DOWN THE THROAT OF A FREE SOILER* (1856)*

After the territory of Kansas was opened to settlement in 1854, Americans flocked to the territory to try to win it for slavery or freedom. The Free Soil supporters quickly outnumbered the proslavery residents, but through a combination of vigilante violence and voter fraud, proslavery men managed to elect a territorial government that endorsed slavery and enacted harsh punishments for anyone who criticized it. To many, the violence in Kansas seemed like a mockery of the "popular sovereignty" solution proposed by Stephen Douglas (1813–1861), a US senator from Illinois. Based on this doctrine, the people of a territory should be able to choose whether to be a free or slave state. In reality, it seemed clear that proslavery forces would never let there be a free choice.

This cartoon by John Magee mocks the Democratic supporters of "popular sovereignty," showing them as a tiny minority overpowering the large Free Soil majority. Senator Douglas and former president Franklin Pierce force-feed slavery in the form of a Black man to a Free Soil man tied to the "Democratic Platform." President James Buchanan and Michigan senator Lewis Cass hold his head back while standing on planks marked "Cuba," "Kansas," and "Central America" to represent their ambition to spread slavery.

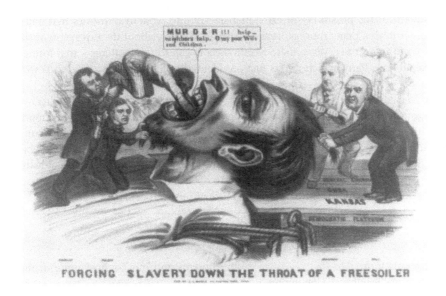

FORCING SLAVERY DOWN THE THROAT OF A FREESOILER

QUESTIONS TO CONSIDER

1. Why did the artist choose to represent the pro-slavery Democrats as tiny figures compared to the large Free Soiler? What is the artist conveying about the conflict in Kansas with this choice?
2. Why might the artist have chosen to depict this scene as a Free Soiler being forced to swallow an enslaved man? Why might that image stick with a viewer?

---

* Courtesy of the Library of Congress

CHAPTER 13

A SLAVEHOLDERS' REBELLION, 1856–1861

13.1 NATIONAL REPUBLICAN PLATFORM (1860)*

The Republican Party was founded as an antislavery coalition in 1854, with the goal of preventing the expansion of slavery in the United States. Following the signing of the 1854 Kansas–Nebraska Act, which allowed for the possibility of extending slavery into western territories that had been guaranteed free territories, many more Northerners began to worry about the expansion of slavery. Over the course of the next two years, these Northerners began to forge alliances that formed the basis for the Republican Party, which ran its first presidential candidate in 1856 and then won the presidency in 1860.

In its early years, the Republican Party was diverse, with its various factions held together by their common opposition to the expansion of slavery. The former Whigs in the party sought support for infrastructure improvements and industry, and the former Democrats sought farmland for common citizens. Abolitionists sought the admission of the free state of Kansas and to continue the ban on slave trading. Former Know Nothings fretted about corruption among the political establishment. To unite their party, Republican leaders had to appeal to each of these constituencies without alienating the others, all while reminding them what had brought them together.

National republican platform.
Adopted by the National Republican Convention Held in Chicago, May 17, 1860.
Resolved, That we, the delegated representatives of the Republican electors of the United States, in Convention assembled, in discharge of the duty we owe to our constituents and our country, unite in the following declarations:

THE REPUBLICAN PARTY.

1. That the history of the nation during the last four years, has fully established the propriety and

* *National Republican Platform. Adopted by the National Republican Convention, held in Chicago* (Chicago: Chicago Press and Tribune Office, 1860), https://www.loc.gov/item/scsm000716/.

necessity of the organization and perpetuation of the Republican party, and that the causes which called it into existence are permanent in their nature, and now, more than ever before, demand its peaceful and constitutional triumph.

ITS FUNDAMENTAL PRINCIPLES.

2. That the maintenance of the principles promulgated in the Declaration of Independence and embodied in the Federal Constitution, "That all men are created equal; that they are endowed by their Creator with certain inalienable rights; that among these are life, liberty, and the pursuit of happiness; that to secure these rights, governments are instituted among men, deriving their just powers from the consent of the governed" is essential to the preservation of our Republican institutions; and that the Federal Constitution, the Rights of the States, and the Union of the States must and shall be preserved.

TRUE TO THE UNION.

3. That to the Union of the States, this nation owes its unprecedented increase of population, its surprising development of material resources, its rapid augmentation of wealth, its happiness at home and its honor abroad; and we hold in abhorrence all schemes for Disunion, come from whatever source they may: And we congratulate the country that no Republican member of Congress has uttered or countenanced the threats of Disunion so often made by Democratic members, without rebuke and with applause from their political associates; and we denounce those threats of Disunion, in case of a popular overthrow of their ascendancy as denying the vital principles of a free government, and as an avowal of contemplated treason, which it is the imperative duty of an indignant People sternly to rebuke and forever silence.

STATE SOVEREIGNTY.

4. That the maintenance inviolate of the Rights of the States, and especially the right of each State to order and control its own domestic institutions according to its own judgment exclusively, is essential to that balance of power on which the perfection and endurance of our political fabric depends; and we denounce the lawless invasion by armed force of the soil of any State or Territory, no matter under what pretext, as among the gravest of crimes.

SECTIONALISM OF THE DEMOCRACY.

5. That the present Democratic Administration has far exceeded our worst apprehensions, in its measureless subserviency to the exactions of a sectional interest, as especially evinced in its desperate exertions to force the infamous Lecompton Constitution upon the protesting people of Kansas; in construing the personal relation between master and servant to involve an unqualified property in persons; in its attempted enforcement, everywhere, on land and sea, through the intervention of Congress and of the Federal Courts, of the extreme pretensions of a purely local interest; and in its general and unvarying abuse of power entrusted to it by a confiding people.

ITS EXTRAVAGANCE AND CORRUPTION.

6. That the people justly view with alarm the reckless extravagance which pervades every department of the Federal Government; that a return to rigid economy and accountability is indispensable to arrest the systematic plunder of the public treasury by favored partisans; while the recent startling developments of frauds and corruptions at the Federal metropolis, show that an entire change of administration is imperatively demanded.

A DANGEROUS POLITICAL HERESY.

7. That the new dogma that the Constitution, of its own force, carries Slavery into any or all of the Territories of the United States, is a dangerous political heresy, at variance with the explicit provisions of that instrument itself, with cotemporaneous exposition, and with legislative and judicial precedent;

is revolutionary in its tendency, and subversive of the peace and harmony of the country.

FREEDOM, THE NORMAL CONDITION OF TERRITORIES.

8. That the normal condition of all the territory of the United States is that of Freedom: That as our Republican fathers, when they had abolished slavery in all our national territory, ordained that "no person should be deprived of life, liberty, or property, without due process of law," it becomes our duty, by legislation, whenever such legislation is necessary, to maintain this provision of the Constitution against all attempts to violate it; and we deny the authority of Congress, of a territorial legislature, or of any individuals, to give legal existence to slavery in any Territory of the United States.

THE AFRICAN SLAVE TRADE.

9. That we brand the recent re-opening of the African Slave Trade, under the cover of our national flag, aided by perversions of judicial power, as a crime against humanity and a burning shame to our country and age; and we call upon Congress to take prompt and efficient measures for the total and final suppression of that execrable traffic.

DEMOCRATIC POPULAR SOVEREIGNTY.

10. That in the recent vetoes, by their Federal Governors, of the acts of the Legislatures of Kansas and Nebraska, prohibiting Slavery in those Territories, we find a practical illustration of the boasted Democratic principle of Non-intervention and Popular Sovereignty embodied in the Kansas-Nebraska Bill, and a demonstration of the deception and fraud involved therein.

ADMISSION OF KANSAS.

11. That Kansas should, of right, be immediately admitted as a State under the Constitution recently formed and adopted by her people, and accepted by the House of Representatives.

ENCOURAGEMENT OF AMERICAN INDUSTRY.

12. That, while providing revenue for the support of the general government by duties upon imports, sound policy requires such an adjustment of these imports as to encourage the development of the industrial interests of the whole country; and we commend that policy of national exchanges, which secures to the working men liberal wages, to agriculture remunerating prices, to mechanics and manufacturers an adequate reward for their skill, labor and enterprise, and to the nation commercial prosperity and independence.

FREE HOMESTEADS.

13. That we protest against any sale or alienation to others of the Public Lands held by actual settlers, and against any view of the Free Homestead policy which regards the settlers as paupers or suppliants for public bounty; and we demand the passage by Congress of the complete and satisfactory Homestead Measure which has already passed the House.

RIGHTS OF CITIZENSHIP.

14. That the Republican party is opposed to any change in our Naturalization Laws or any State Legislation by which the rights of citizenship hitherto accorded to emigrants from foreign lands shall be abridged or impaired; and in favor of giving a full and efficient protection to the rights of all classes of citizens, whether native or naturalized, both at home and abroad.

RIVER AND HARBOR IMPROVEMENTS.

15. The appropriations by Congress for River and Harbor improvements of a National character, required for the accommodation and security of an existing commerce, are authorized by the Constitution, and justified by the obligation of Government to protect the lives and property of its citizens.

A PACIFIC RAILROAD.

16. That a Railroad to the Pacific Ocean is imperatively demanded by the interests of the whole country; that the Federal Government ought to render immediate and efficient aid in its construction; and that, as preliminary thereto, a daily Overland Mail should be promptly established.

CO-OPERATION INVITED.

17. Finally, having thus set forth our distinctive principles and views, we invite the co-operation of all citizens, however differing on other questions, who substantially agree with us in their affirmance and support.

QUESTIONS TO CONSIDER

1. What policies in this platform are aimed toward specific Republican factions?
2. What does the platform say about slavery? What danger does slavery pose according to the Republicans?

13.2 FRANCES ELLEN WATKINS, "A FREE BLACK WOMAN WRITES TO IMPRISONED JOHN BROWN" (1859)*

Frances Ellen Watkins (1825–1911) was one of the first Black women writers in the United States who had her work published. Born free in Baltimore in 1825, Watkins started writing poetry and contributing to antislavery newspapers as a young woman. Her second book of poetry was published in 1854 to great success and was reprinted repeatedly throughout her life. Over the course of a fifty-year career, she published several poetry collections and works of prose, and she was an outspoken voice in favor of abolition throughout the antebellum era.

In 1859 Watkins wrote to John Brown following his capture during his failed raid on the federal arsenal at Harper's Ferry, Virginia. She thanked Brown for his actions against slavery and encouraged him by stating that his sacrifice would inspire future abolitionists.

Kendallville, Indiana

Dear friend: Although the hands of Slavery throw a barrier between you and me, and it may not be my privilege to see you in the prison house, Virginia has no bolts or bars through which I dread to send you my sympathy. In the name of the young girl sold from the warm clasp of a mother's arms to the clutches of a libertine or profligate (a completely immoral and shameless person), - in the name of the slave mother, her heart rocked to and fro by the agony of her mournful separations—I thank you that you have been brave enough to reach out your hands to the crushed and blighted of my race. You have rocked the bloody Bastille (a famous prison stormed and liberated during the French Revolution in 1789); and I hope from your sad fate great good may arise to the cause of freedom. Already from your prison has come a shout of triumph against the giant sin of our country. . . .

We may earnestly hope that your fate will not be a vain lesson, that it will intensify our hatred of Slavery and love of Freedom, and that your martyr grave will be a sacred altar upon which men will record their vows of undying hatred to that system which tramples on man and bids defiance to God. I have written to your dear wife, and sent her a few dollars, and I pledge myself to you and I will continue to assist her. . . .

QUESTIONS TO CONSIDER

1. What did Watkins write to Brown? What encouragement does she offer him?
2. Why does Watkins invoke the image of an enslaved girl sold away from her mother? What does this capture about the evils of slavery for Watkins?

13.3 ALEXANDER H. STEPHENS, EXCERPTS FROM "CORNERSTONE SPEECH" (1861)*

Alexander H. Stephens (1812–1883) was a longtime Georgia congressman and slaveholder who served as the first and only vice president of the Confederate States of America from 1861 to 1865. Although Stephens voted against secession at Georgia's secession convention, he supported the new government once the Confederacy became a reality.

Weeks after being named vice president, Stephens delivered a speech in Savannah, Georgia, on the origins and future of the Confederacy. Often known as the "cornerstone speech" due to Stephen's declaration that the Confederacy's "foundations are laid, its cornerstone rests, upon the great truth that the negro is not equal to the white man; that slavery . . . is his natural and normal condition," the speech has become notable in the years since the Civil War as explicit evidence from a Confederate leader at the time of secession of the central importance of slavery and white supremacy to the Confederate project. Stephens was briefly arrested for treason following the Civil War, but later went on to serve as both a congressman and governor of Georgia.

. . . I was remarking that we are passing through one of the greatest revolutions in the annals of the world. Seven States have within the last three months thrown off an old government and formed a new. This revolution has been signally marked, up to this time, by the fact of its having been accomplished without the loss of a single drop of blood.

This new constitution, or form of government, constitutes the subject to which your attention will be partly invited. In reference to it, I make this first

* Alexander H. Stephens, "Cornerstone Speech," Savannah, Georgia, March 21, 1861, American Battlefield Trust, https://www .battlefields.org/learn/primary-sources/cornerstone-speech.

general remark: it amply secures all our ancient rights, franchises, and liberties. All the great principles of Magna Charta are retained in it. No citizen is deprived of life, liberty, or property, but by the judgment of his peers under the laws of the land. The great principle of religious liberty, which was the honor and pride of the old constitution, is still maintained and secured. All the essentials of the old constitution, which have endeared it to the hearts of the American people, have been preserved and perpetuated. Some changes have been made. Some of these I should have preferred not to have seen made; but other important changes do meet my cordial approbation. They form great improvements upon the old constitution. So, taking the whole new constitution, I have no hesitancy in giving it as my judgment that it is decidedly better than the old.

. . . Another change in the constitution relates to the length of the tenure of the presidential office. In the new constitution it is six years instead of four, and the President rendered ineligible for a re-election. This is certainly a decidedly conservative change. It will remove from the incumbent all temptation to use his office or exert the powers confided to him for any objects of personal ambition. The only incentive to that higher ambition which should move and actuate one holding such high trusts in his hands, will be the good of the people, the advancement, prosperity, happiness, safety, honor, and true glory of the confederacy.

But not to be tedious in enumerating the numerous changes for the better, allow me to allude to one other though last, not least. The new constitution has put at rest, forever, all the agitating questions relating to our peculiar institution African slavery as it exists amongst us the proper status of the negro in our form of civilization. This was the immediate cause of the late rupture and present revolution. Jefferson in his forecast, had anticipated this, as the "rock upon which the old Union would split." He was right. What was conjecture with him, is now a realized fact. But whether he fully comprehended the great truth upon which that rock stood and stands, may be doubted. The prevailing ideas entertained by him and most of the leading statesmen at the time of the formation of the old constitution, were that the enslavement of the African was in violation of the laws of nature; that it was wrong in principle, socially, morally, and politically. It was an evil they knew not well how to deal with, but the general opinion of the men of that day was that, somehow or other in the order of Providence, the institution would be evanescent and pass away. This idea, though not incorporated in the constitution, was the prevailing idea at that time. The constitution, it is true, secured every essential guarantee to the institution while it should last, and hence no argument can be justly urged against the constitutional guarantees thus secured, because of the common sentiment of the day. Those ideas, however, were fundamentally wrong. They rested upon the assumption of the equality of races. This was an error. It was a sandy foundation, and the government built upon it fell when the "storm came and the wind blew."

Our new government is founded upon exactly the opposite idea; its foundations are laid, its cornerstone rests, upon the great truth that the negro is not equal to the white man; that slavery subordination to the superior race is his natural and normal condition. This, our new government, is the first, in the history of the world, based upon this great physical, philosophical, and moral truth. This truth has been slow in the process of its development, like all other truths in the various departments of science. It has been so even amongst us. Many who hear me, perhaps, can recollect well, that this truth was not generally admitted, even within their day. The errors of the past generation still clung to many as late as twenty years ago. Those at the North, who still cling to these errors, with a zeal above knowledge, we justly denominate fanatics. All fanaticism springs from an aberration of the mind from a defect in reasoning. It is a species of insanity. One of the most striking characteristics of insanity, in many instances, is forming correct conclusions from fancied or erroneous premises; so with the anti-slavery fanatics. Their conclusions are right if their premises were. They assume that the negro is equal, and hence conclude that he is entitled to equal privileges and rights with the white man. If their premises were correct, their conclusions would be logical and just but their premise being wrong, their whole argument fails. I recollect once of having heard a gentleman from one of the northern States, of great power and ability, announce in the House of Representatives, with imposing effect, that we of the South would be compelled, ultimately, to yield upon this subject of slavery, that it was as impossible to war successfully against a principle in politics, as it was in physics or mechanics. That the principle would ultimately prevail. That we, in maintaining slavery as it exists with us, were warring against a principle, a principle founded in nature, the principle of the equality of men. The reply I made to him was, that upon his own grounds, we should, ultimately, succeed, and that he and his associates, in this crusade against our institutions, would ultimately fail. The truth announced, that it was as impossible to war successfully against a principle in politics as it was in physics and mechanics, I admitted; but told him that it was he, and those acting with him, who were warring against a principle. They were attempting to make things equal which the Creator had made unequal.

. . . But to return to the question of the future. What is to be the result of this revolution?

. . . We have intelligence, and virtue, and patriotism. All that is required is to cultivate and perpetuate these. Intelligence will not do without virtue. France was a nation of philosophers. These philosophers become Jacobins. They lacked that virtue, that devotion to moral principle, and that patriotism which is essential to good government Organized upon principles of perfect justice and right-seeking amity and friendship with all other powers—I see no obstacle in the way of our upward and onward progress. Our growth, by accessions from other States, will depend greatly upon whether we present to the world, as I trust we shall, a better government than that to which neighboring States belong. If we do this, North Carolina, Tennessee, and Arkansas cannot hesitate long; neither can Virginia, Kentucky, and Missouri. They

will necessarily gravitate to us by an imperious law. We made ample provision in our constitution for the admission of other States; it is more guarded, and wisely so, I think, than the old constitution on the same subject, but not too guarded to receive them as fast as it may be proper. Looking to the distant future, and, perhaps, not very far distant either, it is not beyond the range of possibility, and even probability, that all the great States of the north-west will gravitate this way, as well as Tennessee, Kentucky, Missouri, Arkansas, etc. Should they do so, our doors are wide enough to receive them, but not until they are ready to assimilate with us in principle.

. . . The surest way to secure peace, is to show your ability to maintain your rights. The principles and position of the present administration of the United States the republican party present some puzzling questions. While it is a fixed principle with them never to allow the increase of a foot of slave territory, they seem to be equally determined not to part with an inch "of the accursed soil." Notwithstanding their clamor against the institution, they seemed to be equally opposed to getting more, or letting go what they have got. They were ready to fight on the accession of Texas, and are equally ready to fight now on her secession. Why is this? How can this strange paradox be accounted for? There seems to be but one rational solution and that is, notwithstanding their professions of humanity, they are disinclined to give up the benefits they derive from slave labor. Their philanthropy yields to their interest. The idea of enforcing the laws, has but one object, and that is a collection of the taxes, raised by slave labor to swell the fund necessary to meet their heavy appropriations. The spoils is what they are after though they come from the labor of the slave. . . .

QUESTIONS TO CONSIDER

1. What does Stephens predict for the future of the Confederacy?
2. What does Stephens say about secession? How will the Confederate government be different from that of the Union?

13.4 ARIZONA TERRITORY ORDINANCE OF SECESSION (1861)*

Following the end of the Mexican–American War in 1848, what are now the states of Arizona and New Mexico were organized under the US federal government as the territories of New Mexico. The desert territory was sparsely populated and attracted relatively little interest from Americans west of the Mississippi. Those Americans who did emigrate there, however, came from slaveholding states and settled in and around the Rio Grande Valley in the far south of the territory. Following the secession of several Deep South states over the winter of 1860–1861, residents of Mesilla in modern New Mexico issued an ordinance of secession of their own, declaring the southern portion of the territory, an area including the modern cities of Tucson and Las Cruces, to be the Territory of Arizona.

The territory saw little action during the Civil War. Many of the white residents had more conflicts with the Navajo and Apache who lived throughout the Southwest than they did with Union soldiers. In 1863 the US Congress declared their own territory of Arizona, which roughly conforms to Arizona's modern borders.

People of Arizona in Convention
Adopted March 16, 1861

WHEREAS, a sectional party of the North has disregarded the Constitution of the United States, violated the rights of the Southern States, and heaped wrongs and indignities upon their people; and WHEREAS, the Government of the United States has heretofore failed to give us adequate protection against the savages within our midst and has denied us an administration of the laws, and that security for life, liberty, and property which is due from all governments to the people; and WHEREAS, it is an inherent, inalienable right in all people to modify, alter, or abolish their form of government whenever it fails in the legitimate objects of its institution, or when it is subversive thereof; and WHEREAS, in a government of federated, sovereign States, each State has a right to withdraw from the confederacy whenever the treaty by which the league is formed, is broken; and WHEREAS, the Territories belonging to said league in common should be divided when the league is broken, and should be attached to the separating States according to their geographical position and political identity; and WHEREAS,

Arizona naturally belongs to the Confederate States of America (who have rightfully and lawfully withdrawn from said league), both geographically and politically, by ties of a common interest and a common cause; and WHEREAS we, the citizens of that part of New Mexico called Arizona, in the present distracted state of political affairs between the North and the South, deem it our duty as citizens of the United States to make known our opinions and intentions; therefore be it . . .

RESOLVED, That our feelings and interests are with the Southern States, and that although we deplore the division of the Union, yet we cordially indorse the course pursued by the seceded Southern States.

RESOLVED, That geographically and naturally we are bound to the South, and to her we look for protection; and as the Southern States have formed a Confederacy, it is our earnest desire to be attached to that Confederacy as a Territory.

RESOLVED, That we do not desire to be attached as a Territory to any State seceding separately from the Union, but to and under the protection of a Confederacy of the Southern States.

---

* "Arizona Territory Ordinance of Secession," March 16, 1861, Wikisource, https://en.wikisource.org/wiki/Arizona_Territory_Ordinance_of_Secession.

RESOLVED, That the recent enactment of the Federal Congress, removing the mail service from the Atlantic to the Pacific States from the Southern to the Central or Northern route, is another powerful reason for us to ask the Southern Confederate States of America for a continuation of the postal service over the Butterfield or El Paso route, at the earliest period.

RESOLVED, That it shall be the duty of the President of this Convention to order an election for a delegate to the Congress of the Confederate States of America, when he is informed that the States composing said Confederacy have ordered an election for members of Congress.

RESOLVED, That we will not recognize the present Black Republican Administration, and that we will resist any officers appointed to this Territory by said Administration with whatever means in our power.

RESOLVED, That the citizens residing in the western portion of this Territory are invited to join us in this movement.

RESOLVED, That the proceedings of this Convention be published in the Mesilla Times, and that a copy thereof be forwarded to the President of the Congress of the Confederate States of America, with the request that the same be laid before Congress.

QUESTIONS TO CONSIDER

1. Which of Arizona's grievances are specific to their region or their territory? Which ones are more general nation-wide problems?
2. How do the rebel Arizonans justify secession? What are their goals?

13.5 VISUAL SOURCE: DISTRIBUTION OF THE ENSLAVED POPULATION OF THE SOUTHERN STATES OF THE UNITED STATES (1860)*

This map, produced in 1861, shows the percentage of the residents who are enslaved for every county in all fifteen states where enslavement was legal. At the time, only four of these states—Missouri, Kentucky, Maryland, and Delaware—still considered themselves part of the United States. The others were at war with the US as the Confederate States of America. This map makes clear that, although all fifteen states were often grouped together as the slave South, there were many areas of the South in which there were very few enslaved people and other areas where enslaved people were the majority.

Most enslaved people were concentrated in the "cotton belt," a region stretching across the Deep South from South Carolina to Texas. Enslaved people were particularly concentrated along the Mississippi River, where the ease of water transportation to a major market at New Orleans made plantation farming particularly profitable. However, almost every slave state also had large regions where enslavement was much less common, these often being hillier and mountainous regions of the Appalachians.

* Library of Congress, Geography and Map Division

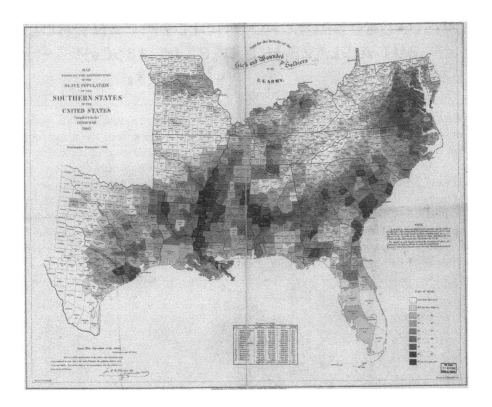

QUESTIONS TO CONSIDER

1. What patterns in this map stand out to you? Which states seem to have the largest and smallest percentage of enslaved people?

2. What differences do you notice between the states that did not secede (Missouri, Kentucky, Maryland, Delaware), those that seceded after Lincoln's inauguration (Virginia, Tennessee, North Carolina, Arkansas), and the Deep South?

13.6 VISUAL SOURCE: POT HOLDER: "ANY HOLDER BUT A SLAVE HOLDER" (c. 1860s)*

Going back to at least the 1760s, when American colonists boycotted British imports, Americans have made political statements with their purchases. This pot holder from the 1860s combines a play on words about rejecting enslavers with a simple picture of a Black couple dancing. While the joke is easy to grasp and the artistry simple, this novelty kitchen implement speaks to Unionist Americans' hostility to the slaveholding class. Throughout the Civil War, Unionist Americans believed that a relatively small clique of slaveholders was responsible for starting the conflict. Most white Southerners would still support the Union, Northerners believed, if only they had not been misled by the slaveholders. Many Northerners, even those who had not been abolitionists before the war, came to believe that the Southern slaveholders were the real enemy and that to break their power, their enslaved people had to be freed.

QUESTIONS TO CONSIDER

1. Why might a nineteenth-century American purchase this pot holder? What statement might they have been trying to make?
2. What is the purpose of the illustration of the dancing Black couple?

* Division of Culture and the Arts, National Museum of American History, Smithsonian Institution

CHAPTER 14

THE WARS OF THE REBELLION, 1861–1863

14.1 EDWIN V. SUMNER, LETTER TO HON. SIMON CAMERON (1861)*

Edwin V. Sumner (1797–1863) was an officer in the US Army who commanded the Department of the Pacific for much of 1861, during the American Civil War. This assignment included the territory of New Mexico, which was composed of modern New Mexico and Arizona. Although New Mexico had experienced some immigration in the ten years since its annexation by the United States, the territory was still very much a frontier, with few large settlements and frequent conflict between white settlers and the Apache and Navajo living in the region.

In early 1861, New Mexican Confederate sympathizers in the town of Mesilla declared that the southern portion of New Mexico would secede and become the Territory of Arizona. The self-declared Arizonans then soon joined the Confederacy. General Sumner wrote to Secretary of War Simon Cameron to describe the unrest in New Mexico and warn him of the problems in the territory.

FORT FAUNTLEROY, N. MEX, *September 27, 1861.*
Hon. SIMON CAMERON:

SIR: As an old printer and soldier of the line in the grand Union Army, I exercise the privilege of addressing you this communication. Having resided sufficiently long in New Mexico and Arizona to become measurably acquainted with the wants and wishes of the people, of acquiring a practical knowledge of the geographical, physical, and moral condition of the

country, and learning to a considerable extent the peculiarities of the inhabitants who are spread over this vast Territory, a region nearly four times as large as the State of Missouri, I feel that I can with some degree of safety and accuracy describe to you the present political condition and standing of the community. . . .

In 1850 New Mexico had a population of 50,000 souls, now (1860), according to the census returns, the white inhabitants, or those free born, exclusive of U. S.

---

* US Army Brigadier-General E. V. Sumner, Letter to Hon. Simon Cameron, *The War of the Rebellion: Official Records*, ser. I, vol. L, part 1 (September 27, 1861), 635–41.

soldiers and Indians, number some 93,000. To govern this country requires a greater degree of administrative ability, comprehensive sagacity and research, matured judgment, and wise forecast, energy, and decision of character than is required to govern the great States of New York or Pennsylvania. . . .

The governors of New Mexico somehow or other never have paid the slightest attention to the will or wishes or wants of the people of the district of Arizona, and hence the citizens of that expansive region, under the political teachings of Philemon T. Herbert, Judge Edward McGowan, Samuel J. Jones, Lieut. S. Mowry, Judge Lucas, Governor Owings, Granville H. Oury, Colonel Ewell (of the U. S. Army), and others, sought to erect, a little over a year ago, a provisional government, embracing the region lying between La Mesilla on the Rio Grande and extending north to the Gila, west to the Colorado, and south to the Sonora line. Our country, stretching more than 1,000 miles along the Mexican frontier, requires a vigilant eye to be kept upon the machinations of the secession forces who are now straining every nerve, using every device, pulling every cord with might and main to circumvent the supporters of our glorious Union, and incorporating the States of Nuevo Leon, Coahuila, Chihuahua, Durango, and Sonora, Mexico, into the Government of the Confederate States of the South. For this purpose Jeff. Davis, the rebel chief, has dispatched secret agents to the governors of the States above enumerated to induce them to secede from the Republic of Anahuac and join the standard of the seceshers. While all this is going on, or has been transpiring under their very eyes and noses, what have the governors of New Mexico been doing to avert the fatal catastrophe? Listless and apathetic, if not secessionists at heart, they are the next thing to them, and have remained as dormant and passive as old Mrs. Partington with her door mop. The time has arrived when a "Sir Forcible Feeble" policy will not answer for the region of the Rio Grande. The Texas rebels and Arizona cut-throats, like the ancient Goths and Vandals, are at the very gates, the portals of the Union, ready with battering cannons to demolish the fairest fabric of freedom ever devised by the wit of man. And what has been done or is doing to prevent them from realizing their ardent longing and desires? The demolition of a free Republic and the erection in

its stead of a military slavery, extending empire, is the ultimate object of the leaders. The restless eye of Jeff. Davis is particularly bent on Arizona. That country was purchased by him of Santa Anna. I say by Davis, for it was by his influence in the Cabinet, the identical man who swayed the councils of President Pierce, who originated the measure and urged it forward until its final completion. He had an object of no ordinary consideration to accomplish. He is the owner of "Empresario grants," in Chihuahua, purchased many years ago of Iturbide and others, which cover extensive silver mines. Arizona was his beau ideal of a railroad route to the Pacific. It was to him the terra incognita of a grand scheme of intercommunication and territorial expansion more vast and complicated than was ever dreamed of by Napoleon Bonaparte in his palmiest days of pride and power. With an eye that never winked and a wing that never tired has Jeff. Davis for more than ten years past turned his thoughts and desires to the Mexican line for indefinite expansion. Hence all the appointments in New Mexico (civil and military) under Fillmore, Pierce, and Buchanan were made solely and exclusively with reference to future operations in this quarter of the Union. With him were banded Benjamin, Gwin, Slidell, and Toombs. No nominations during this period were sent to the Senate or passed by that body without undergoing his scrutiny. I have seen letters from him to some of his present allies written years ago, which shed light on his present movements. . . .

I speak it more in sorrow than in anger when I say that the governing power in New Mexico for the period since it has been under the jurisdiction and subject to the American Union has been anything than possessing a vigorous grasp and characterized by energy and ability. The numerous Indian wars, the disregard of law and open defiance of courts and legislative enactments, the murders and robberies which are perpetrated with impunity all over the country, the demoralization of the U. S. Army, and the abandonment of their duty and of the Union in solemn contravention of their oath of officers high on the roll of military fame have all measurably proceeded from want of vigor and decisive action on the part of the executive head. Where there is no power to curb or restrain the populace, mob law and irresponsible rule will run riot over the land. Nothing is plainer and more certain. Sir, the frontier Territories, like Utah and New Mexico, Colorado and Nevada, &c., require men of brains and nerve to govern them. In the persons of Governor Nye and Governor Gilpin (of Nevada and Colorado) there are men appointed fit to be governors. Such has not been the case either in Utah or New Mexico. Hence polygamy and slavery and peonage, twin relics of barbarism and the offspring of an oligarchy, have had sway and are held up as an example of patriarchal observance for the guidance of the masses, instead of bringing them up to an enlightened standard of civilization, of progress, and improvement. It is about time that these institutions, relics of a dark age and of a deleterious tendency upon the customs and manners of the people, were swept out of existence. I thought this was part of the task to which the Republican party had pledged itself not to overlook.

I undertake to say that four-fifths of the voting population of New Mexico are utterly opposed to the incorporation of the slave code in the statutes of this Territory. Yet there it is, by virtue of the slave power exercising its influence through the accredited agents (civil and military) of the Federal Government. The office-holders, the tools of Jeff. Davis and company, put the slave code in the statutes of New Mexico and not the people, but in utter violation of their will and desire. . . .

There must be a change, a radical change, or the country is undone. . . .

Very respectfully, your obedient servant,
E. V. SUMNER,
Brigadier-General, U. S. Army, Commanding.
[Indorsement.]
WAR DEPARTMENT, *October* 28, 1861.
Approved:
SIMON CAMERON,
Secretary of War.

SPECIAL ORDERS, HDQRS. DEPARTMENT OF THE PACIFIC,

No. 182. *San Francisco, September 28,* 1861.

1. Capt. Edward O. C. Ord, Third Artillery, having been appointed brigadier-general of U. S. Volunteers, is relieved from duty in this department and will comply with instructions received from the Adjutant-General. The command of Light Company C, Third Artillery, will be turned over to First Lieut. Edward R. Warner, who will receipt for all property pertaining to C Company.

3. First Lieut. La Rhett L. Livingston, Third Artillery, will relieve Capt. E. O. C. Ord in command of Light Company C, Third Artillery, giving the usual receipts for all property pertaining thereto.

By order of Brigadier-General Sumner:
RICHD. C. DRUM,
Assistant *Adjutant-General.*

HEADQUARTERS OF THE ARMY,
Washington, September 30, 1861.

Brig. Gen. GEORGE WRIGHT, U. S. Army,
Commanding, &c., San Francisco, Cal.:

SIR: The General-in-Chief directs me to say that, according to the importance of the frontiers and the temper of the Indians, you station in Oregon and Washington Territory a portion of the volunteer force called out on the Pacific Coast. You can best judge, being on the spot, of the proper disposition to be made of the force.

I am, sir, very respectfully, your obedient servant,
E. D. TOWNSEND,
Assistant Adjutant-General.

QUESTIONS TO CONSIDER

1. What has caused the problems that face New Mexico, according to Sumner?
2. What does Sumner think of the Confederate sympathizers in New Mexico? What danger does he believe they pose to the Union?

14.2 FREDERICK DOUGLASS, "HOW TO END THE WAR" (1861)*

Frederick Douglass was a well-known abolitionist author, journalist, and speaker. After escaping enslavement in 1838, he toured both the United States and Britain as an abolitionist speaker, wrote several autobiographies describing his life in slavery and freedom, and published two newspapers in upstate New York. Although Douglass began his career as a disciple of the pacifist William Lloyd Garrison, Douglass came to believe that abolitionists and enslaved people would have to fight back against slaveholders' violence in order to achieve freedom.

Like most abolitionists, Douglass believed that the slaveholders were responsible for the Civil War and pushed the Lincoln administration to do more to end slavery. Cautious of offending conservative Northerners, President Lincoln did not initially support emancipating people enslaved by rebels or enlisting Black soldiers to fight for the Union cause. Douglass was a vocal proponent of Black enlistment and encouraged Lincoln's government to actively embrace emancipation as a goal of the war. Once Lincoln agreed to accept Black soldiers in 1863, Douglass participated in the recruitment effort and two of his sons served in the Union Army.

To our mind, there is but one easy, short and effectual way to suppress and put down the desolating war which the slaveholders and their rebel minions are now waging against the American Government and its loyal citizens. Fire must be met with water, darkness with light, and war for the destruction of liberty must be met with war for the destruction of slavery. *The simple way, then, to put an end to the savage and desolating war now waged by the slaveholders, is to strike down slavery itself,* the primal cause of that war.

Freedom to the slave should now be proclaimed from the Capitol, and should be seen above the smoke and fire of every battle field, waving from every loyal flag! The time for mild measures is past. They are pearls cast before swine, and only increase and aggravate the crime which they would conciliate and repress. The weak point must be found, and when found should be struck with the utmost vigor. Any war is a calamity; but a peace that can only breed war is a far greater calamity. A long and tame war, waged without aim or spirit, paralyzes business, arrests the wheels of civilization, benumbs the national feeling, corrodes the national heart, and diffuses its baleful influence universally. Sharp, quick, wise, strong and sudden, are the elements for the occasion. The sooner this rebellion is put out of its misery, the better for all concerned. A lenient war is a lengthy war, and therefore the worst kind of war. Let us stop it, and stop it effectually—stop it before its evils are diffused throughout the Northern States—stop it on the soil upon which it originated, and among the traitors and rebels who originated the war. This can be done at once, by *"carrying the war into Africa." Let the slaves and free colored people be called into service, and formed into a liberating army,* to march into the South and raise the banner of Emancipation among the slaves. The South having brought revolution and war upon the country, and having elected and consented to play at that fearful game, she has no right to complain if some good as well as calamity shall result from her own act and deed.

The slaveholders have not hesitated to employ the sable arms of the Negroes at the South in erecting the fortifications which silenced the guns of Fort Sumter, and brought the star-spangled banner to the dust. They

* Phillip Foner, ed., *Frederick Douglass: Selected Speeches and Writings* (Chicago: Chicago Review Press, 2000), 447–49.

often boast, and not without cause, that their Negroes will fight for them against the North. They have no scruples against employing the Negroes to exterminate freedom, and in overturning the Government. They work with spade and barrow with them, and they will stand with them on the field of battle, shoulder to shoulder, with guns in their hands, to shoot down the troops of the U.S. Government.—They have neither pride, prejudice nor *pity* to restrain them from employing Negroes *against white men, where slavery is to be protected and made secure.* Oh! that this Government would only now be as true to liberty as the rebels, who are attempting to batter it down, are true to slavery. We have no hesitation in saying that ten thousand black soldiers might be raised in the next thirty days to march upon the South. One black regiment alone would *be*, in such a war, the full equal of two white ones. The very fact of color in this case would be more terrible than powder and balls. The slaves would learn more as to the nature of the conflict from the presence of one such regiment, than from a thousand preachers. Every consideration of justice, humanity and sound policy confirms the wisdom of calling upon black men just now to take up arms in behalf of their country.

We are often asked by persons in the street as well as by letter, what our people will do in the present solemn crisis in the affairs of the country. Our answer is, would to God you would let us do something! We lack nothing but your consent. We are ready and would go, counting ourselves happy in being permitted to serve and suffer for the cause of freedom and free institutions. But you won't let us go. Read the heart-rending account we publish elsewhere of the treatment received by the brave fellows, who broke away from their chains and went through marvelous suffering to defend Fort Pickens against the rebels.—They were instantly seized and put in irons and returned to their guilty masters to be whipped to death! Witness Gen. Butler's offer to put down the slave insurrection in the State of Maryland. The colored citizens of Boston have offered their services to the Government, and were refused. There is, even now, while the slaveholders are marshaling armed Negroes against the Government, covering the ocean with pirates, destroying innocent lives, to sweep down the commerce of the country, tearing up railways, burning bridges to prevent the march of Government troops to the defence of its capital, exciting mobs to stone the Yankee soldiers; there is still, we say, weak and contemptible tenderness towards the blood thirsty, slaveholding traitors, by the Government and people of the country. Until the nation shall repent of this weakness and folly, until they shall make the cause of their country the cause of freedom, until they shall strike down slavery, the source and center of this gigantic rebellion, they don't deserve the support of a single sable arm, nor will it succeed in crushing the cause of our present troubles.

QUESTIONS TO CONSIDER

1. Why does Douglass believe that advocating emancipation will help the Union win the Civil War?
2. Why does Douglass believe it is important for Black Americans to participate in the war effort?

14.3 *NEW YORK WORLD,* DRAFT RIOT (1863)*

The New York Draft Riots were four days of civil unrest in New York City that left over a hundred people dead and thousands injured. The riots were sparked by opposition to the Enrollment Act of 1863, a law that mandated a military draft in communities that did not meet a certain quota of

---

* *Public Opinion: A Comprehensive Summary of the Press Throughout the World on All Important Current Topics* (London: 1863), 3:124–25.

enlistments in the Union Army. The possibility of exemptions for those who were rich enough to pay a commutation fee or hire a substitute caused significant frustration and anger among working class Americans. The widespread belief that the war was being fought on behalf of Black Americans also exacerbated existing racial tensions between poor Irish and Black New Yorkers.

Much of the violence during the riots was targeted at Black New Yorkers. Black civilians and homes were attacked, and an orphanage for Black children was burned down. Order was only restored after the arrival of several regiments of the US Army who had been fighting at Gettysburg in nearby Pennsylvania. This account of the first day of the riots comes from the *New York World*, a newspaper affiliated with the Democratic Party that generally opposed President Lincoln.

(*New York World, July 14*)

NEW YORK yesterday saw the saddest sight that she has ever seen since her first foundation stone was laid. The shameful history of the day is written on another page. The stigma will cling to her name and her fair fame long after the printed page has perished. Last night the northern sky was red with lurid fires lit by the hands of an infuriated mob; nothing but the smoking walls remain of an asylum for negro orphans; men, a score and more, who saw the morning sun, lie stark and dead; work-hops were deserted, and the passion of the labourer becoming as it ever does the opportunity of the ruffian, a saturnalia of pillage, murder, and rapine threatened again and again to set in upon the commercial metropolis of the Union. Crowds all day marched hither and thither along the streets, reckless, unguided, with a burning sense of wrong towards the Government which has undertaken to choose at random from among them the compulsory soldiers of a misconducted war—with a sense of wrong, we say, but wreaking their wrath cowardly and meanly on defenceless, inoffensive negroes, blindly on property owners whose buildings chanced to be hired by Government officials, senselessly on the policemen whose discipline and power day by day insure them that security and order which guards their labour and lives. The law-abiding citizen hangs his head with shame that a Government can so mismanage a struggle for the life of the nation, so wantonly put itself out of harmony and sympathy with the people, so deny itself the support of those whom it represents and serves, as that, in a peaceful city, whose sons have gone to a joyful death for the nation's life by the hundreds and by the thousands, and whose teeming lap has been emptied

of its treasure for the nation's sake—here, in the chief city and very heart of the nation, such scenes as those of yesterday can shock the sight—that these brawny men, whom we counted among the nation's stalwart defenders, can today be shaking the foundations of society—overriding all government and order and law, so that every good citizen who has children and wife to love, and property to guard, wishes that they may be shot down dead in their tracks by the hundred, rather than that order and law shall not be re-established.

The men who have gone from among us to the war, who today guard the capital, and hold Lee and his men at bay among the Maryland hills, are just such men as these who have struck terror through our peaceful streets, of like passions, swayed by like motives, to be kindled with the same patriotic fire. . . .

Will the insensate men at Washington now at length listen to our voice? Will they now give ear to our warnings and adjurations? Will they now believe that defiance of law in the rulers breeds defiance of law in the people? Does the doctrine proclaimed from the Capitol, that in war laws are silent, please put them in practice in the streets of New York? Will they continue to stop their ears and shut their eyes to the voice and will of a loyal people, which for three long years has told them by every act and every word that this war must be nothing but a war for the Union and the Constitution?

Does Mr. Lincoln now perceive what alienation he has put between himself and the men who three years ago thundered out with one voice in Union Square—"The Union, it must and shall be preserved?" These are the very men who his imbecility, his wanton exercise of arbitrary power, his stretches of ungranted authority have transformed into a mob. At the beginning hundreds of thousands of men went willingly to risk their lives at his and the nation's call. Was it impossible for him so to have rested upon the nation's heart, so to have obeyed the nation's will, that if need were still other hundreds of thousands would have gone forth willingly at his bidding? Who believes it? It was not impossible. What has he and his infatuated party done instead? They have framed a Conscription Act, never tolerable to a free people, unconstitutional beyond any manner of doubt in its provisions if not in its very nature, offensive and most unwise in the method of its enforcement, discriminating between rich and poor, unfair, onerous, and most oppressive here where the attrition of discontent was at its height. Does any man wonder that poor men refuse to be forced into a war mismanaged almost into hopelessness, perverted almost into partisanship? Did the President and his Cabinet imagine that their lawlessness could conquer, or their folly seduce, a free people?

QUESTIONS TO CONSIDER

1. What caused the rioting according to the *World*? Who were the rioters and who were the victims of the violence?
2. Why does the *World* argue that President Lincoln is partially responsible for the violence? Do you find their reasoning convincing?

14.4 SPOTTSWOOD RICE, LETTER TO SLAVEHOLDER KITTY DIGGS (1864)*

Spottswood Rice (1819–1907) was an American soldier and clergyman who served in the Union Army during the Civil War. For most of his life before the war, Rice had been enslaved on a tobacco plantation in Missouri, but following the announcement of the Emancipation Proclamation, he escaped and enlisted in the Union Army. At the time of his enlistment Rice had been married for over ten years to Orry Ferguson, and the couple had several children together. Ferguson and their children were enslaved in a different household than Rice, which likely contributed to their not escaping with him. While recovering from rheumatism in an army hospital, Rice wrote several letters, including this one to Kitty Diggs, who enslaved his wife and children. Because Missouri had remained in the Union, enslaved Missourians had not been freed by the Emancipation Proclamation. Rice condemns Diggs for enslaving his children and warns her that the Black soldiers in Missouri have little sympathy for slaveholders and rebel sympathizers.

---

* Ira Berlin, ed., *Freedom: A Documentary History of Emancipation, 1861–1867*, ser. II: The Black Military Experience (Cambridge, UK: Cambridge University Press, 1993), 689–90.

[*Benton Barracks Hospital, St. Louis,
Mo. September 3, 1864*]

I received a leteter from Cariline telling me that you say I tried to steal to plunder my child away from you now I want you to understand that mary is my Child and she is a God given rite of my own and you may hold on to hear as long as you can but I want you to remembor this one thing that the longor you keep my Child from me the longor you will have to burn in hell and the qwicer youll get their for we are now makeing up a bout one thoughsand blacke troops to Come up tharough and wont to come through Glasgow and when we come wo be to Copperhood rabbels and to the Slaveholding rebbels for we dont expect to leave them there root neor branch but we thinke how ever that we that have Children in the hands of you devels we will trie your [vertues?] the day that we enter Glasgow I want you to understand kittey diggs that where ever you and I meets we are enmays

to each orthere I offered once to pay you forty dollers for my own Child but I am glad now that you did not accept it Just hold on now as long as you can and the worse it will be for you you never in you life befor I came down hear did you give Children any thing not eny thing whatever not even a dollers worth of expencs now you call my children your pro[per]ty not so with me my Children is my own and I expect to get them and when I get ready to come after mary I will have bout a powrer and autherity to bring hear away and to exacute vengencens on them that holds my Child you will then know how to talke to me I will assure that and you will know how to talk rite too I want you now to just hold on to hear if you want to iff your conchos-ence tells thats the road go that road and what it will brig you to kittey diggs I have no fears about geting mary out of your hands this whole Government gives chear to me and you cannot help your self

Spottswood Rice

QUESTIONS TO CONSIDER

1. What is the purpose of Rice's letter? What does he want Diggs to know?
2. How does Rice feel about the US government? How does he feel about being a soldier?

14.5 VISUAL SOURCE: *THE NEWS FROM MINNESOTA* (1862)*

In the summer of 1862, in the midst of the Civil War, a second war broke out in Minnesota. The Dakota had been forced to cede much of their land in exchange for promises of money and supplies, but when Indian Agents for the federal government were unable to fulfill these promises, tensions between the Dakota and white settlers rose quickly. Over the course of four weeks of fighting, over three hundred white settlers were killed, along with over a hundred Dakota. Following the American defeat of the Dakota, the federal government executed thirty-eight Dakota men for alleged war crimes in the largest mass execution in US history.

---

* Image published with permission of ProQuest LLC. Further reproduction is prohibited without permission. Image produced by ProQuest LLC as part of ProQuest® HarpWeek Archive. www.proquest.com

This illustration from the popular magazine *Harper's Weekly* portrays violence by the Dakota in stereotypical racialized caricatures and blames the Confederacy for provoking the Dakota attack. A quotation from Confederate president Jefferson Davis noting that the Indians were at peace is combined with an overturned liquor jug marked "C.S.A." The implication is that the Dakota and the United States were at peace until the Confederacy bribed the Dakota to attack the US. While the accusation is false, it may have sounded true to white Northerners who viewed both slaveholders and Native Americans as duplicitous.

"I am happy to inform you that, in spite both of blandishments and threats, used in profusion by the agents of the government of the United States, the Indian nations within the confederacy have remained firm in their loyalty and steadfast in the observance of their treaty engagements with this government."

(The above Extract from JEFF DAVIS'S *last Message will serve to explain the News from Minnesota.)*

QUESTIONS TO CONSIDER

1. Who is responsible for the outbreak of violence in Minnesota according to this illustration? How does the artist depict this visually?
2. What stereotype about Native Americans does the illustrator employ?

14.6 VISUAL SOURCE: *SOWING AND REAPING* (1863)*

This illustration from the popular *Frank Leslie's Illustrated Newspaper* portrayed Southern women's suffering during the Civil War as the consequence of their own misdeeds. In the spring of 1863, conditions in some Southern cities had become dire due to a variety of war-related difficulties. Food production had decreased due to military destruction and the recruitment of working men. The Union blockade and numerous refugees in urban areas made food especially scarce, and rampant inflation made it difficult to buy what food there was. As a result, bread riots broke out in Richmond, Virginia, and other Southern cities, in which thousands of women broke into shops and made off with food and other essential items. The bread riots were a stark reminder that while the Confederate armies were holding their own, many on the home front were suffering.

This illustration contrasts the wealthy Southern women who supposedly urged their husbands and brothers to treasonous rebellion, with the poor, famished people they had become as a result of the war. The title "Sowing and Reaping" implies that the suffering Southern women had brought this fate upon themselves by supporting secession.

SOWING AND REAPING.

QUESTIONS TO CONSIDER

1. How does the artist use dress and physical features to contrast the rich antebellum women with the poor wartime women?
2. Is this a fair characterization of Southern women as a whole? Which factors might the artist be overlooking?

---

* Courtesy of the Library of Congress

CHAPTER 15

ENDING THE WAR AND (RE)CONSTRUCTING THE NATION, 1863–1865

15.1 ABRAHAM LINCOLN, PROCLAMATION OF AMNESTY AND RECONSTRUCTION (1863)*

Throughout 1863 the Confederate armies suffered a series of significant defeats across the country. Hoping to appeal to wavering Confederates, President Abraham Lincoln (1809–1865) announced his Proclamation of Amnesty and Reconstruction (sometimes called the Ten Percent Plan) in December of that year. Lincoln presented lenient terms, offering a pardon and the restoration of rights and property (except enslaved persons) to any individual who swore their future loyalty to the Union. Only Confederate leaders were ineligible for amnesty. Lincoln also announced that Confederate states could form new loyal state governments and rejoin the Union once 10 percent of the 1860 electorate took a loyalty oath. Lincoln hoped to use Union loyalists in occupied states such as Arkansas, Louisiana, and Tennessee to model that he would allow former Confederate states to peacefully return to the Union. The proclamation was printed in large legible type and circulated throughout the South.

Lincoln's proclamation was popular in the Union states, where many saw it as an important step to weaken the rebellion, restore the Union, and quicken the end of the war. Most rebels scorned the proclamation, however, unwilling to give up on the Confederate nation despite its misfortunes.

* Abraham Lincoln, *Proclamation of Amnesty and Reconstruction*, Tuesday, December 8, 1863. Abraham Lincoln papers: ser. 1, General Correspondence, 1833 to 1916. Manuscript/Mixed Material, Library of Congress, https://www.loc.gov/resource/mal.284 9300/?sp=1&st=text&r=-0.359,-0.086,1.719,1.719,0.

Dec. 8, 1863
Proclamation.[1]

Whereas in and by the Constitution of the United States, it is provided that the President "shall have power to grant reprieves and pardons for offences against the United States, except in cases of impeachment," and

Whereas a rebellion now exists whereby the loyal State governments of several States have for a long time been subverted, and many persons have committed, and are now guilty of treason against the United States, and

Whereas, with reference to said rebellion and treason, laws have been enacted by Congress, declaring forfeitures, and confiscations of property, and liberation of slaves, all upon terms and conditions therein stated, and also declaring that the President was thereby authorized at any time thereafter, by proclamation, to extend to persons who may have participated in the existing rebellion, in any State or part thereof, pardon and amnesty, with such exceptions, and at such time, and on such conditions, as he may deem expedient for the public welfare, and

Whereas the Congressional declaration for limited and conditional pardon, accords with well established judicial exposition of the pardoning power, under the British, and American Constitutions, and

Whereas, with reference to said rebellion, the President of the United States has issued several proclamations, with provisions in regard to the liberation of slaves, and

Whereas it is now desired by some persons heretofore engaged in said rebellion, to resume their allegiance to the United States, and to re-inaugurate loyal State governments within and for their respective States, therefore

I, Abraham Lincoln, President of the United States, do proclaim, declare, and make known, to all persons who have, directly or by implication, participated in the existing rebellion, except[2] that a full pardon is hereby granted to them and each of them, with restoration of all rights of property, except as to slaves, and upon the condition that every such person shall take and subscribe an oath, and thenceforward keep and maintain said oath inviolate; and which oath shall be registered for permanent preservation and shall be of the tenor and effect following, towit:

> I do solemnly swear in presence of Almighty God, that I will henceforth faithfully support, protect, and defend the Constitution of the United States, and the Union of the States thereunder; and that I will, in like manner, abide by, and faithfully support all Acts of Congress passed during the existing rebellion, with reference to slaves, so long, and so far, as not repealed, modified, or held void by Congress, or by decision of the Supreme Court; and that I will, in like manner, abide by and faithfully support, all proclamations of the President made during the existing rebellion, having reference to slaves, so long, and so far as not modified, or declared void by decision of the Supreme Court, so help me God.*[3]

*[The following paragraph was written out as an addition on a separate slip] The persons excepted from the benefits of the foregoing provisions are all who are, or shall have been civil or diplomatic officers or agents of the so-called Confederate government; all who have left judicial stations under the United States to aid the rebellion; all who are, or shall have been military or naval officers of said so-called confederate government, above the rank of Colonel in the Army, or of lieutenant in the Navy; all who left seats in the United States Congress to aid the rebellion; all who resigned commissions in the army or navy of the United States, and afterwards aided the rebellion; and all who have engaged in any way, in treating colored persons, or white persons in charge of such, otherwise than lawfully as prisoners of war, and which persons may have been found in the United States service as soldiers, seamen, or in any other capacity.

---

1   Both the date and the heading "Proclamation" appear to be in another hand, not Lincoln's.

2   In the official copy, the words "as hereinafter excepted," follow at this point.

3   The asterisk indicates the insertion point for a paragraph written out as an addition on a separate slip. The list of exceptions is based on War Department, Memoranda for Proclamation of Amnesty and Reconstruction, December, 1863 (q. v.), a document which was provided Lincoln to aid in preparing this proclamation.

And I do further proclaim, declare, and make known that whenever, in any of the States of Arkansas, Texas, Louisiana, Mississippi, Tennessee, Alabama, Georgia, Florida, South-Carolina, and North Carolina, a number of persons, not less than one tenth in number of the votes cast at in such state, at the Presidential election of the year of our Lord, one thousand eight hundred and sixty, each having taken the oath aforesaid, and not having since violated it, and being a qualified voter by the election law of the state, existing immediately before the so-called act of secession, and excluding all others, shall re-establish a State government, which shall be republican, and in no wise contravening said oath, such shall be recognized as the true government of the State, and the State shall receive thereunder the benefits of the Constitutional provision which declares that "The United States shall guaranty to every State in the Union a republican form of government, and shall protect each of them against invasion, and on application of the legislature, or the executive (when the legislature can not be convened against domestic violence)."

And I do further proclaim, declare, and make known that any provision which may be adopted by such State government in relation to the freed people of such State, which shall recognize and declare their permanent freedom, provide for their education, and which may yet be consistent, as a temporary arrangement, with their present condition as a laboring, landless, and homeless class, shall not be objected to by the national executive.*[4]

*[The following paragraph was written out as an addition on a separate slip] And it is suggested as not improper that in constructing a loyal State government in any State, the name of the State, the boundary, the subdivisions, the Constitution, and the general code of laws, as before the rebellion, be maintained, subject only to the modifications made necessary by the conditions hereinbefore stated, and such others, if any, not contravening said conditions, and which may be deemed expedient by those framing the new State government.

To avoid misunderstanding it may be proper to say that this paper proclamation, so far as it relates to State governments, has no reference to States wherein loyal State governments have all the while been maintained. And for the same reason it may be proper to further say that whether members sent to Congress from any State shall be admitted to seats constitutionally rests exclusively with the respective Houses, and not to any extent with the executive.

And still further that this proclamation is intended to present the people of the States wherein the national authority has been suspended, and loyal State governments have been subverted, a mode in and by which the national authority and loyal States governments may be re-established within said States, or in any of them; and, while the mode presented is the best the executive can present suggest, with his present impressions, it must not be understood that no other possible mode would be acceptable.

Given under my hand at the City of Washington, the 8th of December, A. D. one thousand eight hundred and sixty three, and of the independence of the United States of America the eightyeighth.

Abraham Lincoln

---

4   The asterisk indicates the insertion point for the addition to the text that follows. For preliminary drafts of this passage, see the memorandum on the reverse side of Lincoln's draft of a letter to George Opdyke, December 2, 1863.

QUESTIONS TO CONSIDER

1. Lincoln made important exceptions in his offer of amnesty. What are these exceptions and why did Lincoln make them?
2. By requiring only 10 percent of 1860 voters to declare their loyalty before a new government could be formed, Lincoln set a low threshold for a rebellious state to rejoin the Union. What was his purpose in allowing former Confederates to rejoin the Union so easily?

15.2 NANCY JOHNSON, TESTIMONY BY A GEORGIA FREEDWOMAN ABOUT HOW UNION TROOPS STOLE HER PROPERTY (1873)*

As Union armies made their way through Georgia in 1864, soldiers removed or destroyed anything of military value, which often included food and livestock. In 1871 Congress established the Southern Claims Commission with the purpose of reimbursing loyal Americans whose property had been taken or destroyed by the Union Army during the war. Over a hundred special commissioners fanned out across the South to hold hearings, and they eventually forwarded twenty-two thousand cases with testimony from more than two hundred thousand witnesses to Washington for judgment.

Neither Congress nor the commissioners expected formerly enslaved people to bring many cases, as they understood them to have been deprived of any opportunity to own property during their enslavement. However, hundreds of formerly enslaved people did bring cases, describing how the livestock, foodstuffs, and other possessions they had accrued through their hard work had been seized by Union soldiers. Contrary to the expectations of white Northerners, many enslaved people had been industrious, shrewd, and proud of the personal possessions they had acquired.

Testimony by a Georgia Freedwoman before the Southern Claims Commission

[Savannah, Ga., March 22, 1873]

General Interrogatories by Special Com'r—My name is Nancy Johnson. I was born in Ga. I was a slave and became free when the army came here. My master was David Baggs. I live in Canoochie Creek. The claimant is my husband. He was a good Union man during the war. He liked to have lost his life by standing up for the Union party. He was threatened heavy. There was a Yankee prisoner that got away & came to our house at night; we kept him hid in my house a whole day. He sat in my room. White people didn't visit our house then. My husband slipped him over to a man named Joel Hodges & he conveyed him off so that he got home. I saw the man at the time of the raid & I knew him. He said that he tried to keep them from burning my house but he couldn't keep them from taking everything we had. I was sorry for them though a heap. The white people came hunting this man that we kept over night; my old master sent one of his own grandsons & he said if he found it that they must put my husband to death, & I had to tell a story to save life. My old master would have had him killed. He was bitter. This was my master David Baggs. I told him that I had seen nothing of him. I did this to save my husbands life. Some of the rebel soldiers deserted & came to our house & we fed them. They were opposed to the war & didn't own slaves & said they would die rather than fight. Those who were poor white people, who didn't own slaves were some of them Union people. I befriended them because they were on our side. I don't know that he ever did any thing more for the Union; we were way back in the country, but his heart was right & so was mine. I was served mighty mean before the Yankees came here. I was nearly frostbitten: my old

* Testimony of Nancy Johnson, March 22, 1873. GA case files, Approved Claims, series 732, Southern Claims Commission, 3rd Auditor, US General Accounting Office, Record Group 217, National Archives. (Published in Ira Berlin, ed., *Freedom: A Documentary History of Emancipation*, ser. I, vol. 1: The Destruction of Slavery (Cambridge, UK: Cambridge University Press, 2010), 150–54, http://www.freedmen.umd.edu/NJohnson.html.

Missus made me weave to make clothes for the soldiers till 12 o'clock at night & I was so tired & my own clothes I had to spin over night. She never gave me so much as a bonnet. I had to work hard for the rebels until the very last day when they took us. The old man came to me then & said if you won't go away & will work for us we will work for you; I told him if the other colored people were going to be free that I wanted to be. I went away & then came back & my old Missus asked me if I came back to behave myself & do her work & I told her no that I came to do my own work. I went to my own house & in the morning my old master came to me & asked me if I wouldn't go and milk the cows: I told him that my Missus had driven me off–well said he you go and do it—then my Mistress came out again & asked me if I came back to work for her like a "nigger"—I told her no that I was free & she said be off then & called me a stinking bitch. I afterwards wove 40 yds. Of dress goods for her that she promised to pay me for; but she never paid me a cent for it. I have asked her for it several times. I have been hard up to live but thank God, I am spared yet. I quit then only did a few jobs for her but she never did anything for me except give me a meal of victuals, you see I was hard up then, I was well to do before the war.

Second Set of Interrogatories by Spec'l Com'r.

1 I was present when this property was taken.
2 I saw it taken.
3 They said that they didn't believe what I had belonged to me & I told them that I would swear that it belonged to me. I had tried to hide things. They found our meat, it was hid under the house & they took a crop of rice. They took it out & I had some cloth under the house too & the dishes & two fine bed-quilts. They took them out. These were all my own labor & night labor. They took the bole of cloth under the house and the next morning they came back with it made into pantaloons. They were starved & naked almost. It was Jan & cold, They were on their way from Savannah. They took all my husbands clothes, except what he had on his back.
4 These things were taken from David Bagg's place in Liberty County. The Yankees took them. I should think there were thousands of them. I could not count them. They were about a day & a night.

5 There were present my family, myself & husband & this man Jack Walker. He is way out in Tatnal Co. & we can't get him here.
6 There were what we called officers there. I don't know whether they ordered the property taken. I put a pot on and made a pie & they took it to carry out to the head men. I went back where the officers camped & got my oven that I cooked it in back again. They must have ordered them or else they could not have gone so far & they right there. They said that they stood in need of them. They said that we ought not to care what they took for we would get it all back again; that they were obliged to have something to eat. They were mighty fine looking men.
7 They took the mare out of the stable; they took the bacon under the house, the corn was taken out of the crib, & the rice & the lard. Some of the chickens they shot & some they run down; they shot the hogs.
8 They took it by hand the camp was close by my house.
9 They carried it to their camps; they had lots of wagons there.
10 They took it to eat, bless you! I saw them eating it right there in my house. They were nearly starved.
11 I told one of the officers that we would starve & they said no that we would get it all back again, come & go along with us; but I wouldn't go because the old man had my youngest child hid away in Tatnal Co: he took her away because she knew where the gold was hid & he didn't want her to tell. My boy was sent out to the swamp to watch the wagons of provisions & the soldiers took the wagons & the boy, & I never saw him anymore. He was 14 yrs. old. I could have got the child back but I was afraid my master would kill him; he said that he would & I knew that he would or else make his children do it: he made his sons kill 2 men big tall men like you. The Lord forgive them for the way they have treated me. The child could not help them from taking the horses. He said that Henry (my boy) hallooed for the sake of having the Yankees find him; but the Yankees asked him where he was going & he didn't know they were soldiers & he told them that he was going to Master's mules.

12 I didn't ask for any receipt.

13 It was taken in the day time, not secretly.

14 When they took this property, the army was en-camped. Some got there before the camps were up. Some was hung up in the house. Some people told us that if we let some hang up they wouldn't touch the rest, but they did, they were close by. They commenced taking when they first came. They staid there two nights. I heard a heap of shooting, but I don't think that they killed anybody. I didn't know any of the officers or quartermasters.

15 This horse was as fine a creature as ever was & the pork &c were in good order.

16 Item No. 1. I don't know how old the mare was. I know she was young. She was medium sized. She was in nice order, we kept a good creature. My hus-band bought it when it was a colt, about 2 years old. I think he had been using it a year & a little better. Colored people when they would work always had something for themselves, after work-ing for their masters. I most forgot whether he paid cash or swapped cows. He worked & earned money, after he had done his masters work. They bridled & carried her off; I think they jumped right on her back

Item No. 2. We had 7 hogs & we killed them right there. It was pickled away in the barrel: Some was done hung up to smoke, but we took it down & put it into the barrels to keep them from getting it. He raised the hogs. He bought a sow and raised his own pork & that is the way he got this. He did his tasks & after that he worked for himself & he got some money & bought the hogs and then they increased. He worked Sundays too; and that was for our-selves. He always was a hardworking man. I could not tell how much these would weigh; they were monstrous hogs, they were a big breed of hogs. We had them up feeding. The others were some two years old, & some more.

It took two men to help hang them up. This was the meat from 7 hogs.

Item No. 3. I had half a barrel of lard. It was in gourds, that would hold half a bushel a piece. We had this hid in the crib. This was lard from the hogs.

Item No. 4 I could not tell exactly how much corn there was but there was a right smart. We had 4 or 5 bushels ground up into meal & they took all the corn besides. They carried it off in bags and my children's undershirts, tied them like bags & filled them up. My husband made baskets and they toted some off in that way. They toted some off in fanners & big blue tubs.

Item No. 5. I don't know exactly how much rice there was; but we made a good deal. They toted it off in bundles, threshed out—It was taken in the sheaf. They fed their horses on it. I saw the horses eating it as I passed there. They took my tubs, kettles &c. I didn't get anything back but an oven.

Item No. 7. We had 11 hogs. They were 2 or 3 years old. They were in pretty good order. We were intending to fatten them right next year—they killed them right there.

Item No. 8. I had 30 or 40 head of chickens. They took the last one. They shot them. This property all belonged to me and my husband. None of it belonged to Mr. Baggs I swore to the men so, but they wouldn't believe I could have such things. My girl had a changable silk dress & all had [talanas?] & they took them all—It didn't look like a Yankee person would be so mean. But they said if they didn't take them the whites here would & they did take some of my things from their camps after they left.

her
Nancy X Johnson
mark

QUESTIONS TO CONSIDER

1. How did the war impact the lives of Nancy Johnson and her family members?

2. How does Johnson's description of her interactions with her former masters compare to her ex-perience with the Union soldiers?

15.3 EXCERPT FROM THE VIRGINIA BLACK CODES (1866)*

After the end of the Civil War, new state governments in the former Confederate states passed a series of laws to define the rights of freedpeople, commonly called "Black Codes." While these laws often granted freedpeople new rights they had not had while enslaved—such as to marry and make contracts—the primary focus of these laws was to control the working conditions of Black Southerners. Although the laws varied from state to state, they generally required freedpeople to sign months-long contracts for plantation labor and forbade them from changing employers if someone offered them better wages or working conditions. These laws defined freedpeople who would not sign these contracts as "vagrants," and allowed anyone detained for vagrancy to be forcibly set to work. "Black Codes" ran contrary to many Black Southerners' hopes and expectations of freedom. Many freedpeople desired to cease working on plantations and move around as they wished throughout their county and state, choices that had been denied to them while enslaved. By forcing them into plantation labor and denying their choice in whether or where to work, lawmakers tried to re-create the antebellum conditions of slave labor as closely as they could.

AN ACT to regulate contracts for labor between white and colored persons, and to impose a fine on persons enticing laborers from the service of their employers under such contracts.

1. *Be it enacted by the general assembly,* That no contract between a white person and a colored person for the labor or service of the latter for a longer period than two months shall be binding on such colored person, unless the contract be in writing, signed by such white person, or his agent, and by such colored person duly acknowledged before a justice or notary public, or clerk of the country or corporation court, or overseer of the poor, or two or more credible witnesses in the county or corporation in which the white person may reside, or in which the service or labor is to be performed. And it shall be the duty of the justice, notary, clerk, or overseer of the poor, or the witnesses, to read and explain the contract to the colored person before taking his acknowledgment thereof, and to state that this has been done in the certificate of the acknowledgement of the contract.

2. If any person shall entice away from the service of another any laborer employed by him under a contract as provided by this act, knowing of the existence of such contract, or shall knowingly employ a laborer bound to service to another under such contract, he shall forfeit to the party aggrieved not less than ten nor more than twenty dollars for every such offence, to be recovered by warrant before any justice of the peace.

---

* Excerpts from Virginia Black Codes (1866), in "Laws in Relation to Freedmen," US Senate 39th Congress, 2nd Session, Senate Executive Doc. No. 6 (Washington, DC: War Department, Bureau of Refugees, Freedmen, and Abandoned Lands, 1866–67), 227–29, Library of Congress, https://memory.loc.gov/cgi-bin/ampage?collId=ody_llmisc&fileName=ody/ody0517/ody0517 page.db&recNum=226&itemLink=r%3Fammem%2Faaodyssey%3A%40field%28NUMBER%2B%40band%28llmisc%2Body 0517%29%29&linkText=0.

3. This act shall be in force from and after the first day of April, eighteen hundred and sixty-six, and the first section shall not apply to any contract made prior to that date.

Passed February 20, 1866.

AN ACT to amend and re-enact the 14th section of chapter 108 of the code of Virginia for 1860, in regard to registers of marriage and to legalize the marriages of colored persons now cohabiting as husband and wife.

1. *Be it enacted by the general assembly*, That the fourteenth section of chapter one hundred and eight of the code of Virginia for eighteen hundred and sixty, be, and the same is hereby, amended and re-enacted so as to read as follows, to wit: "Henceforth, it shall be the duty of every minister, or other person, celebrating a marriage, and of the clerk or keeper of the records of any religious society which solemnizes marriages, by the consent of the parties, in open congregation, at once to make a record of every marriage between white persons, or between colored persons, solemnized by or before him, stating in such record whether the persons be white or colored, and, within two months after such marriage, to return a copy thereof, signed by him, to the clerk of the county or corporation in which the same is solemnized. The clerk issuing any marriage license shall at the time ascertain from the party obtaining such license a certificate setting forth, as near as may be, the date and place of the proposed marriage, the full names of both the parties, their ages and condition before marriage, whether single or widowed, the places of their birth and residence, the names of their parents, and the occupation of the husband."

2. That where colored persons, before the passage of this act, shall have undertaken and agreed to occupy the relation to each other of husband and wife, and shall be cohabiting together as such at the time of its passage, whether the rites of marriage shall have been celebrated between them or not, they shall be deemed husband and wife, and be entitled to the rights and privileges, and subject to the duties and obligations of that relation, in like manner as if they had been duly married by law; and all their children shall be deemed legitimate, whether born before or after the passage of this act. And when the parties have ceased to cohabit before the passage of this act, in consequence of the death of the woman, or from any other cause, all the children of the woman, recognized by the man to be his, shall be deemed legitimate.

3. This act shall be in force from its passage.

Passed February 27, 1866.

AN ACT to amend and re-enact the 9th section of chapter 103 of the code of Virginia for 1860, defining a Mulatto, providing for the punishment of offences by colored persons, and for the admission of their evidence in legal investigations, and to repeal all laws in relation to slaves and slavery, and for other purposes.

1. *Be it enacted by the general assembly*, That every person having one-fourth or more of negro blood, shall be deemed a colored person: and every person, not a colored person, having one-fourth or more of Indian blood, shall be deemed an Indian.

2. All laws in respect to crimes and punishments, and in respect to criminal proceedings, applicable to white persons, shall apply in like manner to colored persons and to Indians, unless when it is otherwise specially provided.

3. The following acts and parts of acts are hereby repealed, namely: All acts and parts of act relating to slaves and slavery; chapter one hundred and seven of the code of eighteen hundred and sixty, relating to free negroes; chapter two hundred of said code, relating to offences by negroes; chapter two hundred and twelve of said code, relating to proceedings against negroes; chapter ninety-eight of said code, relating to patrols; sections twenty-five to forty-seven, both inclusive, of chapter one hundred and ninety-two of said code; sections twenty-six to thirty, both inclusive, and sections thirty-three to thirty-seven, both inclusive, of chapter one hundred and ninety-eight of said code; the fifth paragraph, as enumerated in section two of chapter two hundred and three of said code; all acts and parts of acts imposing on negroes the penalty of stripes, where the same penalty is not imposed on white persons; and all other acts and parts of acts inconsistent with this act.

4. This act shall be in force from its passage.
   Passed February 27, 1866.

AN ACT in relation to the testimony of colored persons.

1. *Be it enacted by the general assembly*, That colored persons and Indians shall, otherwise competent and subject to the rules applicable to other persons, shall be admitted as witnesses in the following cases:

1. In all civil cases and proceedings at law and in equity in which a colored person or an Indian is a party, or may be directly benefited or injured by the result.
2. In all criminal proceedings, in which a colored person or an Indian is a party or which arise out of an injury done, attempted or threatened to person, property, or rights of a colored person or Indian, or in which it is alleged in the presentment, information or indictment, or in which the court is of opinion, from the other evidence, that there is probable cause to believe that the offence was committed by a white person in conjunction or co-operation with a colored person or Indian.
3. The testimony of colored persons shall in all cases and proceedings, both at law and in equity, be given *ore tenus* and not by deposition; and in suits in equity and in all other cases in which the deposition of the witness would be regularly part of the record, the court shall, if desired by any party or if deemed proper by itself, certify the facts proved by such witness or the evidence given by him as far as credited by the court, and one or the other may be proper, under the rules of law applicable to the case; and such certificate shall be made part of the record.
4. This act shall be in force from its passage.
   Passed February 28, 1866.

AN ACT providing for the punishment of vagrants.

1. *Be it enacted by the general assembly*, That the overseers of the poor, or other officers having charge of the poor, or the special county police, or the police of any corporation, or any one or more of such persons, shall be and are hereby empowered and required, upon discovering any vagrant or vagrants within their respective counties or corporations, to make information thereof to any justice of the peace of their county or corporation, and to require a warrant for apprehending such vagrant or vagrants, to be brought be before him or some other justice; and if upon due examination it shall appear that the person or persons are within the true description of a vagrant, as hereinafter mentioned, such justice shall, by warrant, order such vagrant or vagrants to be employed in labor for any term not exceeding three months, and, but any constable of such county or corporation to be hired out for the best wages that can be procured; to be applied, except as hereafter provided, for the use of the vagrant or his family, as ordered by the justice. And if any such vagrant or vagrants shall, during such time of service, without sufficient case, run away from the person so employing him or them, he or they shall be apprehended on the warrant of a justice, and returned to the custody of such hirer, who shall have, free of any further hire, the services of said vagrant for one month in addition to the original term of hiring; and said employer shall then have the power, if authorized by the justice, to work said vagrant confined with ball and chain; or should said hirer decline to receive again said vagrant, then said vagrant shall be taken by the officer, upon the order of a justice, to the poor or work house, if there be any such in said county or corporation; or, if authorized by the justice, to work him, confined with ball and chain, for the period for which he would have had to serve his late employer, had he consented to receive him again; or should there be, when said runaway vagrant is apprehended, any public work going on in said county or corporation, then said vagrant, upon the order of a justice, shall be delivered over by said officer to the superintendent of such public work, who shall, for the like last mentioned period, work said vagrant on said public works, confined with ball and chain, if so authorized by the justice. But if there be no poor or work house in said county or cooperation, and no public work then in progress therein, then, in that event, said justice, may cause said vagrant to be delivered to any person who will take charge of him, said person to have his services free of charge. . . .

QUESTIONS TO CONSIDER

1. What rights do the Virginia Black Codes grant to freedpeople and what restrictions do they impose on those rights?
2. The Black Codes were a series of laws governing several different aspects of Black Southerners' social, legal, and familial lives. How do these several laws work together to limit and control the living conditions of Black Southerners?

15.4 VISUAL SOURCE: BATTLEGROUND RUINS IN CHARLESTON, SOUTH CAROLINA (c. 1860–1865)*

Charleston, South Carolina, held particular significance for Americans on both sides of the Civil War. As one of the largest cities in the Confederacy, the home of some outspoken proslavery ideologues, and the location of Fort Sumter where the war had begun, Charleston represented the heart of slavery and the secession. South Carolina, spurred on by a hotbed of secessionists in Charleston, had been the first state to secede in 1860. The Union government hoped to capture the city, both to close the port and to seize this important Confederate symbol. The Union Navy blockaded Charleston for over eighteen months between July 1863 and February 1865, when Confederate forces eventually evacuated, retreating ahead of a Union Army advancing north from Georgia.

Over a year of naval bombardment reduced much of the city to ruins. The building pictured in the foreground of this photograph was a church; one of its remaining columns stands prominently in the center of the image, while to the right a hole in the wall exposes the brickwork of the crumbling building. Though no people appear in the picture, signs of human habitation are evident in the path through the debris.

---

* Courtesy National Archives, photo no. 111-B-4667

QUESTIONS TO CONSIDER

1. The column at the center of the image is relatively undamaged compared to the ruins all around it. What thoughts or feelings was the photographer trying to evoke by focusing his image on this architecture?

2. Many towns were captured during the Civil War without experiencing significant physical damage. What would the capture and destruction of Charleston have meant to those on different sides of the war?

15.5 VISUAL SOURCE: THOMAS NAST, *PARDON AND FRANCHISE* (1865)*

In the wake of the Civil War, the United States had to determine how to integrate former Confederates and Black Americans into the body politic. In this image published in *Harper's Weekly*, famous cartoonist Thomas Nast (1840–1902) juxtaposes former rebels seeking pardons from a disdainful feminine Columbia (representing an idealized United States) with Columbia's praise for a Black veteran wounded in battle.

_____

* Courtesy of the Library of Congress

In May 1865, President Andrew Johnson (1808–1875) issued an amnesty proclamation for all former Confederates who would swear loyalty to the Union. However, Confederate leaders and major landholders were excepted and had to apply to Johnson personally for a pardon. Thanks to Johnson's pardon, many former rebels could participate in postwar elections and help guide the course of early reconstruction efforts. In contrast, no state had expanded voting opportunities for Black Americans by the end of the war, although Lincoln had endorsed the expansion of voting rights to some Black Americans, including soldiers. With former rebels allowed to vote in Southern states, where the overwhelming majority of Black people lived, the likelihood of a meaningful expansion of Black voting rights looked slim. Unable to vote themselves, Black veterans faced the prospect of having their rights curtailed by governments elected by the former rebels they had fought against.

QUESTIONS TO CONSIDER

1. The concept of loyalty is central to the contrast Nast draws in this image. What hypocrisy is he trying to highlight with this illustration?
2. Political cartoons in the nineteenth century frequently used Columbia to represent a civilized, idealized, and virtuous United States. How does Nast use this character to make his opinions clear to the reader?

CHAPTER 16

THE PROMISE AND LIMITS OF RECONSTRUCTION, 1865–1877

16.1 THADDEUS STEVENS, SPEECH TO CONGRESS (1867)*

Following the Confederate surrender at Appomattox, Virginia, in April 1865, President Andrew Johnson (1808–1875) and Republican lawmakers such as Thaddeus Stevens (1792–1868) disagreed over how to integrate former rebels into the Union. Johnson claimed that the authority to reconstruct the seceded states fell under his power as chief executive. He issued blanket pardons to many former rebels and installed governors of his own choosing in former Confederate states. Johnson made no attempt to enfranchise the millions of freedpeople who lived in the former Confederacy. In opposition to this approach, Stevens argued that Congress, as the legislative body elected by the American people, was the correct authority to determine the course of reconstruction. He feared that Johnson's pardons and refusal to grant Black Southerners the vote would lead the new Southern state governments to be dominated by former Confederates, endangering Black and white Southerners who had remained loyal to the Union throughout the war.

In the wake of the Civil War, Johnson, himself a white Southerner, thought it best to re-establish the Union as quickly as possible, with as little change as possible. Stevens argued that unless significant changes were instituted to prevent those who launched the rebellion from taking power again, then the war would have been fought for nothing.

---

* Thaddeus Stevens, "Speech on Reconstruction," January 3, 1867, Teaching American History, https://teachingamericanhistory .org/document/speech-on-reconstruction-2/.

This is a bill designed to enable loyal men, so far as I could discriminate them in these States, to form governments which shall be in loyal hands, that they may protect themselves from . . . outrages. . . . In states that have never been restored since the rebellion from a state of conquest, and which are this day held in captivity under the laws of war, the military authorities, under this decision and its extension into disloyal states, dare not order the commanders of departments to enforce the laws of the country. . . .

Since the surrender of the armies of the confederate States of America a little has been done toward establishing this Government upon the true principles of liberty and justice. . . . But in what have we enlarged their liberty of thought? In what have we taught them the science and granted them the privilege of self-government? . . . Call you this a free Republic when four millions are subjects but not citizens? . . . I pronounce it no nearer to a true Republic now when twenty-five million of a privileged class exclude five million from all participation in the rights of government. . . .

What are the great questions which now divide the nation? In the midst of the political Babel which has been produced by the intermingling of secessionists, rebels, pardoned traitors, hissing Copperheads, and apostate Republicans, such a confusion of tongues is heard that it is difficult to understand either the questions that are asked or the answers that are given. Ask, what is the "President's policy?" and it is difficult to define it. Ask, what is the "policy of Congress?" and the answer is not always at hand.

A few moments may be profitably spent in seeking the meaning of each of these terms. Nearly six years ago a bloody war arose between different sections of the United States. Eleven States, possessing a very large extent of territory, and ten or twelve million people, aimed to sever their connection with the Union, and to form an independent empire, founded on the avowed principle of human slavery and excluding every free State from this confederacy. . . . The two powers mutually prepared to settle the question by arms. . . .

President Lincoln, Vice President Johnson, and both branches of Congress repeatedly declared that the belligerent States could never again intermeddle with the affairs of the Union, or claim any right as members of the United States Government until the legislative power of the Government should declare them entitled thereto. . . . For whether their states were out of the Union as they declared, or were disorganized and "out of their proper relations" to the Government, as some subtle metaphysicians contend, their rights under the Constitution had all been renounced and abjured under oath, and could not be resumed on their own mere motion. . . .

The Federal arms triumphed. The confederate armies and government surrendered unconditionally. The law of nations then fixed their condition. They were subject to the controlling power of the conquerors. No former laws, no former compacts or treaties existed to bind the belligerents. They had all been melted and consumed in the fierce fires of the terrible war. The United States . . . appointed military provisional governors to regulate their municipal institutions until the law-making power of the conqueror should fix their condition and the law by which they should be permanently governed. . . . No one then supposed that those States had any governments, except such as they had formed under their rebel organization. . . . Whoever had then asserted that those States [were] entitled to all the rights and privileges which they enjoyed before the rebellion and were on a level with their loyal conquerors would have been deemed a fool. . . .

In this country the whole sovereignty rests with the people, and is exercised through their Representatives in Congress assembled. . . . No Government official, from the president and the Chief Justice down, can do any one single act which is not prescribed and directed by the legislative power. . . .

. . . This I take to be the great question between the President and Congress. He claims the right to reconstruct by his own power. Congress denies him all power in the matter, except those of advice, and has determined to maintain such denial. . . .

. . . [President Johnson] desires that the States created by him shall be acknowledged as valid States, while at the same time he inconsistently declares that the old rebel States are in full existence, and always have been, and have equal rights with the loyal States. . . .

Congress refuses to treat the States created by him as of any validity, and denies that the old rebel States have any existence which gives them any rights under the Constitution. . . . Congress denies that any State lately in rebellion has any government or constitution known to the Constitution of the United States. . . .

It is to be regretted that inconsiderate and incautious Republicans should ever have supposed that the slight amendments already proposed to the Constitution, even when incorporated into that instrument, would satisfy the reforms necessary for the security of the Government. Unless the rebel States, before admission, should be made republican in spirit, and placed under the guardianship of loyal men, all our blood and treasure will have been spent in vain. I waive now the question of punishment which, if we are wise, will still be inflicted by moderate confiscations, both as a reproof and example. Having these States, as we all agree, entirely within the power of Congress, it is our duty to take care that no injustice shall remain in their organic laws. Holding them "like clay in the hands of the potter," we must see that no vessel is made for destruction. Having now no governments, they must have enabling acts. . . . Impartial suffrage, both in electing the delegates and ratifying their proceedings, is now the fixed rule. There is more reason why colored voters should be admitted in the rebel States than in the Territories. In the States they form the great mass of the loyal men. Possibly with their aid loyal governments may be established in most of those States. Without it all are sure to be ruled by traitors; and loyal men, black and white, will be oppressed, exiled, or murdered. There are several good reasons for the passage of this bill. In the first place, it is just. I am now confining my arguments to Negro suffrage in the rebel States. Have not loyal blacks quite as good a right to choose rulers and make laws as rebel whites? In the second place, it is a necessity in order to protect the loyal white men in the seceded States. The white Union men are in a great minority in each of those States. With them the blacks would act in a body; and it is believed that in each of said States, except one, the two united would form a majority, control the States, and protect themselves.

Now they are the victims of daily murder. They must suffer constant persecution or be exiled. . . .

Another good reason is, it would insure the ascendancy of the Union party. Do you avow the party purpose? exclaims some horror-stricken demagogue. I do. For I believe, on my conscience, that on the continued ascendancy of that party depends the safety of this great nation. If impartial suffrage is excluded in the rebel States then everyone of them is sure to send a solid rebel representative delegation to Congress, and cast a solid rebel electoral vote. They, with their kindred Copperheads of the North, would always elect the President and control Congress. While slavery sat upon her defiant throne, and insulted and intimidated the trembling North, the South frequently divided on questions of policy between Whigs and Democrats, and gave victory alternately to the sections. Now, you must divide them between loyalists, without regard to color, and disloyalists, or you will be the perpetual vassals of the free-trade, irritated, revengeful South. For these, among other reasons, I am for Negro suffrage in every rebel State. If it be just, it should not be denied; if it be necessary, it should be adopted; if it be a punishment to traitors, they deserve it.

But it will be said, as it has been said, "This is Negro equality!" What is Negro equality. . .? It means . . . just this much, and no more: every man, no matter what his race or color; every earthly being who has an immortal soul, has an equal right to justice, honesty, and fair play with every other man; and the law should secure him these rights. The same law which condemns or acquits an African should condemn or acquit a white man. The same law which gives a verdict in a White man's favor should give a verdict in a black man's favor on the same state of facts. Such is the law of God and such ought to be the law of man. This doctrine does not mean that a Negro shall sit on the same seat or eat at the same table with a white man. That is a matter of taste which every man must decide for himself. . . . If there be any who are afraid of the rivalry of the black man in office or in business, I have only to advise them to try and beat their competitor in knowledge and business capacity, and there is no danger that his white neighbors will prefer his African rival to himself. . . .

QUESTIONS TO CONSIDER

1. According to Stevens, what are some of the "great questions" Americans must decide in the wake of the Civil War?
2. Stevens is very conscious of white Americans' prejudice against freedpeople and other Black Americans. How does he address this issue in his speech?

16.2 TESTIMONY OF MERVIN GIVENS TO CONGRESS ABOUT KU KLUX KLAN ACTIVITY IN SOUTH CAROLINA (1871)*

Beginning in 1866, Republicans in the United States Congress passed a series of laws and constitutional amendments meant to reconstruct former Confederate states. These policies established temporary military governorships in those states, enfranchised all men including freedmen, and barred some rebel leaders from holding political office. In response, many white Southerners engaged in violent campaigns of terror, primarily targeting Black Southerners as well as white Unionists. These attacks were often carried out by white supremacist groups such as the Ku Klux Klan, the White League, and the Red Shirts. Often attacking at night and in disguise, the terrorists would intimidate, harass, assault, mutilate, and kill men and women who they believed supported Republican, Unionist, or racially egalitarian policies. Although these groups were relatively unorganized at first, in the early 1870s they grew in size, incorporating Confederate veterans and adopting a more paramilitary character. In response to the testimony of people like Mervin Givens, Congress passed Enforcement Acts in 1870 and 1871, which President Ulysses S. Grant (1822–1885) used to effectively, if temporarily, curtail white supremacist terrorism in the South.

SPARTANBURG, SOUTH CAROLINA, July 12, 1871 MERVIN GIVENS (colored) sworn and examined. By Mr. Stevenson:

QUESTION: Your name in old times was Mery Moss?
ANSWER: Yes, sir; but since freedom I don't go by my master's name. My name now is Givens.
QUESTION: What is your age?
ANSWER: About forty I expect.
QUESTION: Where do you live?
ANSWER: With Silas Miles.

QUESTION: Where is that?
ANSWER: Five miles from here on the straight Columbia road.
QUESTION: Is it at General Bates's place?
ANSWER: No sir; it is on the road by Cedar Springs.
QUESTION: Did you not live on General Bates's place?
ANSWER: No, sir.
QUESTION: Have you ever been visited by the Ku-Klux?
ANSWER: Yes, sir.
QUESTION: When?

* *Report of the Joint Select Committee to Inquire into the Condition of Affairs in the Late Insurrectionary States, made to the two Houses of Congress, February 19, 1872*, Internet Archive, 698–700, https://archive.org/details/reportofjointsel04unit/page/698/mode/2up?q=givens.

ANSWER: About the last of April.

QUESTION: Tell what they said and did.

ANSWER: I was asleep when they came to my house, and did not know anything about them until they broke in on me.

QUESTION: What time of night was it?

ANSWER: About twelve o'clock at night. They broke in on me and frightened me right smart, being asleep. They ordered me to get up and make a light. As quick as I could gather my senses I bounced up and made a light, but not quick enough. They jumped at me and struck me with a pistol, and made a knot that you can see there now. By the time I made the light I catched the voice of them, and as soon as I could see by the light, I looked around and saw by the size of the men and voice so that I could judge right off who it was. By that time they jerked the case off the pillow and jerked it over my head and ordered me out of doors. That was all I saw in the house. After they carried me out of doors I saw nothing more. They pulled the pillow-slip over my head and told me if I took off they would shoot me. They carried me out and whipped me powerful.

QUESTION: With what?

ANSWER: With sticks and hickories. They whipped me powerful.

QUESTION: How many lashes?

ANSWER: I can't tell. I have no knowledge at all about it. May be a hundred or two. Two men whipped me and both at once.

QUESTION: Did they say anything to you?

ANSWER: They cursed me and told me I had voted the radical ticket, and they intended to beat me so I would not vote it again.

QUESTION: Did you know any of them?

ANSWER: Yes, sir; I think I know them.

QUESTION: What were their names?

ANSWER: One was named John Thomson and the other was John Zimmerman. Those are the two men I think it was.

QUESTION: How many were there in all?

ANSWER: I didn't see but two. After they took me out, I was blindfolded; but I could judge from the horse tracks that there were more than two horses there. Some were horses and some were mules. It was a wet, rainy night; they whipped me stark naked. I had a brown undershirt on and they tore it clean off.

QUESTION: Could you not judge whether there were more than two?

ANSWER: No, sir; they would not give me time. They whirled me right around and told me to go when they got through whipping, and I just split right off without trying to see anything more.

QUESTION: How far did you live from General Bates's place then?

ANSWER: I expect it was five miles.

QUESTION: Did you know what the Ku-Klux had done there?

ANSWER: No, sir. I didn't live in the settlement at all. I heard a heap, but I didn't know it.

QUESTION: Did you know whether the people were driven off of his place?

ANSWER: I think a good many were.

QUESTION: Did you know any of them who lived there?

ANSWER: I used to know them in old times, but I have almost forgotten, people have changed about so.

By Mr. Van Trump:

QUESTION: There were, then, two men who came to your house?

ANSWER: Yes, sir; that was all I could see.

QUESTION: Were they disguised?

ANSWER: Yes, sir.

QUESTION: How?

ANSWER: They had on some sort of gray-looking clothes, and much the same sort of thing over their face. One of them had a sort of high hat with tassel and sort of horns.

QUESTION: How far did John Thomson live from there?

ANSWER: I think it is two or three miles.

QUESTION: Were you acquainted with him?

ANSWER: Yes, sir.

QUESTION: Where?

ANSWER: At my house. My wife did a good deal of washing for them both. I was very well-acquainted with their size and their voices. They were boys I was raised with. John Zimmerman is a play-boy I have been with all my life.

QUESTION: How old is John?

ANSWER: About twenty-five years.

QUESTION: A married man?

ANSWER: No, sir, single.

QUESTION: How old is John Thomson?

ANSWER: I don't know his age. They lived farther below. The way I got acquainted with him, they kept a grocery shop.

QUESTION: Does living below make any difference about your knowing his age?

ANSWER: I never got acquainted with him until last winter.

QUESTION: Can you not form an idea of his age?

ANSWER: He may be the same age; he is a young gentleman.

QUESTION: Not married?

ANSWER: No, sir.

QUESTION: Were their faces completely covered?

ANSWER: Yes, sir; I could not see them.

QUESTION: Then it is only by judging their voices and size that you believe it was them?

ANSWER: Yes, sir.

QUESTION: Did you tell anybody else it was John Thomson?

ANSWER: I have never named it.

QUESTION: Why?

ANSWER: I was afraid to.

QUESTION: Are you afraid now?

ANSWER: I am not afraid to own the truth as nigh as I can.

QUESTION: Is there any difference in owning to the truth on the 12th of July and on the 1st of April?

ANSWER: The black people have injured themselves very much by talking, and I was afraid.

QUESTION: Are you not afraid now?

ANSWER: No, sir; because I hope there will be a stop put to it.

QUESTION: Why do you hope so?

ANSWER: Because I believe that gentlemen have got it in hand that is coming to do something for us.

QUESTION: Do you think we three gentlemen can stop it?

ANSWER: No, sir; but I think you can get some help.

QUESTION: Has anybody been telling you that?

ANSWER: No, sir; nobody told me that.

QUESTION: You did not see any horses when Thomson and Zimmerman came up to the house in the night?

ANSWER: No, sir; but over where they whipped, I went down next morning after my shirt, and the horses were hitched within about ten steps of the fence.

QUESTION: You thought there were more than Thomson and Zimmerman, judging by the horse tracks?

ANSWER: Yes, sir.

QUESTION: You said some were horse and some were mule tracks; can you tell the difference?

ANSWER: Yes, sir; I can tell the difference in the size of a horse's track and a mule's.

QUESTION: Is there much difference?

ANSWER: Yes, sir.

QUESTION: If both are shod?

ANSWER: Yes, sir; there is a great difference in the shape, and I have shod horses and mules, and I am very well acquainted with both kinds of feet.

QUESTION: Why did you not commence a prosecution against Thomson and Zimmerman?

ANSWER: I am like the rest, I reckon; I am too cowardly.

QUESTION: Why do you not do it now; you are not cowardly now?

ANSWER: I shouldn't have done it now.

QUESTION: I am talking about bringing suit for that abuse on that night. Why do you not have them arrested?

ANSWER: It ought to be done.

QUESTION: Why do you not do it?

ANSWER: For fear they would shoot me. If I were to bring them up here and could not prove the thing exactly on them, and they were to get out of it, I would not expect to live much longer.

QUESTIONS TO CONSIDER

1. Givens believed he knew the men who attacked him, despite their efforts to blindfold him. What does Givens's previous relationship with his attackers indicate about the postwar South and white supremacist violence there?

2. Givens and his questioners allude to other similar incidents of violence in nearby areas. How has Givens's life been impacted by this violence in his community?

16.3 VISUAL SOURCE: DISTINGUISHED MEMBERS, RECONSTRUCTED CONSTITUTION OF LOUISIANA (1868)*

Between 1867 and 1869, former Confederate states held conventions to establish new state constitutions that would codify political and civil rights for Black Americans. Over 250 Black delegates were elected to these conventions, and they constituted a majority in states such as Louisiana and South Carolina. This was a remarkable change from the antebellum period in which free and enslaved Black people made up a substantial minority, or even the majority, of state populations but were not considered part of the body politic. These representatives came from a variety of backgrounds. Most were ministers, craftsmen, teachers, or farmers; only a few had been manual laborers. Unusually, almost all Black convention delegates in Louisiana had been born free.

The constitutions these delegates helped write codified substantial changes to the prewar state governments. Many existing property qualifications (such as for jury service) were abandoned, punishments reminiscent of slavery such as whipping were outlawed, and government-funded public schools were established where there had been none. Although Black delegates were divided over some issues, such as whether to disenfranchise former rebels, they formed a solid bloc throughout the South in favor of expanded civil rights and public education.

* Courtesy of the Library of Congress

QUESTIONS TO CONSIDER

1. The delegates pictured here are surrounded by martial imagery such as battle flags, cannons, and bayonets. What is the illustrator trying to convey about the delegates with these symbols?
2. This image was included with a printing of the constitution the delegates eventually produced. What might have been the purpose of including this picture in the publication?

16.4 VISUAL SOURCE: PHILADELPHIA MAYORAL ELECTION POSTER ON RACIAL SEGREGATION ON PUBLIC TRANSIT (1868)*

While the national political focus remained on the former Confederacy and the fate of the freed-people there, Black communities in Northern states campaigned for equal treatment by their local governments. Although the Northern states had abolished slavery decades previously, many still had a variety of restrictive statutes that controlled when, where, and how Black Americans could work, travel, and live. The purpose of many of these laws was to keep Black Americans on the margins of society, to segregate Black communities from their white neighbors.

For decades Philadelphia housed one of the largest and most politically active Black communities in the Northern states. Following the Civil War, Black Philadelphians began to challenge racial segregation on the city's trolley car line. Segregation on the trolley cars not only curtailed Black Philadelphians' ability to travel but was a public rebuke of Black claims to social equality. For three years, Black Philadelphians protested these restrictions until an 1867 law finally forbade racial segregation on public transport in Pennsylvania. Segregation in public spaces remained a salient political issue, as this poster from the 1868 Philadelphia mayoral election demonstrates.

* Courtesy of the Library of Congress

1868? Phila

NEGROES TO RIDE

IN CITY RAILWAY

PASSENGER CARS!

MORTON McMICHAEL

Declines to say whether he is in favor of, or against, Negroes riding in the City Passenger Railway Cars.

DANIEL M. FOX

Declares himself in OPPOSITION to all such privileges. See his manly, direct Letter, in which he declares against all social and political equality with the Negro Race, and in favor of cars exclusively for themselves. Read the Letter in the "Ledger" and "Inquirer" of to-day.

QUESTIONS TO CONSIDER

1. How does the author use fonts and phrasing to frame the issue of segregation on municipal public transport?

2. The poster says Fox not only opposes integration on public transport but also "all social and political equality" with Black Americans. Why is racial equality a concern for Fox and his supporters at this particular moment—in 1868?

16.5 VISUAL SOURCE: THOMAS NAST, *UNCLE SAM'S THANKSGIVING DINNER* (1869)*

The German-born American cartoonist Thomas Nast (1840–1902) designed this idealistic portrayal of prosperity and racial equality for the Thanksgiving holiday in 1869. Following the ratification of the Fourteenth Amendment in 1868, which established equal citizenship for those born or naturalized in the United States, Nast's illustration portrays many different American ethnic groups participating in a shared feast. White, Black, Chinese, and Native American people of all ages feast together, seated at a table below portraits of presidents Washington, Lincoln, and Grant. The centerpiece of the table displays the slogans "Self Government" and "Universal Suffrage," while captions in the corner offer an invitation reading "Come One, Come All, Free and Equal."

Here Nast offers a deliberately aspirational portrayal of a truly egalitarian American society. The US government had attacked, enslaved, and proscribed all of the non-white groups represented, but here at "Uncle Sam's Thanksgiving Dinner" past wrongs are forgotten or forgiven. Nast illustrates the radical implications of the equality promised by the Fourteenth Amendment and highlights the hypocrisy of those who clung to racial prejudice while claiming to support the Constitution.

UNCLE SAM'S THANKSGIVING DINNER.

QUESTIONS TO CONSIDER

1. Examine the diners closely. Note which groups Nast depicts and how they interact with one another. How does Nast use the diners to represent his message?
2. What does Nast believe to be core American values? How can you tell this from his illustration?

* Courtesy of the Library of Congress